בס״ד

To Know and To Care

An Anthology of Chassidic Stories
about the
Lubavitcher Rebbe
Rabbi Menachem M. Schneerson

by Eliyahu and Malka Touger

Volume II

Published by:
Sichos In English
788 Eastern Parkway • Brooklyn, New York 11213
(718) 778-5436 • Fax (718) 735-4139

TO KNOW AND TO CARE
Volume II

Published and Copyrighted by
SICHOS IN ENGLISH

788 Eastern Parkway • Brooklyn, N.Y. 11213
Tel. (718) 778-5436

All rights reserved.
No part of this publication may be
reproduced in any form or by any means,
including photocopying and translation,
without permission in writing from the
copyright holder or the publisher.

ISBN 978-1984942616

First Printing — 5756 • 1996
Second Printing — 5766 • 2006
Createspace Edition — 5778 • 2018

Acknowledgments:

Uri Kaploun for his editorial input
Gershom Gale and Dovid S. Pape for copy-editing
Yosef Yitzchok Turner for layout and typography
Rabbi Yonah Avtzon for countless hours of painstaking effort
in making this dream a reality.

Table of Contents

Introduction
Telling Stories 1

Chapter 1
What You Need and What You are Needed For 11

Chapter 2
No Small Matter 37

Chapter 3
A Shepherd of Souls 47

Chapter 4
Reaching Outward 71

Chapter 5
Digging For Roots 85

Chapter 6
Jewels in the Streets 93

Chapter 7
Opening the Iron Fist 105

Chapter 8
Shepherding His Flock 121

Chapter 9
Unveiling Hidden Treasures 135

Chapter 10
Precious Souls 155

Chapter 11
"The Language of the Wise is Healing" (Proverbs 12:18) 161

Chapter 12
"Rejoice O Barren One" (*Isaiah* 54:1) 195

Chapter 13
Beyond Nature's Limits 207

Chapter 14
Sparks of Greatness 231

Chapter 15
More Than During His Lifetime 247

Afterword 267

Glossary and Biographical Index 273

Introduction
Telling Stories

An Original Picture

During the *shivah* mourning for the Rebbe Rashab, one of the vintage chassidim began extolling the Rebbe's character with all kinds of superlatives.

In the middle of the venerable gentleman's talk, the Rebbe Rayatz cut him off. "You're not speaking about my father," he admonished, "you're speaking about yourself!"

Now the speaker had been saying: "The Rebbe was this..., the Rebbe was that...." Why, then, did the Rebbe Rayatz say he was speaking about himself?

He meant that though ostensibly praising the Rebbe Rashab, the chassid was really enumerating those of his own characteristics which he considered good, developing them to the extreme, and crediting them to the Rebbe Rashab.

He was unable to expand his vision beyond his own horizons. He wasn't talking about the Rebbe, because there is something about a Rebbe that transcends our comprehension.

A Rebbe's wisdom is wisdom; his emotions are emotions, and his directives are directives. But when encountering and relating to a Rebbe, there is something that transcends intellect and emotion, something that you can't put your finger on.[1]

The Secret of Attraction

Consider: What distinguishes a masterpiece from a copy? A good copyist may use the same colors and even brushstrokes as the original artist, but there will always be something missing.

---

1. There is, however, a reciprocal effect: The transcendental quality also endows the particular attributes with uniqueness.

The original is vested with a unique vitality and energy that the copy simply does not possess. And it's precisely that vitality and energy that tells us we're in the presence of a masterpiece.

In other words, what makes a painting beautiful is not what we can describe about it — its lines and colors — but what we can't put into words, the inspiration and energy which the artist breathed into it.

To explain this using the language of chassidic thought: The *Kabbalah* teaches that our three primary emotive attributes express *Chessed* (kindness), *Gevurah* (power), and *Tiferes* (beauty).

What is unique about beauty, chassidic thought goes on to explain, is that it is a combination of kindness and power. This is not to imply that kindness is half-beautiful and power, half-beautiful, and true beauty is a composite of them both. Instead, the intent is to point out that kindness and power are opposites that cannot ordinarily be fused. The only factor that can bring them together is a quality that transcends them both.

So the thing that attracts is not what we can describe — the two opposites which we see coming together — but what we *cannot* describe, the transcendent power which brings them together, and which shines forth through their fusion.

The same is true of people. What attracts us in people is not what we can tell about them, the qualities and attributes they possess, but what we can't put into words — the quality we call soul.

A soul is an actual part of G-d,[2] and, like Him, is boundless. What draws us to our fellow man is this transcendent quality, the spark of G-d which glows inside each person.

A Rebbe is a person in whom this spark of G-dliness is revealed without hindrance.

Accordingly, we are not trying to explain the Rebbe or interpret him; that would be presumptuous. We would do no

---

2. *Tanya*, ch. 2.

better than the well-meaning elder chassid we encountered at the outset.

Moreover, the attempt would defeat the purpose. What is special about a Rebbe is not the superlatives people use to describe him: a Torah genius, a visionary leader, a caring and sympathetic listener, or the like. What draws us is the quality that can be described only with the term "Rebbe" — something without limit, a unique energy and vitality that comes from the G-dliness which we all possess, and which a Rebbe reveals in a distinctive way.

Stories are a good way to express this quality. First of all, a story is alive; it breathes in a way that an essay or thesis cannot. In the Torah, it is the stories which we remember, and which have the greatest impact on us. So, too, stories have always been the *Torah Shebichsav*, the Written Torah, of *Chassidus*. For like the Torah itself, these stories convey a multidimensional message which inspires and empowers.

If this is true of an individual story, it surely is true of a collection of stories.

There is no way we can "sum up the Rebbe," but as a person reads one story after another after another, he will come to perceive some of the Rebbe's dimensions, and come to appreciate, recall and relive those unique qualities for which we have no words.

Stories, Not Tales

When we were considering a name for Vol. I of *To Know and To Care*, the subtitle seemed obvious: "Contemporary Chassidic Stories About the Lubavitcher Rebbe."

Then a member of our editorial board said: "Wait! 'Tales' sounds much more literary than 'stories.'"

Another forcefully objected: "Tales," he argued, "are tall! We want to make it clear that these stories *actually happened.* 'Stories' may not sound so literary, but it conveys the point more powerfully."

But what would be so bad about tales? After all, if the point in telling a story is to learn from it, to derive inspiration and direction, is it so important whether it happened or not?

Yes.

Because for a story to make a sincere impression, you have to know it's true.

Any argument is communicated better with a story. That's why the best speeches are rich in allegory, and why a lecturer will often relate an anecdote.

But then his listener knows he is hearing an argument; he understands that this is merely an illustration of the thought the lecturer wants to convey.

When a person actually sees a story happen, however, or hears about it from a trusted friend, it's very different. He's coming face-to-face with reality. And there is nothing more powerful than truth.

Whenever he told a chassidic story, the Rebbe would always emphasize the importance of detail and accuracy, because it is precisely the details that imbue a story with the ring of truth.

Accordingly, every one of the stories related below was heard either from the principals involved or from a reliable source who heard it firsthand. Countless faxes and telephone calls have gone into checking and rechecking the authenticity of these narratives. Our intent is not to convey merely a chassid's feeling of what *could* have happened, but a truthful record of what actually took place.

Inseparable Elements

To end this introduction here would be easy, but it wouldn't be fully honest. To be fully honest, we have to confront a question that for three years has been on the mind of everyone whose life was touched by the Rebbe.

Let me share an experience with you.

The word *farbrengen* literally means "spending time together." Chassidim get together and share, talking forthrightly about their spiritual journeys. *Farbrengens* conducted by a Rebbe or *mashpia* (spiritual mentor) take on a more formal structure, but in essence — and very often in practice — *farbrengens* among chassidim remain a meeting of equals, where questions are posed and wrestled with.

One night, I attended such a *farbrengen*. Several old friends — some *shluchim*, some living in Crown Heights — got together, and spoke seriously about where we were going as Lubavitchers.

As we got to talking, one of the men blurted out: "I think it's time Lubavitch stopped putting so much emphasis on the Rebbe."

It was quite a bombshell; the conversation never really recovered. Some of the people took the speaker to task, and he didn't get the opportunity to explain himself.

What was he saying, and why were his ideas so unpalatable for the others?

I think my friend was trying to say that Lubavitch is an ideology and a way of life.

The Rebbe wants us to be outward directed, to advance, to reach out to others and into ourselves, to continually move towards new horizons in our own Divine service, and in our mission of spreading Torah and *Chassidus*. Too often, focusing just on the Rebbe can catch a person up in pleasant memories of the past, and cause him to forget that there is still a present and a future.

If that was my friend's intent, why did everyone shout him down? Why were they so unwilling to think about *Chassidus* without a Rebbe?

Because a Rebbe is an embodiment of what *Chassidus* stands for. If you want to know what *Chassidus* asks of you, theory has its shortcomings. Looking at the Rebbe, by contrast, provides us with a real-life example of what *Chassidus* demands, where it expects us to go.

To quote a story: One of the gifted students of the Maggid of Mezritch was known as *Der Volpe* by his colleagues. He, however, lapsed into depression, and from depression into alcoholism. Despite his fallen state, he, nevertheless, retained sparks of greatness. In fact, it was when he was drunk that he would reveal his master's teachings without restraint, oblivious to whether or not there was anyone listening.

Der Volpe's story became known throughout White Russia. If a chassid heard a drunkard talking about spiritual concepts, he would not dismiss him, but instead would listen carefully. For perhaps the drunkard was *Der Volpe*, and from the tirade, the listener might discover a gem of wisdom.

Once while visiting an inn, one of the Alter Rebbe's chassidim heard a drunkard holding forth on the Torah's mystic secrets. This chassid had heard of *Der Volpe*, and so he lent an ear.

He knew what to listen for, and how to savor it when he heard it. He drank in *Der Volpe's* words.

After carrying on for a while, *Der Volpe* had to excuse himself briefly. The chassid hurried to check *Der Volpe's* pack, anxious to find a text containing a discourse of the Maggid or another such treasure. All he found were a few rags.

As he put the pack down, two strong hands grabbed him from behind. "What are you looking for in my pack?" *Der Volpe* demanded.

Unnerved, the chassid could do no more than tell the truth: he had been inspired by what *Der Volpe* had said, and was certain that if he saw it on paper, the impression would be even more powerful.

"That's the problem with you chassidim today," *Der Volpe* growled. "For us, the chassidim, the Rebbe and the Rebbe's teachings were all one; we didn't need a written record. Today, the three are each distinct entities; that's why you need a text."

The Rebbe taught us more than any text could. If we were to focus only on his philosophy and not on the Rebbe himself, we would miss the essence of his message. That's why my other friends would not conceive of chassidism without a Rebbe.

In writing this book, my friends' dialogue still echoes in my mind. This volume is not intended to be merely a collection of heartwarming memories. Instead, I wanted to allow every reader the opportunity to live with the Rebbe so that he could understand — and connect with — that dimension which transcends intellect and emotion.

Experiencing this quality as it was expressed through the Rebbe will inspire and empower us to reveal a similar spark in ourselves, and within our surroundings. In doing so, we will further the mission with which the Rebbe charged us:[3] making the world conscious of *Mashiach*, and preparing an environment in which his purpose can be fulfilled.

Eliyahu Touger

Sivan 15, 5756
Pittsburgh, Pa

---

3. See *Sound the Great Shofar*, p. 113.

Chapter 1 —
What You Need and What You are Needed For

As one of the Alter Rebbe's wealthy chassidim advanced in years, he was able to marry off his children and establish them in business. A generous man by nature, when the responsibilities of his immediate family became less pressing, he committed himself to pay for the weddings and dowries of his relatives' children.

Suddenly, however, his business affairs took a sharp turn for the worse, and instead of being affluent, he found himself in debt and unable to meet his commitments. Before his financial situation became public knowledge, he hurried to Liozna to receive advice and blessings from the Alter Rebbe.

At *yechidus,* he poured out his heart to the Rebbe, saying that he was prepared to remain impoverished himself, but he needed to pay his debts and honor the commitments that he had made to his relatives.

The Alter Rebbe responded: "*You are speaking about what you need. But you have not given a thought to what you are needed for.*"

The chassid fainted; the Alter Rebbe's attendant had to help him out of the Rebbe's room. When he came to, he began to devote himself to prayer and study, without thinking of his business concerns.

After the chassid had conducted himself in this fashion for some time, the Alter Rebbe sent for him. Standing before the Rebbe, the vision of his previous *yechidus* flashed in his mind, and he could barely muster the strength to look the Rebbe in the face. This time, however, the Alter Rebbe spoke to him gently: "Now you appreciate G-d's truth.... You can return home...; may G-d grant you success."

The man made his way home and discovered that the gloomy picture he had seen previously could be corrected. A few favorable strokes of fortune had given him the opportunity to right his financial course.

The sequence is noteworthy. Once he was able to appreciate his purpose, he was granted the means to accomplish it.

The Rebbe gives people a sense of mission, enabling them to see what they were needed for. This awareness helps them mold their characters. Commitment to a purpose beyond self empowered them to redefine their sense of self and live fuller and more complete lives.

What You Need and What You are Needed For 13

Rabbi Moshe Feller and his wife Mindy were one of the first couples to begin the tradition of *shlichus*. Before leaving for the twin cities of Minneapolis-S. Paul, they went to *yechidus* to receive the Rebbe's blessing and advice.

At that *yechidus,* Rabbi Feller was a little surprised. The Rebbe spent most of the time speaking to Mrs. Feller, telling her that since she had studied mathematics, graduating *Phi Beta Kappa* from Hunter College, she should continue her studies and try to get a university position. This would not, the Rebbe emphasized, compromise her position as a *shluchah*. On the contrary, having a post at the university would facilitate outreach activities there.

Shortly after arriving in Minnesota, Mrs. Feller was able to secure a position at the University of Minnesota. The head of the mathematics department was Paul Rosenbloom, soon to become famous for developing the "new math."

Besides being a mathematical genius, Prof. Rosenbloom had a vibrant Jewish heart, and a sincere desire for spiritual growth. His discussions with the new faculty member soon went far beyond mathematics, and he established a close relationship with the Feller family and a growing interest in Judaism and Chassidism.

In 1963, Prof. Rosenbloom was called to Brooklyn College for consultation. When he told Rabbi Feller about the upcoming trip, Rabbi Feller suggested that he visit the Rebbe for *yechidus.*

"Why would the Rebbe want to spend time with me?" Prof. Rosenbloom asked.

Rabbi Feller assured him that the Rebbe would find subjects which would interest both of them, and arranged an appointment.

The meeting was scheduled for 11 PM. Prof. Rosenbloom realized that the Rebbe would be seeing many people before and after him. Feeling that the area in which he shared the greatest common interest with the Rebbe was *chinuch* (education), and to save the Rebbe time, he wrote some of his ideas down and gave them to one of the Rebbe's secretaries.

When he gave him the note, Prof. Rosenbloom told the secretary the general thrust of his thinking: that the programs of *limudei kodesh* (Torah studies) and *limudei chol* (secular studies) in Jewish day schools should be integrated.

The secretary reacted with shock. "There must be," he told the professor, "a distinction between the holy and the mundane! A child must know what is sacred and what is not."

When speaking to the Rebbe, however, Prof. Rosenbloom received a different picture. "Children should be taught to appreciate that everything is connected with the Torah," the Rebbe told him. "When they perform an experiment in a science lab, they should know that it is G-d's creative power that is causing the chemical reactions they observe.

"There are some," the Rebbe continued, "who have two sets of bookshelves, one for *seforim* [sacred texts] and another for secular books. That is the wrong approach. If a person thinks of secular wisdom as being unrelated to the Torah, he does not understand the Torah, nor does he truly understand the secular subject he is studying."

This *yechidus* spurred Prof. Rosenbloom to continue his progress in Jewish observance and deepen his connection with Lubavitch. Several years later, when he moved to New York to accept the mathematics chair at Columbia University, Prof. Rosenbloom was an observant Jew with a strong connection to the Rebbe. At first, he rented an apartment close to the university, but he and his family felt the lack of Jewish community there, and he asked the Rebbe if they should move to Crown Heights.

"Absolutely not," the Rebbe answered. "You should live near the university. A Jewish professor on campus should see that he has a colleague who wears a *yarmulke*; a Jewish student should see a young boy who walks proudly with his *tzitzis* hanging out."

Although the Rebbe wanted Prof. Rosenbloom to serve as an example of Jewish practice, he made it clear that this was not to be done at the expense of his professional advancement. On the contrary, he urged Prof. Rosenbloom to forge ahead with his research. At one point, he invited him to bring a new mathematics paper to every *farbrengen* he attended.

Prof. Rosenbloom faithfully adhered to this directive. On *Yud-Tes* Kislev, Purim, and other occasions when some people chose to offer presents to the Rebbe, Prof. Rosenbloom would present him with a mathematics paper.

Once he brought a copy of a paper that had been published in a major journal. The Rebbe gave it a quick perusal and asked if he had not seen the paper before. The professor directed the Rebbe's attention to a footnote on the first page. There it stated that the preliminary draft had been presented to the Lubavitcher Rebbe at a *Yud-Tes* Kislev *farbrengen*.

Prof. Rosenbloom shared a birthday with the Rebbe, *Yud-Alef* Nissan. Year after year, at the *farbrengen* held on that date, he found a unique way to celebrate together. He would present the Rebbe with a mathematical problem which he had devised in the course of weeks of work, then wait a few brief moments until the Rebbe responded with its solution.

As their connection developed, the Rebbe began to entrust Prof. Rosenbloom with projects, some in the field of Jewish outreach and some in mathematics. One day, Prof. Rosenbloom received a package from the Rebbe's office containing a mathematics paper written in German and a note from the Rebbe's secretary, Rabbi Groner. Rabbi Groner stated that the Rebbe would like to know if the professor could find someone who understood German, and who would complete the paper and prepare it for publication.

Prof. Rosenbloom answered that the language was not a problem; most students of higher mathematics knew enough German to appreciate the paper. The problem was that mathematical research was very individualized, and it would be necessary to find someone with an expertise in the particular field which the paper addressed.

Rabbi Groner relayed the professor's answer to the Rebbe, who replied by asking the professor to prepare a summary of the paper so that it could be presented to another person.

As Professor Rosenbloom began writing the summary, he realized that it would be difficult to find someone to complete the paper, and so he chose instead to offer advice to the author as to how he could complete the research himself. Neither the Rebbe nor Rabbi Groner had revealed the author's identity, and Prof. Rosenbloom had not inquired.

At his next visit to a *farbrengen,* Prof. Rosenbloom presented his letter of advice to the Rebbe. The Rebbe asked him if he could find someone to complete the research, but the professor answered that it was unlikely. "Any person who would have the knowledge and ability to think creatively needed to complete this paper would most likely want to work on his own research," he explained. The professor added that he had prepared the summary in a manner that would allow the author to finish the paper himself. This, he felt, would be the best alternative.

The Rebbe answered that this was impossible because the author was no longer living, and again spoke of finding someone else. "Would money make a difference?" asked the Rebbe, offering to pay a generous fee for the work.

"No," answered the professor. "For such a person, the project itself would have to be the inspiration."

"Could you find a graduate student whom you could direct in this work?"

"I'm afraid not," answered the professor, explaining that the subject was too complex for an ordinary student.

Seeing the Rebbe's sharp interest, however, Prof. Rosenbloom offered to complete the paper himself. Initially, the Rebbe refused, saying he did not want to take him away from his own research. But the professor persisted, sensing that the Rebbe genuinely wanted the paper completed.

Ultimately the Rebbe agreed, and allowed him to undertake the project. He then revealed that it was his own brother, Reb Yisrael Aryeh Leib Schneerson, who had begun the paper.

When the project was completed, the Rebbe asked the professor to try to have it published. He requested, however, that it be published under a pseudonym, with no biographical data concerning the author, aside from the fact that he had served as a professor of mathematics at the University of Liverpool.

The Rebbe showed an interest in all the members of the Rosenbloom family. Once the professor's young son was having problems at school, and the guidance counselor suggested that professional counseling be sought for him. Mrs. Rosenbloom was very upset by this suggestion, and arranged a *yechidus* at which the problem could be discussed.

At *yechidus*, the Rebbe explained that there was no need for such an approach. Shifting the focus of discussion, he asked the Rosenblooms what they intended to do with their son on Chanukah. The Rosenblooms answered that they were planning to light candles with him and give presents, but nothing out of the ordinary.

The Rebbe suggested that they throw a Chanukah party for the members of their son's class. Since he was only seven, the Rebbe added, they should invite the girls as well. The Rosenblooms should make sure that their own daughter had other plans for the afternoon, however, so that the boy could be the center of attention.

The party was scheduled for the Sunday of Chanukah. On the preceding Friday, a package arrived at the Rosenbloom home with a copy of the Merkos publication, "The Complete Story of Chanukah" for every member of the class. On Monday, Rabbi Chodakov, the Rebbe's personal secretary, called and asked how the party went.

From that time onward, the child's socialization ceased to be a problem.

At a *yechidus* before the boy's *Bar Mitzvah*, the Rebbe showed an interest in Mrs. Rosenbloom's activities. She told the Rebbe that she was involved with the Speakers Bureau of the Lubavitch Women's Organization, arranging talks at meetings of Hadassah, Bnei Brith and other Jewish organizations in an attempt to heighten the awareness of Torah Judaism.

"And do you speak yourself?" the Rebbe asked.

"Oh no," Mrs. Rosenbloom answered, explaining that she shied away from public speaking.

"That's a shame," the Rebbe told her. "It would be far more effective if women could hear the Torah's message from someone who came from the secular world and understands that perspective."

The Rebbe did not content himself with merely making a suggestion. The following day, the Rosenblooms received a message from his office asking that Mrs. Rosenbloom be the primary speaker at their son's *Bar Mitzvah*, announcing the establishment of a free loan fund in honor of the Rebbe's mother.

After making this speech, Mrs. Rosenbloom found public speaking less daunting, and began speaking at many of the functions arranged by the Lubavitch Women's Organization.

≈

As a youth, Rabbi Naftuli Estulin studied in the underground Lubavitcher *yeshivah* in Russia. The boys lived in constant fear of detection, and dreamed of leaving Russia and going to a place where they could practice Judaism openly.

From time to time, the Rebbe would send *shluchim* to Russia. Posing as tourists, they would have clandestine meetings with members of the Lubavitch underground. Once when a *shliach* came, all the students of the *yeshivah* wrote *pidyonos* (requests for blessings) to the Rebbe, asking that he pray that they be able to leave Russia. Now the *shliach* could not carry the *pidyonos* out as they were, for his luggage might be searched and the notes confiscated. So the chassidim baked a cake and put the *pidyonos* into the batter. The *shliach* packed the cake carefully, thinking that if he were questioned by the authorities, he would tell them that a relative had baked it for his father.

The *shliach* was not questioned, and was able to bring the cake to the Rebbe, who said it was the sweetest cake he had ever received. And the Rebbe's prayers and those of the chassidim bore fruit; shortly afterwards, Naftuli and his fellow students were allowed to leave Russia.

His family settled in Israel, arriving just before Rosh HaShanah, 5727. When Naftuli heard that a group of chassidim were planning to visit the Rebbe for the holidays of Tishrei, he felt an urge to join them. A fine chassidic feeling, but he lacked an Israeli passport, a visa to America, and money for the ticket! Yet Naftuli was not one to let such obstacles stand in his way. Through a succession of minor miracles, on the day before Sukkos, he was standing in 770, waiting to see the Rebbe.

Later, at *yechidus,* the Rebbe greeted Naftuli with a broad smile. He told him to stay in Crown Heights for a month and then return to Israel. After discovering that Naftuli had borrowed money for the trip, the Rebbe gave him the funds to repay the loan.

After studying for a year in *Eretz Yisrael*, Naftuli's parents and teachers decided that he was ready to study in the Rebbe's *yeshivah* in 770, and he made his second trip to the Rebbe.

When Naftuli came to 770, he found it difficult to adjust; he didn't speak the language, the culture was different. But beyond the obvious problems of acclimation to a new setting, Naftuli had trouble finding his place in the *yeshivah*. Although he had grasped the basics of *Talmudic* study in Russia, all the other *yeshivah* students his age had been studying their entire lives. They were already capable of tackling advanced Rabbinic texts, and were busy preparing themselves for ordination. Because of this, Naftuli had difficulty finding a *chavrusa* (study partner). Moreover, while friendly, the American students were more at home with their own, and Naftuli often felt out of place.

One of the elder chassidim whom Naftuli knew from Russia, Reb Avraham, was visiting 770 at the time, and was scheduled to meet the Rebbe at *yechidus.* Naftuli opened his heart to him, telling him of his difficulties, and requesting that he ask the Rebbe for a blessing.

In the course of his *yechidus,* Reb Avraham mentioned Naftuli's plight. The Rebbe looked at him in surprise: "Why is he discouraged? He will be an *atamanom buded* "(a Russian term meaning "heroic leader").

In 5730 (1970), Naftuli became engaged, and sought to go out on *shlichus.* Back then, there were only about 30 people working as *shluchim* in America. The students who had grown up studying at 770 were all enthused with the prospect, but the idea was still on the horizon; there simply were not many opportunities available.

At that time, one of the more colorful Lubavitcher *shluchim* was Rabbi Gershon Mendel Garelik, Chief Rabbi of Milan. Rabbi Garelik was interested in opening a kosher restaurant in his city, and offered Naftuli a *shlichus* position. He would be the *mashgiach* (*kashrus* supervisor) in the restaurant, and would have other duties spreading *Yiddishkeit* throughout the city.

Naftuli was excited. What the opportunity was did not concern him; what was important was that he would be the Rebbe's *shliach.*

He wrote to the Rebbe, asking whether or not he should take the job, but did not receive an answer. Undaunted, he wrote a second time. But although he anxiously awaited the Rebbe's reply, none was forthcoming. When Rabbi Garelik saw that Naftuli had not received a response, he also wrote the

Rebbe, describing the offer he had made and asking whether it was appropriate.

The Rebbe replied that G-d had not worked miracles to take Naftuli out of Russia so that he could become a *kashrus* supervisor!

Naftuli was happy that the Rebbe had greater aspirations for him, and began looking for another offer. His brother-in-law, Rabbi Begun of Brazil, proposed that he join him there, and promised to find him a position. Again, he wrote to the Rebbe asking whether he should accept the offer, but again, the Rebbe did not reply. At that time, Naftuli's sister was visiting the Rebbe, and at *yechidus* she asked whether Naftuli should come to Brazil.

Again, the Rebbe had other plans. "There will be time for him to come to Brazil," he told Mrs. Begun. Naftuli soon understood. It became clear that the Beguns were *hoping* that a place could be found for him, but that there was no job immediately available that fit his personality and training.

So Naftuli spent a year in New York, studying half a day in *kollel* (a higher Rabbinic academy) and teaching Russian children at a new school opened by the Friends of Refugees from Eastern Europe.

In 5731 (1971), Rabbi Shlomo Cunin, the head *shliach* in California, heard rumors that large numbers of Russian Jews would soon be allowed to emigrate. He spoke to several potential sponsors, and found patrons willing to finance an outreach program to connect these Russian Jews to their spiritual heritage. When looking for a rabbi to head the program, Rabbi Cunin could find none more suitable than Naftuli.

Naftuli was excited; this seemed to be exactly what he should be doing. Immediately, he wrote to the Rebbe about the proposal, but again he did not receive an answer! After a few days passed, he wrote a second time, but the Rebbe again did not reply.

Baffled, he went to Rabbi Chodakov (the Rebbe's personal secretary), and requested that he ask the Rebbe to clarify the matter for him.

Rabbi Chodakov told him that he would speak to the Rebbe at 11 that night; Naftuli should come back at about 12 for an answer.

At midnight, Rabbi Chodakov had a broad smile. He told Naftuli: "The Rebbe told me that in your letters you wrote about what you want, what you think is appropriate for you. But your wife was not mentioned at all, nor did she sign."

Naftuli went home and told his wife the Rebbe's answer. She was also happy to go on *shlichus,* and readily agreed. Naftuli wrote another letter, which both he and his wife signed. This time the Rebbe replied immediately, advising him to accept the position.

At *yechidus* before they left for California, the Rebbe told the couple that their first responsibility was to spread *Yiddishkeit* to Jews coming from Russia, Czechoslovakia, and other countries from behind the Iron Curtain, and beyond that, to spread the wellsprings of *Chassidus* throughout California.

Three months after they moved, Mrs. Estulin gave birth. Seeing an opportunity to promote his program, Naftuli wanted to publicize the *bris*. He imagined the headlines: a Russian immigrant whose own *bris* had been performed underground was now making a *bris* for his child in public.

Rabbi Cunin disagreed; he did not see this as an issue on which public attention should be focused.

Convinced that his position was right, Naftuli wrote to the Rebbe, asking whether he should publicize the *bris* or not. The Rebbe answered that with regard to this question, he should listen to Rabbi Cunin, but that there would come a time when Naftuli would publicize circumcisions for Russian children throughout Los Angeles.

The Rebbe's words proved prophetic, as many of the Russian immigrants arriving in Los Angeles had never been circumcised. Reb Naftuli was among the first in America to organize circumcisions for older youths and adults, and had *mohelim* specially trained to perform the surgery. Over 9,000 such circumcisions have been performed in Los Angeles to date, attracting media attention around the world.

The wave of Russian immigrants which Rabbi Cunin expected did not materialize immediately, so in his first years, Naftuli also took on other duties, including the establishment of a *Chabad* Information Center on Fairfax Ave. But by the mid-70s, thousands of Russian Jews had settled in the Los Angeles area, and Naftuli found himself occupied day and night providing for their material and spiritual needs.

In 1978, Naftuli opened a facility for the immigrants on La Brea Ave., where most of them had settled. Two years later, when the center of the Russian Jewish community moved to West Hollywood, Naftuli opened another center there. Not only was Naftuli responsible for the spiritual needs of these Jews, he also had to bear the entire burden of fundraising.

Naftuli's building was only 3,000 sq. feet. That small space housed a *shul,* a kitchen, a library, classrooms for adults and youths, offices and counseling rooms. And in the summer, it also served as the center for a camp for hundreds of children. It was constantly teeming with activity.

On one hand, the close quarters made everyone feel at home. On the other, as Naftuli's work became more successful, the overcrowding became unbearable. There were simply too many people.

From his youth in Russia, Naftuli had dreamed of building a large *shul.* Now he saw this objective, not only as a dream, but as an absolute necessity. But the prospects of acquiring such a building were daunting, for real estate prices in Los Angeles were exorbitant.

Before the holiday of Shavuos 1991, Naftuli wrote to the Rebbe asking for a blessing that he be able to build or acquire a *shul* in the near future, and somehow find $500,000 — the amount he felt would be needed for a down payment. The

Rebbe replied that he would soon receive more than he could possibly have expected!

On the 18th of Tammuz, while the summer camp was in session, a middle-aged man walked into Naftuli's *shul,* apparently looking for a *minyan* for the afternoon services. When told the *minyan* would be later, he stayed and watched the children eating lunch. Naftuli was there at the time, and introduced himself to the visitor, asking if he could be of any help.

The visitor started asking Naftuli about the camp: "Why isn't there a bigger facility? The kids seem to be having a good time, but everything is so crowded!"

Naftuli answered that he would *love* a bigger facility, but couldn't afford it.

"Maybe I can help," the man said. "Come, let's take a walk down S. Monica Blvd. (the main street in the area). We'll see if there is any suitable property."

Naftuli could barely believe what he was hearing. He had never seen this man before and, though neatly dressed, the stranger was far from elegantly clothed. He looked more like a candidate for a donation than a person able to make a large one!

But Naftuli wanted to make the man feel good, was interested in finding a property, and besides, maybe the man *could* help. And so he accompanied him.

As they walked, the man told his story. His name was Harry Rubinfeld. His daughter was being treated in a hospital nearby. After visiting her, he had come to the *shul* looking for a *minyan.*

He had been born in Czechoslovakia. (Naftuli remembered the Rebbe's words in *yechidus* about Jews from Czechoslovakia). As a youth after the war, he had often gone hungry in the post-holocaust communist society.

Afterwards, he had migrated to America, and found work in California as a painter. He had been able to save some money, and had invested in real estate. Slowly but surely, he had been able to amass capital. He had invested this further, and thus put together a considerable nest egg. His wife had recently passed away, and he was thinking of making a large donation in her honor.

When he had seen the immigrant children eating lunch, he had remembered his own days of hunger, and his difficulties in finding a place in American society. It occurred to him that he would like to dedicate a building for these children.

As they were walking, the man noticed a large garage for sale. "This looks like an appropriate location," he told Naftuli. "I will return to the *shul* for *minchah*. Find out what they're asking, and we'll see what we can do."

Naftuli walked into the garage and was impressed. The property was huge, 12,000 square feet. The location was ideal. In his mind, he could picture it renovated and transformed into a perfect facility. But the owners were demanding a high price; as a down payment alone, they were seeking $500,000!

Naftuli returned to his *shul* and conveyed this information to Mr. Rubinfeld. "I was thinking of giving $400,000, but I was impressed by the children and I was impressed by you. Here," Mr. Rubinfeld said, writing out a check for $50,000 on the spot and placing $450,000 in escrow, to be transferred upon completion of the sale.

With the down payment in hand, Naftuli was able to negotiate from a position of strength with regard to the total price of the building. After completing the purchase, he called the many Russian Jews he had helped over the years and told them of the opportunity they had been given. In all, he received pledges of close to one million dollars!

Today, working from the renovated facility, Reb Naftuli exclaims: "My life story is an advertisement for *Mashiach*. It shows that redemption is a possibility, and that by following the Rebbe's vision and accepting the mission with which he has charged us, each one of us can find success that exceeds our highest expectations."

When Rabbi Immanuel Schochet was in his teens, the Central Lubavitcher *yeshivah* in which he studied had a varied student body. Only about half the students came from Lubavitch homes, and many of the others didn't identify themselves as Lubavitcher Chassidim. For them, the *yeshivah* was a Torah academy of high repute, a center for *yiras shamayim* (fear of heaven), which at the same time had an accredited high school. These students were thinking of combining their *yeshivah* studies with a college education in the future, and needed a recognized high-school diploma for admittance to college.

In his senior year, Immanuel also had such plans. He applied to an institution which offered both *yeshivah* and university training, and was accepted subject to his passing a college entrance exam.

On the *Shabbos* of *Yud-Beis* Tammuz, the Rebbe delivered a *sichah* sharply criticizing the attitude which had begun to spread within the American Jewish community, that every youth must attend college.

"For what purpose?" the Rebbe asked. "Why should Torah studies be sacrificed in favor of secular knowledge? It is assumed that a college degree will insure a person a successful livelihood, but that is far from the truth. A person's livelihood is in G-d's hands, and He can provide for a person whether or not he has a degree."

On the days following the *farbrengen*, the *Rosh Yeshivah*, Rabbi Mentlick, spoke to each of the senior students, repeating the Rebbe's message. Almost all of those who had contemplated college agreed to spend the following year studying solely in *yeshivah*.

Immanuel did not make a final decision about the matter. He had already paid for the college entrance exam, and considered postponing his decision until he had completed the test. He wrote the Rebbe a letter explaining his decision. The Rebbe responded, detailing the reasons for his public statements, but he did not apply any pressure, and instead left the decision in Immanuel's hands.

On the *Shabbos* before the scheduled exam, the Rebbe held a *farbrengen* in honor of *Chaf Av*, his father's *yahrzeit.* In the course of the *sichos,* the Rebbe focused on the *Rambam*'s statement (*Mishneh Torah, Hilchos De'os* 6:1) that a person is always influenced by his surroundings, and therefore should seek out a setting conducive to moral and spiritual growth. If he cannot find such a setting, it is preferable to dwell alone in the desert than to live in a morally corrupt environment.

While the Rebbe's words were obviously of general import, Immanuel felt that they were also directed to him personally. This impression was strengthened when he made eye contact with the Rebbe after the *sichah*. At that point, Immanuel decided that he would not take the exam.

Nevertheless, he did not give up his college plans entirely. On the contrary, he felt that there were several reasons for both the private and public attention which the Rebbe had given him. Perhaps one of the factors was the effect his decision might have on other students. The following year, he thought to himself, he would be more private about his plans. He would devote himself to his Torah studies with diligence, but would keep his options open. He had heard about a combined program operated by a renowned *yeshivah* and a recognized university, in which the university gave college credit for one's Rabbinical studies. He thought that after completing one year of full-time *yeshivah* study in Lubavitch, he would enroll in that program.

Everything proceeded according to plan. Immanuel studied diligently, and kept his thoughts about the future to himself. He applied to the joint program, was accepted, and planned to begin his studies the following September.

On Shavuos, the Rebbe delivered a *sichah* in which he focused on the practice of going away to the Catskill

Mountains for summer vacation. "It is important," the Rebbe emphasized, "to pay attention to one's health. But one's vacation should not be a vacation from Torah study, nor a vacation from modesty.

"Too often," he continued, "a vacation is considered a time to relax, and standards are also relaxed. 'After Labor Day,' people say, 'we will return to the city, and then we will return to our pattern of Torah observance.'"

During the singing which followed the *sichah,* the Rebbe sought out Immanuel with his eyes. When he found him, the Rebbe spoke: "Immanuel, you also have plans to fix things up after Labor Day. Say *LeChaim* and forget about them."

Immanuel was stunned. For a moment, he didn't even realize what the Rebbe meant. But the Rebbe kept looking at him with a broad smile. After a few moments, he understood that the Rebbe must be referring to his plans for the following year.

Now Immanuel had kept his plans a secret. For that matter, he hadn't thought about the issue much himself. In his mind, the matter had been resolved, and his life had focused on more immediate concerns. Surely, he hadn't been thinking of his future during the *farbrengen.*

Again, the Rebbe spoke to him: "Say *LeChaim.* Your plans will never work out anyway. Forget about them."

Immanuel said *LeChaim* and heeded the Rebbe's advice. That was the last time he thought about college for many years. Instead, he devoted his energies solely to his *yeshivah* studies.

Several years afterwards, he was serving as Rabbi of a congregation in Toronto and teaching in a local *yeshivah.* He also took several university courses to upgrade his teaching skills. When he became engaged and began to think about earning a livelihood, he wrote to the Rebbe regarding a business opportunity. The Rebbe directed him to ignore the matter. "Your energies," the Rebbe told him, "should be focused solely on Torah study, general knowledge, and writing about these matters."

Rabbi Schochet was thankful for the Rebbe's encouragement, but was unsure of what to do. He had considered the opportunity, not because he was attracted to business, but because he would have to provide for his family. How was he to do that and focus his attention "solely on Torah study, general knowledge, and writing about these matters"?

The Rebbe had an answer for that as well. He hired Rabbi Schochet to translate some of his private correspondence, and to write and translate for several of the Lubavitch outreach organizations. At the same time, he told Rabbi Schochet to enter university to pursue general studies.

In the years that followed, in lectures at college campuses and Lubavitch centers around the world, at the Ivy League Torah Study Program, and in a variety of different outreach programs, Rabbi Schochet has used both his Torah studies and his general knowledge to spread *Yiddishkeit*.

It all started ordinarily enough. Avraham and Tuvia Lerner, two brothers from the Lubavitch community in Montreal, had birthdays only a few days apart. They came to New York for *yechidus* and entered the Rebbe's room together. Avraham approached the Rebbe, gave him the note he had prepared, and listened carefully as the Rebbe gave him a short blessing.

Then Tuvia gave the Rebbe his note. This was the *yechidus* before his *Bar Mitzvah,* and so Tuvia listened attentively as the Rebbe gave him a blessing.

And then the entire nature of the *yechidus* changed; Tuvia spoke up: "Rebbe, you'll have to excuse me. I'm sure you want me to appreciate the blessing you gave me. I want to understand it, and know it well enough so that I can repeat it at my *Bar Mitzvah.* Could you say it again, and then listen while I repeat it back to make sure I'm saying it right? And could you speak a little slower? I wasn't able to understand it the first time."

The Rebbe smiled broadly, leaned forward in his chair, and repeated the blessing, speaking slower and using simpler words. After he finished, he told Tuvia: "Now you say it."

Tuvia began, but made several errors. Before he could finish, the Rebbe interrupted him: "You weren't listening carefully," he told him. "I'll say it for you once more, but this time pay attention."

The Rebbe then repeated the blessing a third time, speaking even more slowly and using even simpler words. He then listened carefully as Tuvia repeated it, correcting him from time to time. When Tuvia was finished, the Rebbe asked him: "Are you happy now?"

Tuvia answered that he was, and the Rebbe concluded: "I'm happy too."

This began a unique relationship that continued for 13 years, until Tuvia's untimely death from cancer. Throughout that time, the Rebbe would frequently call Tuvia to *yechidus,* affording him the opportunity several times a year. (Ordinarily, a *yeshivah* student would have *yechidus* only once a year, on — or near — his birthday.) The Rebbe would also give Tuvia presents of the new Torah texts printed by *Kehot,* the Lubavitch publishing house.

Once, after the Rebbe had given him the newly printed collection of discourses from the year 5666 entitled *Yom Tov Shel Rosh HaShanah,* Tuvia said he did not think himself worthy of such a gift. The text was reputed to be very difficult, and Tuvia did not think he could understand it.

The Rebbe told Tuvia that if he studied only the first page and learned it well, that would be enough to prove him worthy of the present.

Tuvia was not a gifted student. If anything, his abilities were less than ordinary, but he possessed simple faith and great trust. His sincerity was inspiring. The Rebbe took a special interest in his development, offering him encouragement and help.

Once Tuvia came to *yechidus* unhappy. He wanted to advance spiritually, he told the Rebbe, but was not being given the opportunity. His teachers and fellow students considered him too simple to make real progress, and so they gave up on him before he could achieve anything.

The Rebbe reassured him. "Find study partners," he told Tuvia, "and find a *mashpia* (spiritual mentor), and tell me who they are. I'll make sure they give you the help you need."

Indeed, throughout the years, the Rebbe paid special attention to the teachers and students who worked with Tuvia, granting them distinctive blessings.

When Tuvia was 16, he wanted to go to *Eretz Yisrael* to study. Unfortunately, none of the *yeshivos* would accept him. They felt that the difficulties any student feels acclimating to a new environment, Tuvia's modest abilities, and his unfamiliarity with Hebrew would not make it a productive experience.

Tuvia took all the letters of rejection and showed them to the Rebbe at *yechidus.* He told him of his desire to study in *Eretz Yisrael*, and his difficulty at being accepted.

The Rebbe read each letter, commenting each time: "This letter; it's not a problem," and when he completed them, told Tuvia: "Go to *Eretz Yisrael.* You will succeed in your studies there. *Eretz Yisrael* needs a boy like you."

After receiving these blessings, Tuvia was able to prevail on the Lubavitcher *yeshivah* in Kfar Chabad to accept him. The Rebbe made frequent personal inquiries to see how Tuvia was doing, asking for monthly updates on the lad's studies. Tuvia studied in *Eretz Yisrael* for two years, and made significant advances.

After Tuvia returned to America, he wanted to study in the Lubavitcher *yeshivah* in Montreal so that he could be close to his mother; his father had passed away and he felt she needed his help. The *yeshivah*'s administrators, however, felt he should study in New York. "You have a unique relationship with the Rebbe," they told him. "Why not study in the *yeshivah* closest to him?"

Tuvia was not convinced, and took this problem also to the Rebbe. "I too think you should study in Montreal," the Rebbe told him, and so it was.

During the time Tuvia was in Montreal, the Rebbe asked him to keep in contact, requesting that he write at least once a week. And the Rebbe would almost always answer these letters, though not necessarily at length.

Once the Rebbe did not answer a letter, and the following week, Tuvia did not write. Shortly afterwards, he was called to *yechidus*. "Why didn't you write?" the Rebbe asked him.

"Since you didn't answer my previous letter, I thought you were no longer interested," Tuvia replied.

"I was busy," the Rebbe responded, "and I didn't have the opportunity that week. I have many responsibilities. You're a *yeshivah* student; you have more time. Even if I don't have a chance to answer you, you must continue writing."

At one point, the Rebbe asked him: "Do you have a special feeling for a *mitzvah* that I can help you with?"

Tuvia told the Rebbe that he had been looking to purchase *tefillin* prepared according to the views of *Rabbeinu Tam*.[1] He had tried to find a pair that were written and whose compartments were fashioned *behiddur* (with meticulous care, so that the *mitzvah* could be performed in a beautiful and conscientious manner), but had been unsatisfied with the *tefillin* he had been shown.

---

1. There is a difference of opinion between *Rashi* and *Rabbeinu Tam* regarding the order in which the four passages involved should be placed in *tefillin*. The majority of *halachic* authorities follow *Rashi*, and therefore the *tefillin* worn during prayer follow this order. But because a substantial number of authorities advocate following the order suggested by *Rabbeinu Tam*, all G-d-fearing men should wear them also. They are customarily put on after the conclusion of the morning prayers. See *Shulchan Aruch HaRav*, ch. 34.

"I will help you," promised the Rebbe. "I'll find *tefillin* that are written and prepared with the proper care."

"I'm glad you will help me find such a pair," answered Tuvia, "but I want to pay for them myself."

"How can you afford to pay for them?" replied the Rebbe. "You're a *yeshivah* student; you have no income."

But Tuvia was adamant. He would let the Rebbe find the *tefillin* for him, but he wanted to pay for them. The Rebbe contacted Rabbi Aronow, a veteran Lubavitch scribe from Toronto, and gave him precise instructions with regard to how the *tefillin* should be written, and the compartments fashioned. Rabbi Aronow communicated the instructions regarding the compartments to Rabbi Shneur Zalman Gafni in Israel, for it was more likely that the Rebbe's specifications would be met there.

Thus began a four-year effort. The specifications set by the Rebbe were so difficult that the professionals chosen by Rabbi Aronow wanted to give up. They did not see how it was possible to make *tefillin* that met such standards. Over 30 pairs were submitted for the Rebbe's examination, but he rejected them all. "The specifications are too difficult for anyone to meet," Rabbi Aronow told the Rebbe.

"These *tefillin* are for a unique individual," the Rebbe answered. "All the particulars should be adhered to."

When, after four years, an acceptable pair was finally completed, the Rebbe called Tuvia to *yechidus.* He was extremely happy to give him the *tefillin,* and Tuvia was happy to receive them. "But I want to pay for them," Tuvia insisted. "How much do they cost?"

"Ninety dollars," the Rebbe answered.[2]

Shortly afterwards, Tuvia came to the Rebbe with a problem. He wanted to receive *semichah* (rabbinic ordination). At

---

2. At that time, the price of carefully prepared *tefillin* (without any of the unique specifications required by the Rebbe) was approximately $400 a pair.

that time, the Rabbis of the Lubavitcher *yeshivah* would convey this status on a student when he had demonstrated proficiency in the details of the *kashrus* laws. Tuvia knew those laws well, but because his knowledge of *Talmud* as a whole was lacking, the Rabbis did not want to grant him *semichah*.

"So I will test you," said the Rebbe, and he proceeded to ask Tuvia 10 questions with regard to the laws of *kashrus*.

"You know the laws well," concluded the Rebbe. "I am giving you *semichah*."

"Would the Rebbe give it to me in writing?" Tuvia asked.

"Why have it in writing?" the Rebbe replied. "This way, your study is *lishmah*, for the sake of the *mitzvah* itself."

"Studying *lishmah* is very nice," Tuvia answered, "but having it in writing would be even better."

This was one time when Tuvia did not prevail. The Rebbe did not give him a written *semichah*.

Then Tuvia asked the Rebbe if he could help him find *Rashi tefillin* that met all the specifications required for his *Rabbeinu Tam tefillin*. The Rebbe agreed, but told Tuvia that it would take some time. In the interim, he showed Tuvia how to correct the *Rashi tefillin* which he already had.

At one point, the Rebbe told him that he had found a pair of *Rashi tefillin*. "Are they the very best in the world?" Tuvia asked.

"Are you sure you want to wait for the very best?" the Rebbe asked, and looked sad when Tuvia answered affirmatively.

Shortly afterwards, the reason for the sorrow became evident: the cancer that was to claim Tuvia's life began spreading throughout his body. He did not live long enough to have "the best *tefillin* in the world" prepared.

He passed away in Montreal, and there was a question as to whether he should be buried there or in the Lubavitch cemetery in New York, near the Previous Rebbe's grave. Between 3 and 4 a.m., Tuvia's brother Avraham received a call from the Rebbe's office. The Rebbe had advised that Tuvia be buried in New York.

On the following day, the Rebbe went to pray at the Previous Rebbe's graveside, so he was only several yards away from Tuvia's funeral, and at night he held a surprise *farbrengen.*

Perhaps this was the Rebbe's way of saying farewell to this unique *neshamah* in whose development he had shared.

Chapter 2 —
No Small Matter

One of the chassidim of the Maggid of Mezritch approached him with a problem. He had invested a large amount of money in merchandise and had dispatched it with an agent for sale in a distant city. Several months had passed without word from him. He had inquired at the city to which he had originally directed the man, but there was no sign of either him or the merchandise. What should he do? If the merchandise was lost, he would face financial ruin.

The Maggid put on his reading glasses, looked into a volume of the *Zohar* lying on his table for a few moments, and then instructed his chassid to travel to Leipzig. There he would find his agent and his merchandise intact.

The chassid journeyed to Leipzig, met the wayward agent, retrieved his merchandise, and sold it for a profit.

Why was it necessary for the Maggid to look into the *Zohar?* If he had an answer for the chassid, why didn't he give it to him immediately?

Chassidim explain as follows: The light which G-d created on the first day of creation enables a person to see from one end of the world to the other.

Nevertheless, G-d saw that it was not appropriate for this light to shine in an unperfected world, and He therefore concealed it. Where did He conceal it? In the Torah.[1]

By studying the Torah, and particularly the Torah's mystic dimensions, where its spiritual light is revealed, the Maggid was able to gain access to this transcendent light. Having done so, he was able to advise the chassid with regard to his merchandise.

Why did the Maggid employ such a lofty spiritual tool merely to locate merchandise?

Because a Jew's financial resources are connected with his spiritual mission in this world. Everything in the world contains sparks of G-dliness which are concealed by the material substance of the world. Mankind has been given the task of refining the material and revealing this innate G-dliness. Every individual is destined to elevate certain sparks. If these G-dly energies are not elevated, that individual's soul remains incomplete.

The Baal Shem Tov expounded this concept in his interpretation[2] of the verse,[3] "Hungry and also thirsty, their soul longs within them." The Baal Shem Tov asked, "Why are they hungry and thirsty? — Because 'their soul longs within them.' Their souls seek a bond with the G-dly energy contained in the food and drink."

We may be unaware of the spiritual motivation underlying our physical desires and find all sorts of reasons to describe what we want and why we want it. In truth, however, a deeper force motivates our will. Why does a Jew want possessions and material success? — Because his soul has an unarticulated

---

1. *Chagigah* 12a.
2. *Kesser Shem Tov,* sec. 194, p. 25c; see also *Likkutei Sichos,* Vol, I, p. 177; Vol. XIX, p. 182ff.
3. *Tehillim* 107:5.

desire to fulfill the G-dly purpose associated with these seemingly material blessings.

These concepts enable us to explain a problematic passage in *Tanya*,[4] in which the Alter Rebbe issues "an open rebuke, [motivated] by concealed love," reproving his followers for coming to him:

> To ask for advice about worldly concerns, what to do with regard to matters of this material world. [Such counsel was never asked even] of the great Sages of Israel of bygone years... for whom no secret was hidden[5]...

The Alter Rebbe then proceeds to explain the reason why his followers would seek him out regarding such matters: "Love upsets the natural order of conduct."[6] The self-love of the chassidim and their concern for their own material welfare would cloud their vision.

Commenting on this passage, the Rebbe raises an obvious question: Despite the Alter Rebbe's statements, we find that chassidim would ask the Alter Rebbe himself, and similarly, the subsequent Rebbeim, about such matters. And the Rebbeim would not withhold answers. Indeed,[7] at times the Rebbeim would solicit such advice.

Why would the Rebbeim disregard the advice given by the Alter Rebbe?

For the reason, the Alter Rebbe himself gave. Because "Love upsets the natural order of conduct." Out of their great love for the chassidim and their concern for their material and spiritual welfare, the Rebbeim were willing to go beyond their natural

---

4. *Iggeres HaKodesh*, Epistle 22.
5. Par. *Daniel* 4:6; see *Chulin* 59a.
6. *Bereishis Rabbah* 55:8.
7. See the introduction to Ch. 9.

order of conduct and advise their chassidim concerning material affairs.

"Why did I come here?" he kept asking himself. "Here I am, wasting the time of one of the spiritual giants of our generation! I have presented him with an intricate business problem with which he has no way of helping. What's more, I have spent a great deal to come, and most importantly, I've delayed taking the steps needed to solve my problem."

What motivated these thoughts?

In 5727 (1967), a traditional Jew began drawing close to Lubavitch in his local community. As he became more involved, he realized that Lubavitch was more than a local movement. He traveled to *Eretz Yisrael,* and was impressed with the network of educational facilities Lubavitch had established there. He then began to study the Rebbe's thoughts, and was further impressed by his wisdom.

Now, he was a wealthy man and a generous donor to Jewish causes. Suddenly, in the midst of coming close to Lubavitch, he suffered a major financial setback. His business was threatened by bankruptcy and government investigation. When the local Lubavitch representative learned of his difficulties, he advised him to speak to the Rebbe.

"Like a drowning man clutching at a straw," he thought, he had latched onto the idea.

When his local *shliach* had called Rabbi Chodakov, the Rebbe's personal secretary, to arrange *yechidus,* Rabbi Chodakov had explained that the waiting list was full for the next few months. When the *shliach* explained that the issue was urgent, Rabbi Chodakov replied that the list for *yechidus* on the coming Sunday was not that long. "If the man would come and wait until *yechidus* is over," he continued, "I will probably be able to squeeze him in before the Rebbe goes home."

And so the man traveled to New York with one purpose in mind — to see the Rebbe. During the trip, and while waiting to see the Rebbe, he had plenty of time to prepare himself. Most of the time was spent composing a 16-page letter which explained his business difficulties in great detail. When he entered the Rebbe's room, he gave the Rebbe that letter.

The Rebbe looked at him and asked if he could describe the problem in his own words.

He answered that he could, but that it would not do justice to the issue; in the letter, he had explained every aspect clearly. So the Rebbe began to read. Surprisingly, each page took him about three minutes.

It was then, with the only sound being the ticking of the clock, that the man began having the thoughts mentioned at the outset. "For after all," he thought, "the Rebbe is reading without a single pause. He hasn't asked one question. There is no way he can fully comprehend the matter with such a reading. He's just reading to be polite. I should never have come here."

While he was having such thoughts, the Rebbe continued reading with absolute concentration. After slightly less than an hour had passed, he completed the letter and then spoke to his visitor.

First, the Rebbe asked him if he knew the meaning of *bitachon* (usually translated as "trust in G-d"). The visitor answered that he did not, so the Rebbe told him: "*Bitachon* means feeling as confident and happy in the midst of one's problems as one would feel if they had already been solved."

Then the Rebbe told him not to reduce any of his regular donations to charity. For example, if he had always given a *chai* (Hebrew for 18) when he received an *aliyah,* he should continue to do so despite the difficulties he was experiencing.

And then the Rebbe advised him to check his *tefillin.*

When he heard that, the visitor protested: "I just bought a new pair in Kfar Chabad! They were the most expensive available, and supposedly of the highest quality. Must I still check them?"

"Have them checked anyway," the Rebbe responded.

The Rebbe then proceeded to his visitor's business difficulties. He asked him three questions: two rhetorical and one

No Small Matter 43

requiring a piece of information. From these questions, the man realized that the Rebbe had comprehended the matter in its entirety.

The Rebbe then proceeded to give the visitor several sentences of measured advice. The visitor recorded them mentally, sensing that this would be the most accurate appraisal of his situation that he would ever receive.

On the following day, he took his *tefillin* to the aged scribe, Reb Yeshayah Matlin, to have them checked. After a few hours, Reb Yeshayah called and explained that these were perhaps the most perfect pair of *tefillin* he had ever seen. Everything — the calligraphy, the compartments, the straps — was of the highest quality. There was, however, one difficulty; the passages had not been inserted in the proper order, and so the *tefillin* had been defective. Reb Yeshayah had corrected the problem, and now they were acceptable.

The man returned home and hired a team of lawyers to help him overcome his difficulties. To describe the situation to them, he used a copy of the letter he had given the Rebbe. The lawyers' reading took much longer, and was continually punctuated by questions. In the end, he felt their analysis was far less clear than the Rebbe's, so he shared the Rebbe's advice with them and used it to steer a path through his problems.

After two years, he was able to extricate himself from his difficulties and return to his former affluence.

For many years, Reb Avraham Parshan owned a farm on the outskirts of Toronto, in partnership with a real-estate broker. One day, the broker approached Reb Avraham with an offer to purchase his part of the property.

In general, Reb Avraham would not consult the Rebbe about business deals which he considered to be of minor importance. On this occasion, however, he did, and the Rebbe advised him not to sell.

A month later, the broker came with a higher offer. Again, the Rebbe told him not to accept, but instead to suggest a price that could truly be considered astronomical. Furthermore, the Rebbe advised Reb Avraham to say that this offer would stand only until Rosh HaShanah.

On *Erev Rosh HaShanah,* Reb Avraham went out to buy knives, as is customary in certain communities, in keeping with the phrase from the Rosh HaShanah prayers: "He who apportions (lit. 'cuts') life for all the living." When he returned, the agent came in to "cut" a deal; the buyer had accepted the price. It turned out that the buyer was Bramlea, a large British development company, and the property was necessary for one of their projects.

On another occasion, Reb Avraham had a plot of land in North York which he was considering selling. As a general rule, the Rebbe had advised him not to sell land in the same condition he bought it, but instead to develop or improve the property in some way, so it could be sold for a higher sum. In this instance, however, Reb Avraham was pressed for cash and was thinking of selling the property as it stood.

At *yechidus,* without mentioning his financial straits, Reb Avraham asked the Rebbe if he should sell. The Rebbe told him not to.

After *yechidus,* Rabbi Klein, one of the Rebbe's secretaries, told Reb Avraham that Rabbi Chodakov, the Rebbe's personal secretary, would like to see him. Rabbi Chodakov told Reb Avraham that the Rebbe had told him that if a person is thinking of selling property, he probably needs money. With that, he told Reb Avraham that as head of *Machne Israel* (one of the charitable organizations directed by the Rebbe), he had been instructed to offer Reb Avraham an interest-free loan of $50,000 for six months.

On another occasion, Reb Avraham was considering investing a large sum in real estate in *Eretz Yisrael.* At that time, there was a well-known contractor for whom people in the religious community would wait in line to invest. Reb Avraham met with him, and worked out what appeared to be an attractive deal, but with one contingency: the Rebbe would have to approve of the transaction.

The Rebbe answered that he favored another option, and advised Reb Avraham to meet with Reb Ephraim Wolf, director of the Lubavitcher *yeshivah* in *Eretz Yisrael*. Reb Ephraim had just received a parcel of land from the Israeli government near the *yeshivah* in Lod, and was contemplating the construction of a Lubavitch community. Reb Avraham was willing to invest and the community was started.

Ultimately, all the apartments were sold, and so in addition to the merit of constructing a Lubavitch community, Reb Avraham was able to make a tidy profit.

The other contractor, meanwhile, went bankrupt, and all those who had invested with him lost their money.

Chapter 3 —
A Shepherd of Souls

R. Menachem Mendel of Vitebsk was raised by the Maggid of Mezritch. When he was a boy of about 12, the Maggid took him to his Rebbe, the Baal Shem Tov for the first time. On Friday night, the Baal Shem Tov delayed his prayers until the boy reached his *shul,* but other than that showed him no attention throughout the *Shabbos.* On *Motzaei Shabbos,* the Maggid presented the youth to the Baal Shem Tov.

The Baal Shem Tov began telling a long parable involving the journeys of a young man. R. Menachem Mendel, the Maggid, and the other disciples of the Baal Shem Tov (including R. Yaakov Yosef of Polonnoye, author of *Toldos Yaakov Yosef)* listened attentively, sensing that the tale contained a message of significant import.

Years passed. Both the Baal Shem Tov and the Maggid passed away, and R. Menachem Mendel assumed the leadership of the chassidic movement in White Russia. In 1777, he led a group of chassidim on *aliyah* to *Eretz Yisrael.* Before he left for the Holy Land, he went to visit R. Yaakov Yosef in Polonnoye.

"Do you remember the parable the Baal Shem Tov told you?" R. Yaakov Yosef asked.

47

"Yes," replied R. Menachem Mendel. "That is why I'm here. For implicit in the allusions of the parable was that on my way to *Eretz Yisrael* I would visit you."

R. Menachem Mendel would later say that at each phase in his life, he was able to understand the insinuations the parable had for him.

The implication is that each of our lives is a story, a Divinely inspired mission which we are destined to fulfill. Another implication is that the souls of certain individuals like the Baal Shem Tov are cognizant of the missions of others, and able to guide them in accomplishing their purpose.

Reb Yoel Kahan has always been known for his unique teaching skills. Even while still a *yeshivah* student, he demonstrated an outstanding ability to explain chassidic concepts. For this reason, he was chosen to deliver a series of underground *shiurim* on the *Tanya* in the Lakewood *yeshivah*.

Why underground? Well, Lakewood is one of the foremost *yeshivos* in the country, but it favors the Lithuanian approach to Torah study. Needless to say, *Chassidus* is not on the curriculum, and the entire mystic dimension of Jewish knowledge is not emphasized. While the administration knew of Reb Yoel's weekly *shiur*, it wanted no official association with it.

Reb Yoel's teaching skills soon attracted a following. There were many students who enjoyed the ideas of *Chassidus*. Others felt intimidated by the thought of attending the *shiur*, but would speak to Reb Yoel before or afterwards.

Among the latter was one of the *yeshivah*'s more advanced students, a brilliant young man who would often ask Reb Yoel questions regarding *Talmudic* passages. Although Reb Yoel tried to convince him to attend the *shiur*, he refused.

The students who *did* attend told Reb Yoel that this student was well respected, and that his presence would greatly enhance the other students' respect for the *shiur*, and so Reb Yoel persevered. But there was no way he could change the student's mind.

One day the student asked Reb Yoel if an audience with the Rebbe could be arranged for him. Reb Yoel agreed; he was certain that after *yechidus*, the student would be willing to study *Chassidus*.

The student wanted to see the Rebbe urgently, but appointments for *yechidus* had been arranged months in advance. Nevertheless, Reb Yoel prevailed upon Rabbi Chodakov, the Rebbe's personal secretary, to allot one minute of the Rebbe's time at midnight the following Monday.

When Reb Yoel told the student that he had been able to arrange *yechidus*, but only for a minute, the student replied that a minute would be sufficient.

Shortly before midnight that Sunday, he arrived to see the Rebbe. Reb Yoel was waiting for him, and advised him of the procedure for *yechidus.* Shortly afterwards, he entered *yechidus.*

The minute passed... and so did five minutes... ten minutes....

Rabbi Groner, the Rebbe's secretary, entered the room several times to see if perhaps the student was taking the Rebbe's time unnecessarily, but each time the Rebbe motioned to him not to interfere.

After an hour, the student emerged, still deep in thought. Despite Reb Yoel's request for an explanation of what had transpired, the student offered a polite but brief good-bye and headed back to Lakewood.

In the subsequent weeks, Reb Yoel tried to engage him in conversation, but he was avoided, or would receive only terse replies. Understanding that for some reason the student no longer desired his company, Reb Yoel turned his attention elsewhere. Ultimately, he lost touch with him entirely.

Years passed.

One day, while Reb Yoel was walking down the street, he heard a car beeping and someone calling his name. He looked around, but saw no one he recognized. A driver was obviously trying to get his attention, but Reb Yoel could not understand why. And how did the driver know his name?

The stranger had long curly hair, and if he was wearing a *yarmulke,* it wasn't obvious. How did he know Reb Yoel? And what did he want from him?

Reb Yoel approached out of courtesy.

"Do you remember me, Reb Yoel?" the driver asked.

"No," confessed Reb Yoel.

"From Lakewood ... years ago. My name is .... We used to talk. You arranged for me to come to the Rebbe."

Reb Yoel remembered.

"Can we arrange a time to study *Chassidus?*" the driver asked. Reb Yoel agreed.

And so they studied once a week for several months. Reb Yoel hesitated to pry into his student's private life, and the man did not volunteer information. Their time together focused strictly on the ideas of *Chassidus* and their application in our Divine service.

After Reb Yoel saw that his student was becoming absorbed in the learning, he felt it appropriate to speak a little more personally.

"There's something that's been puzzling me," Reb Yoel told him. "I'm not asking you about what happened between Lakewood and the present time, but I am still curious about that *yechidus* years back. What happened? And why didn't you want to speak to me afterwards?"

The student explained that he had discovered a difficulty with a particular *Talmudic* passage, and that no one in Lakewood had been able to resolve the question. He had heard that the Rebbe was a Torah genius, and hoped that the Rebbe would be able to help him.

"That's why," he said, "I was happy with a minute of the Rebbe's time. I figured that if he could resolve the difficulty, it would be possible in a minute, and if not, then anything longer would be a waste of time.

"It didn't even take the Rebbe a minute to resolve the question," he continued. "Within 45 seconds, I was getting ready to leave, perfectly satisfied with the answer I had been given. But the Rebbe called me by name.

"'...,' he said, 'Do you study *Chassidus?*'

"I explained that I did not. Not that I had anything against *Chassidus*, but it just wasn't for me. I was doing well in the study of the *Talmud* and its commentaries, and saw no need to change my pattern."

"The Rebbe explained that the study of *Chassidus* is important, for it leads to *Yiras Shamayim*, 'the awe of G-d,' which is necessary to protect one's Torah study. 'Without the study of *Chassidus*,' the Rebbe explained, 'a person can lose sight of the G-dliness of the Torah. And if that happens, his entire pattern of observance can erode.'

"I told the Rebbe that I could appreciate his premise in theory, but was not worried. With G-d's help, I had been successful in my studies. My observance was steadfast. I could see where I was going, and did not understand why I should change path in midstream. And most important, learning any new discipline takes time. Why should I take time away from Torah and invest in a new path?

"The Rebbe continued to press his point, but I remained unmoved. I was doing well and saw no reason to change."

"Then the Rebbe paused, a faraway look in his eye. He said: 'When a *yeshivah* student does not learn *Chassidus*, it might happen that one day he will walk into the study hall and take offense at another student's petty remark. It will disturb him, and he won't be able to concentrate on his studies. In his idle time, he will do such and such [a mild transgression]. That will lead him further, and the next day, he will do such and such [a more severe transgression].'

"The Rebbe continued, describing a chain of ten different transgressions. 'And then,' the Rebbe went on, 'being an honest person, the student will not be able to reconcile his conduct with study at a *yeshivah*, and he will depart. From that point, it will not be long before he loses contact with his Jewish roots entirely.'

"I was aware that I had taken an hour of the Rebbe's time, and didn't see the point of going further. I told the Rebbe I would think about the matter and left.

"That's why I didn't speak to you afterwards. I felt that if I was going to think honestly about the Rebbe's words, I didn't want anyone pressuring me into accepting them.

"After thinking the matter through, I decided to stick with my original position. I was doing well in my studies. Why should I start a different course?

"And so I continued to avoid you. I knew that you would not let me ignore the Rebbe's words, and would bring up the matter continually. I didn't want that. I wanted to get on with my studies."

Reb Yoel had been listening attentively, but didn't know whether to pursue the matter further.

Without prompting, the student continued: "Several months afterwards, I confronted a particularly difficult passage in the *Talmud.* I labored on it for days. Finally, I thought I had a resolution. Satisfied with myself, I went from the library to the study hall. There I saw two other students discussing the same passage. 'I'll try my explanation on them,' I thought.

"I did, and they didn't accept it. One of them even ridiculed my whole approach.

"That was hard for me to accept. I had labored on the subject for days, and not only was my explanation not appreciated, it was rudely dismissed. I left the study hall in a huff.

"Afterwards, I couldn't get my mind back on my studies. Maybe I was tired after having worked so long, or maybe I was still agitated about what the other student had said, but I felt I needed to take the night off. And that night I committed the first of the transgressions the Rebbe had mentioned.

"From that night on, my life wasn't the same. The pattern the Rebbe described unfolded. Each of the ten transgressions he had mentioned occurred, just as he had said they would. And then I left *yeshivah.* And from there ... well, I don't have to go on. You can see my lifestyle."

Reb Yoel didn't know whether to ask him why he had suddenly decided to study *Chassidus*. Sometimes a story has to be given time.

But the student went on. "I had strayed so far from *Yiddishkeit* that although I married a Jewish girl, we didn't raise our children with any knowledge of their heritage. In our house, there was neither *Shabbos* nor *Yom Tov*. We didn't even go to *shul* on Rosh HaShanah or Yom Kippur.

"One day, my son came home from school upset. 'Daddy,' he told me, 'somebody called me a dirty Jew. What's that? Are we Jewish? What does it mean?'

"I was at a loss to answer him. Yes, somewhere in the attic, I still had some volumes of the *Talmud*. I could probably still explain some of the arguments to him. But those were laws about damages and rituals; they wouldn't answer his question.

"I told him that we would find time to talk about the matter, and changed the subject. But it bothered me. Why couldn't I think of something to tell my son about being Jewish?

"The next day, when I went to the newsstand, I saw *The Jewish Press*. I thought maybe I would be able to find something there that I could tell my son.

"While flipping through the pages, I saw an announcement of a *farbrengen* with the Rebbe. Maybe I would find an answer there. I jotted down the address, and noted the date and time. It was late, but I resolved to stop in for at least half an hour.

"I remembered 770 when I entered. I took a place in the back of the room and focused on the Rebbe. Although it had been years, I still understood Yiddish, and was able to follow what he was saying. And I was surprised. He was repeating the same concepts that he had told me at *yechidus*! He was saying how even a person who is proficient in the study of *Talmud* should study *Chassidus*, for *Chassidus* endows a person with the fear of G-d. 'Without the study of *Chassidus*,' the Rebbe explained, 'a person can lose sight of the G-dliness of the

Torah. And if that happens, his entire pattern of observance can be easily eroded.'

"After half an hour, I left. It was late, and I wanted to get home, but I knew I was going to come back. There was something about the Rebbe that attracted me. And I couldn't help but marvel at the coincidence of hearing the same words that I had heard years before.

"I kept buying *The Jewish Press*, waiting to see when there would be another *farbrengen*. When I saw the advertisement, I set aside the date.

"Again I found a place in the crowd of chassidim. I could see the Rebbe, but I doubted he could see me. Again, his message was familiar. 'A student may protest that he is doing well in his study of Talmud. Why then should he begin the study of a new discipline?' And he continued, using the same arguments he had used years before to emphasize the contribution *Chassidus* can make to a person's Divine service.

"I felt that this was more than coincidence. Twice I had come to see the Rebbe, and twice he spoke about the same subject he had spoken about years before, using almost the same words! I felt he was speaking to me personally, but I couldn't understood how he could have picked me out in the crowd, or how he could have recognized me, considering the way I now looked."

"The next time I went to a *farbrengen* was the last night of Pesach. This time there was no microphone, so I had to work my way in among the chassidim to hear. As I reached a place from which the Rebbe's voice was audible, I heard him say: 'When a *yeshivah* student does not learn *Chassidus,* it might happen that one day he will walk into the study hall and take offense at another student's petty remark. This will disturb him and he won't be able to concentrate on his studies. In his idle time, he will do such and such. That will lead him further and the next day, he will do such and such.' The Rebbe went on, mentioning the same ten sins he had mentioned then.

"I felt that it was far more than coincidence. But I still was not sure. How could the Rebbe have seen me? And why would he speak directly to me among so many people?

"I made up my mind to wait until the *farbrengen* was over and join the line to receive *kos shel berachah* from the Rebbe. I resolved that if I could detect any sign of recognition in his face, I would start studying *Chassidus*.

"As I came before the Rebbe, his face broke out in a wide smile. '...,' he called me by name, 'Maybe the time has come for you to begin studying *Chassidus?*'

"That's why," he said, looking Reb Yoel in the face, "I sought you out."

※

In the 1960s, Reb Avraham Parshan was able to influence two girls to become observant and visit the Rebbe. One of the girls came from a traditional family, and her parents were less than enthusiastic about her attraction to Lubavitch. On many occasions, they caused Reb Avraham considerable discomfort.

Reb Avraham mentioned the matter to the Rebbe. The Rebbe replied: "It is not only two girls whom you brought closer. It's two chains that will go on for generations."

Both girls married chassidic husbands and raised observant families.

※

After several years of studying at the *Tiferes Bachurim* program of the Rabbinical College of America, Yoel Zimmerman married and began to raise a family. He spent a year studying in *kollel* (a program for married students), and afterwards began to plan his future. Personable, intelligent and energetic, with knowledge of the American culture and a talent for communicating Torah to people, Yoel seemed a natural for

Lubavitch outreach activities. And indeed, he received attractive employment offers from several *Chabad* Houses.

He soon narrowed his choices to three: one in California (where he had begun his *teshuvah*), one in Cleveland (where he had worked for a summer in outreach activities for youth), and a third in Buffalo, New York. He favored the California option, but wanted to consult the Rebbe before making a decision.

While Yoel was preparing his letter to the Rebbe, he remembered that before leaving California to study in Morristown, his father had asked him to go into the family business, and he had told him that he would consider the matter.

Now the idea of becoming a businessman was foreign to Yoel, and yet, as a gesture of respect to his father, he also included that option in the letter, telling the Rebbe that he did not think he had business acumen, and was worried that working with his father might strain their relationship.

When Yoel received the Rebbe's answer, he was startled. The Rebbe had circled the words "enter the family business," indicating it was the right choice, and had added a proviso: "If the business will provide a sufficient livelihood, and if its operation will allow for the observance of *Shabbos* and the festivals in a desirable manner."

The Zimmerman business was open only from Monday to Friday, so there was no problem with *Shabbos*. The observance of the festivals, however, presented a problem. Yoel wanted the business closed entirely, but his father argued that the loss would be too great. The older man asked the Rebbe what they should do.

The Rebbe answered that the son should be flexible, and that the Zimmermans should seek Rabbinic guidance in composing a *shtar mechirah* — a formal contract selling the business to a gentile for the holidays — so they would not be the official owners on those days.

Yoel began to appreciate the path the Rebbe was charting for him. He settled in Chicago, becoming one of the pillars of the growing Lubavitch community there. Over the years, his business acumen proved itself, and his relationship with his father didn't suffer.

Nor have his business activities kept him from involvement in Jewish outreach. His efforts and support are indispensable elements in the success of the Lubavitch *cheder* in that city. One of the *shluchim* said of him: "We don't consider him merely one of our supporters; he is an indispensable member of our team!"

~

In 1953, a student left his Orthodox home in Chicago to study in the Telshe *Yeshivah* in Cleveland. Although New York is not on the route from Chicago to Cleveland, he stopped over to visit relatives and receive the blessings of several Torah giants living there. His family were by no means Lubavitchers, but had established a connection with the Previous Rebbe during the latter's visit to Chicago in 1942. And so the prospective student also went to receive a blessing from the Rebbe before undertaking this new phase of life.

At *yechidus,* the Rebbe gave him warm blessings and told him: "In Cleveland lives Rabbi Zalmen Katzenellenbogen (Kazen). He can help you with regard to the study of both Torah law and *Pnimiyus HaTorah,* the Torah's spirit and soul. You would profit from studying with him."

The student promised to look up Rabbi Katzenellenbogen in Cleveland, and the *yechidus* ended.

As soon as he arrived in Cleveland, the student went to the post office to send a telegram to his parents, notifying them of his safe arrival. While he was waiting in line, a distinguished looking Jew with a beard and broad smile entered the post office. The young man had never met Rabbi Katzenellenbogen, nor seen a picture of him, but without thinking twice, he walked up and greeted him: "*Shalom Aleichem*, Reb Zalmen! The Rebbe advised me to study with you."

The Rabbi and his family had just settled in Cleveland, and he was somewhat startled at being greeted by an unknown youth. Nonetheless, he listened closely to the student's description of his *yechidus,* and the two established a relationship that continued throughout the student's stay in Cleveland.

~

As a youth, Jonathan Sacks received a grant one summer from the Hillel Foundation in London to observe the activity of outlying Jewish communities in North America. In the process of his research, he met many representatives of Lubavitch, stayed at several *Chabad* Houses and observed their activities. While visiting London, Ontario, he met Prof. Yitzchak Block and was deeply impressed.

Prof. Block convinced Jonathan to spend a week studying at *Yeshivas Hadar HaTorah* in Crown Heights at the end of the summer. During that week, Jonathan had the opportunity to attend a *farbrengen* with the Rebbe. He was taken by the Rebbe, and in the middle of the *farbrengen* thanked him for the hospitality he had received from Lubavitch representatives during his travels. In response, the Rebbe asked Jonathan to stay in Crown Heights for Rosh HaShanah.

At first, Jonathan was not sure whether to accept the invitation. He had a full scholarship to Cambridge, and was due back there. After many discussions with chassidim, however, he decided to stay.

The highlight of Rosh HaShanah with the Rebbe was *tekios*. No one who witnessed the Rebbe sounding the *shofar* will ever forget the sight.

Now, as awesome as *tekios* were, there was also an awesome striving to see the Rebbe. Young *bachurim* and elder chassidim would press to draw close to the Rebbe and watch him as he sounded the *shofar*. Occasionally people would even faint from the crush.

Jonathan had never experienced anything like this. But with many polite requests, and much firm resolve and youthful energy, he managed to secure a place from which he could see the Rebbe.

What he saw left a profound impression on him, inspiring him to deepen his commitment to Jewish studies and maintain his connection to the Rebbe.

Years afterwards, when he became Dean of Jews College and later Chief Rabbi of England, he would point to that Rosh HaShanah as a turning point in his life. He would say: "The Rebbe took a young man with questions and made him into a Chief Rabbi."

Although raised in a secular home, Sarah had been a Lubavitcher for many years. In the summer of 1985, she was planning to visit Israel and organize Shabbatons for Americans living there. Before leaving, she wrote to ask the Rebbe for a blessing for success in her outreach activities, and also in finding a *shidduch*. The Rebbe answered with a blessing and gave her two bills to give to charity. Without examining the bills, she folded them and put them in her purse.

On her way to Israel, Sarah stopped off in London to visit relatives. There she unfolded the bills the Rebbe had given her. The top bill was an Israeli ten *shekel* note, but the second was an English pound!

Sarah had not told the Rebbe anything about a trip to England. And indeed, the stopover proved providential, for it was there that she was introduced to her future husband.

A Shepherd of Souls

He was an exceptional student, showing prodigious energy and aptitude. All the teachers at the *yeshivah* foretold great things for him.

But his energies were not controlled. True, he could study for hours without rest, but he could also party the night away without rest!

His teachers never suspected there was anything amiss. They could not fathom how anyone who could apply himself to the *Talmud* and its commentaries so diligently could have anything but Torah study on his mind.

How wrong they were! After the *yeshivah* day was over, he would go to night spots and participate in activity that was most unbefitting for a *yeshivah* student.

This schizophrenic existence might have continued endlessly, except that the young man became infatuated with a woman. A short while after they met, they were standing together outside the Civil Court — married!

The young man knew his parents would never consent to such a match. They were from a traditional family, and would want him to marry a girl from a similar background, perhaps the daughter of a Rabbi. A woman off the street?! That would break their hearts.

Rather than tell his parents the truth, the young man devised a plan. He would explain to his father that he needed to earn money, and was leaving *yeshivah* for a year to work. During that time, he could remain married, and over the course of the year he would find a way to communicate the news to his parents in a way that would hurt them least.

So he called his father and told him that he had been in an auto accident. Thank G-d, he had escaped without injury, but he had destroyed a car belonging to a friend. Unfortunately, the car had not been insured. He could not, he told his father, bear to cause his friend such a loss. Nor would he be willing to accept the money from his parents, for he knew they were not wealthy. There were other children in the family, and soon there would be weddings and other expenses to think of.

Hard as it was, he continued, he would have to make a sacrifice. He would leave *yeshivah* for a year and work to repay the debt.

His father wouldn't hear of it. Yes, the debt would have to be paid, but somehow the older man would find a way. His son was a promising *yeshivah* student, and he wanted nothing more than for him to live up to his potential. He would not consent to his leaving *yeshivah*.

At this point, the son had another idea. His father was nurturing a growing respect for the Lubavitcher Rebbe. The young man reasoned that the Rebbe, though a traditional religious leader, was also a modern man. After all, he had attended university, hadn't he? He was, the young man thought, the type of Rabbi who might agree to his scheme. And so the son suggested that the question be put to the Rebbe. If the Rebbe told him to remain in *yeshivah,* he would. But if the Rebbe consented to his getting a job, his father would have to accept that decision.

The father was willing to have the Rebbe decide, and dispatched the young man, together with an older brother, to 770. Apparently, the two thought they would be able to arrange *yechidus.* When this proved impossible, the young man wrote a letter to the Rebbe instead, repeating the tall tale he had told his father, and asking whether he should remain in *yeshivah* or go to work.

Shortly after submitting his letter, he returned to see if there was an answer. As was his custom, the Rebbe had written a reply at the bottom of the letter.

The answer surprised the young man. The Rebbe had ignored the two suggested alternatives, and instead wrote briefly: "Go home."

Now this was the furthest thing from the young man's mind. He quickly surveyed the situation. No one else had seen the Rebbe's answer; perhaps even the secretary had not noticed what the Rebbe had written. The practice in 770 was not to take the note with the Rebbe's handwriting, but to copy the answer down on another piece of paper.

So the young man wrote that the Rebbe had told him to go to work!

His brother was waiting for him outside 770. He listened to the answer his brother had purportedly received, and the two turned to depart. Suddenly, the brother remembered that he had several acquaintances studying in 770. "Wait a moment," he told his brother, "I just want to say hello."

When the brother entered 770, he was met by Rabbi Chodakov, the Rebbe's personal secretary. "The Rebbe sent me to look for you," he told the brother. "He would like to see you after the evening prayers."

Not knowing what to expect, the older brother waited outside the Rebbe's room that evening. The Rebbe was direct and to the point: "Take your brother home; be careful not to let him out of your sight."

"Wait! Didn't the Rebbe tell my brother to go work?" the brother asked.

"Whatever was answered before is not important," the Rebbe replied diplomatically. "Now take your brother home."

When the older brother conveyed the Rebbe's message to his brother, the young man was shaken. For the first time in weeks, he came face to face with reality, and it wasn't a pleasant experience. He looked at his spiritual state, and began to appreciate how low he had fallen. And to make matters worse, he had *formalized* the descent; according to the law of the land, he was married!

He understood now who the Rebbe was, and that he had seen through his facade. And he appreciated the fact that the Rebbe hadn't criticized him, but allowed him to come to this realization himself. He knew that he desperately needed advice and direction.

Asking his brother to wait, he wrote another letter to the Rebbe. This time, he told the truth. With tears of remorse, he told the Rebbe everything and asked what he should do.

The Rebbe told him to go home and tell his father his entire story. Yes, it would be painful, but the reward he would receive would outweigh the pain. Afterwards, the father should contact the Rebbe, and the Rebbe would advise him with regard to finding a lawyer to annul the marriage.

The remorseful young man followed the Rebbe's advice. Through ongoing contact with the Rebbe, he was able to find a way to reverse his conduct, and grew to become a G-d-fearing Torah scholar.

Rabbi Yosef Wineberg served as a *shliach* for the Previous Rebbe and continues to serve in that capacity for the Rebbe. The Rebbe told him on several occasions: "Your mission is to sow spirituality, and to reap material returns." For although Rabbi Wineberg raises funds for the Lubavitcher *Yeshivah*, he never saw his mission as merely collecting money. Instead, his intent is to spread Judaism and *Chassidus*, to connect Jews to their heritage and give them practical means to express that connection. Far before Jewish observance had become common in the outer reaches of our people's far-flung diaspora, Rabbi Wineberg undertook missions to South Africa, Brazil, and other countries, reaching out to Jews and inspiring identity and observance.

In the early years of the Rebbe's *nesius*, Rabbi Wineberg went for *yechidus* before traveling to South Africa on behalf of the Lubavitcher *Yeshivah*. At the *yechidus*, the Rebbe asked him: "Do you stop in any other countries on your way to South Africa?"

Rabbi Wineberg told him that the plane made occasional stops for refueling, but these were for brief intervals. To this the Rebbe replied: "Do you not stay in any place for a day or two?"

Rabbi Wineberg answered him that this was not the plan. Toward the end of the *yechidus,* the Rebbe again asked Rabbi Wineberg if he was planning to stop in any other countries on the way.

Rabbi Wineberg had been working with the Rebbe long enough to appreciate that this was not ordinary curiosity. When he came home, he told his wife that although he was scheduled to arrive in South Africa on Wednesday, she should not be disappointed if a telegram does not arrive before *Shabbos,* for from the Rebbe's words, it appeared that he would be delayed for a day or two and would not necessarily have the opportunity of communicating before *Shabbos* began.

As Rabbi Wineberg prepared to board the plane, he noticed that one of his acquaintances, Rabbi Lenger of Ganeles-Lenger wines, was also planning to board the flight. They both appreciated the advantage of having another *heimishe* person for company on the long journey.

One of the refueling stops for the journey to South Africa was Dakar, a small country on the West African coast. As they were preparing to deplane there, the crew announced that the stay would be prolonged slightly because they were experiencing certain technical difficulties.

They deplaned at 10 PM. As Rabbi Wineberg was sitting in the lobby, he noticed a young man looking at him intently. When Rabbi Wineberg took off his hat and revealed a *yarmulka,* the man approached him and introduced himself as Mr. Pinto, a Sephardic Jew from Egypt. He had been in Dakar for six months and hadn't seen a Jewish face. He missed the Jewish involvement which he had experienced at home, and he was worried about the effect living in such a Jewish wasteland would have on his children.

Rabbi Wineberg explained to him that he could maintain a stronger sense of Jewish identity by intensifying his Jewish observance. "Do you have *tefillin* here?" Rabbi Wineberg asked him.

"Yes," Mr. Pinto answered. He did have *tefillin,* but unfortunately, he had fallen out of the habit of putting them on each day.

"When your children see you putting on *tefillin* daily," Rabbi Wineberg told him, "the concept of being Jewish will mean much more to them. They will have a tangible example of what being Jewish means."

Mr. Pinto promised to put on tefillin daily. He and Rabbi Wineberg talked for a few more minutes, and then Rabbi Wineberg was called back to his plane. Rabbi Wineberg felt that perhaps his conversation with Mr. Pinto was the reason for the delay and with that he would have fulfilled whatever intent the Rebbe had in mind when speaking about a stop on the way to South Africa.

Apparently, this was not the case. After a few hours of flying, the crew announced that they were experiencing engine trouble and would have to return to Dakar. After they deplaned, the passengers were informed that one of the plane's engines had burnt out and it would be two or three days before it could be replaced.

Rabbi Wineberg's companion, Mr. Lenger, was worried. It was already past midnight Wednesday morning. If the delay was more than two days, it would be questionable whether they would arrive before *Shabbos.* Rabbi Wineberg calmed him; the Rebbe had spoken to him about a delay for a day or two, no longer.

After being placed in a local hotel and resting for several hours, Rabbi Wineberg set out to look for Jews. That was not an easy task in Dakar, for there were few in the country. Many of the people had not even heard what a Jew was.

He was able, however, to locate a store whose owner was reputed to be Jewish. Rabbi Wineberg entered the store and asked for the owner. He was introduced to a young man named Clement. Was he the owner of the store?

No, he was the owner's nephew.

Was he Jewish?

Yes, he was.

Clement talked freely with Rabbi Wineberg. He came from Lebanon. He felt the financial opportunities open for him in Dakar were worth undertaking the difficulties of leaving home and a familiar environment. He and his uncle know of four other Jewish families.

Rabbi Wineberg spoke to him about Jewish involvement and practice. Clement acknowledged that he had been lax in this area.

"Do you have *tefillin* here?" Rabbi Wineberg asked.

Clement admitted that he had left his in Lebanon.

"Would you put on *tefillin* if I sent them to you?"

Clement promised that he would.

They talked for a while longer, and Rabbi Wineberg sensed a genuine warmth on Clement's part. "Today is also a day," he told him. "Come with me and put on *tefillin* now."

Clement agreed and went with Rabbi Wineberg to his hotel room. As they were returning to the store, they met Mr. Pinto, who expressed his surprise at seeing Rabbi Wineberg still in the city.

Rabbi Wineberg explained about the engine trouble his plane had experienced and then introduced Clement. "You had complained of being in Dakar for six months without meeting another Jew," he told Mr. Pinto. "I've been here less than a day, and I have been able to find one."

Rabbi Wineberg spent the majority of the next day with Clement, developing a relationship with him. Clement took him sight-seeing and they talked freely. One subject bothered Rabbi Wineberg and as the connection between them grew, he felt free to broach the issue. "What about marriage?" he asked Clement. "What chance is there of you finding a Jewish girl here in Dakar?"

Clement had to admit that there was almost no opportunity. "Promise me that you will never marry out of the faith," Rabbi Wineberg told Clement. Clement made the promise, telling Rabbi Wineberg that the time they had spent together had made an indelible impression upon him.

Rabbi Wineberg's plane was fixed in time for him to arrive in South Africa before *Shabbos.* At his first opportunity, he wrote a letter to the Rebbe describing his experiences in Dakar. The Rebbe sent *tefillin* and *Siddurim* for the community there.

Throughout the months that followed, Rabbi Wineberg maintained a connection with Clement and Mr. Pinto, sending them cards for Rosh HaShanah and letters from time to time. Before Pesach, the Rebbe instructed his personal secretary, Rabbi Chodakov, to send *matzos* to Dakar.

When the *matzos* arrived, Clement and Mr. Pinto decided to make a communal *seder.* At the *seder,* they spoke emotionally of the Rebbe's commitment to Jews throughout the world, how sitting in New York, he senses the longing within the heart of a Jew in Africa to maintain contact with his Jewish roots. After Pesach, they wrote the Rebbe a moving letter thanking him and describing the *seder.*

The following summer, Rabbi Wineberg had *yechidus* with the Rebbe before leaving on a mission to Brazil and South Africa. "You will be stopping in Dakar," the Rebbe said with a smile. "Why not spend a few days there even if the plane is in order? This time, you can notify the people before you come."

Rabbi Wineberg notified his friends in Dakar, and they arranged a get-together of the entire community. Significantly, it was held on *Yud-Beis* Tammuz, the anniversary of the Previous Rebbe's release from prison in Russia.

There was only one unpleasant element of the trip; Rabbi Wineberg saw that Clement was still single. "Do you remember your promise?" Rabbi Wineberg reminded him. Clement answered affirmatively. He explained that he had traveled to France to look for a Jewish girl to marry, but had not met anyone. "But," he assured Rabbi Wineberg, "there is no reason to worry. I will never marry out of the faith."

Several months afterwards, Rabbi Wineberg received a wedding invitation in the mail from Clement (and a second invitation to forward to the Rebbe). Clement had gone back to Lebanon to look for a wife. He had found a Jewish girl whom he would be marrying and then they would return to Dakar. "When I received that letter," Rabbi Wineberg explained, "I felt that my mission in Dakar had been completed."

Chapter 4 —
Reaching Outward

"You do your Rebbe a disservice by telling so many miracle stories about him," a friend once told me.

"What do you mean?" I responded.

"The Rebbe changed the direction of traditional Jewry," my friend began to explain. "Before he assumed leadership of Lubavitch, religious Jewry was on the defensive. He turned the tables and enabled it to advance. For this, every observant Jew, whether or not he is his chassid, owes the Rebbe a debt.

"In cities and countries where Jewish observance would never have been given a chance, the Rebbe made it a reality. These are the Rebbe's true miracles. Whatever private salvation he was able to achieve for individuals detracts from these greater achievements."

For the Rebbe, these efforts have never been looked at as private matters, and he has inspired thousands of young men and women to devote themselves to these goals.

This is the point of this chapter: To shed some light on the personal side of the Rebbe's efforts to inspire the spread of Jewish awareness and practice throughout the world.

In 5732 (1972), the Rebbe celebrated his 70th birthday. On that occasion, he called for the establishment of 70 new *Chabad* institutions. Rabbi Shlomo Cunin, director of *Chabad* activities in California, undertook to establish 10 of these by setting up 10 new *Chabad* Houses in that state.

At the same *farbrengen,* Rabbi Cunin brought several of the donors to the Rebbe to present him with the key to the *Chabad* House that had recently been established on the UCLA campus. The Rebbe told them: "If you're giving me the key, then it becomes my house. And if it's my house, I want its doors to be open 24 hours a day, seven days a week, for anyone in need."

And he added: "This is going to start a pattern. It will be like a chain-store. Soon there will be *Chabad* Houses all over the country."

Before Rabbi and Mrs. Sholom Ber Lipskar departed for *shlichus* in Miami, Florida, they went to the Rebbe for *yechidus.* The Rebbe showered unique blessings on them, wishing them success in both their outreach efforts and their personal lives. He told them: "I am going with you."

Inspired by these blessings, the Lipskars dedicated themselves to increasing Jewish awareness and practice, and met with extraordinary success. They were able to inspire many individuals to adopt a deeper Jewish identity and increase their Jewish practice.

A year later, the Lipskars again went to *yechidus,* and Rabbi Lipskar gave the Rebbe a detailed written report of his activities throughout the year. The Rebbe bent over and read it with concentration. While he was doing so, Rabbi Lipskar felt a certain pride. After all, it had been a good year, and he was certain that his achievements would bring the Rebbe satisfaction.

In the middle of reading, the Rebbe looked up at Rabbi Lipskar. "What about that young girl concerning whom you wrote to me?"

At first, Rabbi Lipskar did not recall the girl to whom the Rebbe was referring. And then he remembered. Several months earlier, on their way to *shul* one *Shabbos*, he and his wife had met a young Jewish girl who had become involved in a religious cult. They had established a relationship with the girl, and helped wean her away from the cult. In the course of their discussions, the girl had mentioned that she came from a broken home. The Lipskars had written to the Rebbe describing the girl's situation and asking for a blessing. In the letter, they had mentioned her mother's status.

The Rebbe had replied with a blessing, but had asked Rabbi Lipskar to make sure that the mother had received a Rabbinically acceptable *get* (bill of divorce).

Rabbi Lipskar had made preliminary inquiries about the matter, but had been unable to locate the mother. The demands of his schedule eventually pushed the matter entirely out of his thoughts. But although he had forgotten, the Rebbe had remembered, and wanted an answer.

After the *yechidus* was over, Rabbi Lipskar set out to verify the status of the girl's mother. After 48 hours of intensive effort, he was able to assure the Rebbe that the woman had in fact received an acceptable *get*.

Rabbi Lipskar understood the Rebbe's question as a lesson to him. Even though a person may achieve success in many spheres, he must also pay close attention to the details affecting the life of every Jewish child whom one has touched.

~

Rabbi Moshe Hecht, the veteran *shliach* in New Haven, Connecticut, once found himself $100,000 short of the amount needed to cover the budget for the school he directed. Rabbi Hecht had a plan to raise the sum by finding 100 "friends" who would each donate $1,000. He told the Rebbe of his idea, asking for a blessing that his efforts should succeed.

The Rebbe replied with a blessing, and added : "From one such friend you have certainly not yet received a donation. His name is Menachem Schneerson. Check for participation enclosed."

Together with the letter was a check for $1,000.

※

Reb Sholom Posner, the Rebbe's *shliach* in Pittsburgh for many years, once told the Rebbe at *yechidus* of the purchase and renovation of a building to serve as a school and community center. He concluded by asking the Rebbe if he would like to become a partner in the effort, not only through his blessings and advice, but also by making a monetary contribution.

The Rebbe agreed, and told Rabbi Posner: "I would be happy if other *shluchim* would learn from you and make such requests."

※

George Rohr is a businessman who had often been inspired by the Rebbe, and who supports many Lubavitch activities. Once, when receiving *lekach* before Yom Kippur, it occurred to him that he should give something *to* the Rebbe and not merely take from him. With that thought in mind, he told the Rebbe that for Rosh HaShanah, he had organized a *minyan* for over 130 Jews who had no Jewish background.

The Rebbe immediately became serious. "With no background?" he repeated, looking at Rohr intently.

Not understanding what he had said wrong, Rohr could only say it again: "With no background."

"Go back and tell them," the Rebbe said, "that they *have* a Jewish background! They have the background of Avraham, Yitzchak and Yaakov."

❦

"A hearty *yasher koach*," said Rabbi Chodakov (the Rebbe's personal secretary) to Rabbi Mendel Baumgarten.

Rabbi Baumgarten was surprised. Rabbi Chodakov was not prone to emotional expressions. It's true that the Rebbe had just given Rabbi Baumgarten and his wife a broad smile as he left 770, but why was Rabbi Chodakov so excited?

It was about 2 AM Monday morning. Rabbi Baumgarten and his wife had just returned from conducting a *Shabbaton* with university students in College Park, Maryland. His chassidic sixth sense told him that since participation in such outreach efforts was encouraged by the Rebbe, he should stop in at 770 before going home.

When he arrived, the Rebbe had just finished seeing people for *yechidus* that night, so Rabbi Baumgarten decided to stay and watch as the Rebbe left the building. As the Rebbe was leaving, he saw Rabbi Baumgarten and his wife waiting in the corridor, and gave them a broad smile.

Why was Rabbi Chodakov so happy? "Throughout the week, the Rebbe has been earnest, intense, you could almost say upset," he told Rabbi Baumgarten. "Even at the *farbrengen* on *Shabbos*, he spoke in a demanding tone, asking why the chassidim were not doing more outreach work. This is the first time he has smiled all week!"

❦

On entering the Rebbe's room for *yechidus*, a Lubavitch communal leader noticed that the Rebbe had an almost sad expression on his face. With some boldness, he asked the Rebbe what was troubling him.

The Rebbe replied that there was a family in Crown Heights with six children, five boys and one girl. The boys had already grown up, married and assumed positions in *shlichus* in cities around the world. A while ago, the girl had also married. Recently, she and her husband wrote asking the Rebbe to let them accept a *shlichus* position in a distant city.

The Rebbe gave his approval contingent on the consent of the woman's parents. Although this would mean that the elder couple would be alone, they willingly agreed.

"At the present moment," the Rebbe concluded, "the parents and their daughter are at the airport saying farewell, and many tears are being shed. It's true that they are tears of joy, but nevertheless, when they are crying, how can I not cry?"

―

In 1941, while fleeing from the Nazis, the Rebbe spent about a year in the city of Nice in Southern France. Almost 40 years later, Rabbi Yosef Yitzchak Pinson arrived in Nice as the Rebbe's *shliach,* determined to bring *Yiddishkeit* to that city.

Rabbi Pinson's activities were blessed with success from the beginning, and he soon had to look for a building to serve as a school and a center for *Chabad's* outreach activities.

On four different occasions, he found what he thought was an appropriate spot, and each time he asked the Rebbe whether he should purchase the site. The Rebbe replied by referring him to Rabbi Binyamin Gorodetsky, who served as the Rebbe's chief representative in Europe and North Africa. On each occasion, Rabbi Gorodetsky took the question back to the Rebbe, who then explained why he thought the location was unsuitable.

Rabbi Pinson is by no means an idle dreamer. And yet, like all of us, there are times when he too can become smitten by a particular vision. On a road leading to the home in which the Rebbe had stayed, there was a large building with ample grounds. "The Rebbe must have looked at this building several times each day," Rabbi Pinson thought to himself. "This is the perfect location for my school!"

He tried to find the owner of the building, but without success. After several months of searching, while on a visit to New York one summer, he asked the Rebbe for a blessing to help him purchase the building. The Rebbe consented at once.

When he returned to France, Rabbi Pinson realized that the lease on the building he was renting for the school was up; he *had* to find a different location. One ad in the "For Rent" section of the newspaper attracted his attention. He inquired about it, and it turned out to be precisely the property on which his attention had become fixed.

He offered to buy the property, but the owner explained that he had recently inherited it, and that his accountant had advised him that for tax purposes, it was preferable for him to rent it out.

Not seeing any alternative, Rabbi Pinson agreed to rent the property. Feeling that the gentile owner would have difficulty understanding the Rebbe-chassid relationship, he phrased his agreement in the following manner: "There is, however, one condition. My school is a local branch of an international organization with headquarters in New York. Before I enter into any binding commitment, I must receive approval from the head of the organization."

The owner was willing to give Rabbi Pinson several days, so Rabbi Pinson phoned the Rebbe's secretary, Rabbi Klein, and requested that he ask the Rebbe if he should rent the building or not. The Rebbe responded within an hour that Rabbi Pinson should *buy* the building.

Rabbi Pinson was unsure of what to do. He thought, however, that if he could negotiate a rental agreement, perhaps he could have an option to buy added to the contract. With these thoughts in mind, he contacted the owner again.

When he told the owner that the head in New York had agreed to the rental, the owner told him: "I've changed my mind. I spoke to my accountant, and he says he can arrange for me to sell the property after all. Are you interested? If not, I'll look for someone else."

Rabbi Pinson told the owner that he would be happy to buy the property. As the negotiations grew serious, Rabbi Pinson realized that he would not be able pay the entire price, and would have to take out a mortgage. Now, obtaining a mortgage in France takes time, particularly for a charitable organization. Since it would be impossible to make all the arrangements before the school year began, Rabbi Pinson decided it would be necessary to rent the property for at least several months.

Before their next meeting, Rabbi Pinson withdrew a large amount of cash from his bank. Shortly after they began speaking, he put the money on the table and offered to rent the property for three months.

"But we spoke about buying," the owner of the property said.

Rabbi Pinson explained that he was even more interested in buying than the owner was in selling, but that he was experiencing difficulty in arranging a mortgage, and needed to open the school in time for the fall term.

Reluctantly, the owner agreed. When his secretary typed out the rental contract, she mistakenly made it for six months instead of three. Rabbi Pinson was very happy, since it would have been very difficult to complete the process in three months, and now he would have ample time.

After making several applications for a mortgage, Rabbi Pinson was told that as a representative of a charitable organization that had just begun activities in the city, the only way that he would be granted a mortgage would be if the city council agreed to serve as a guarantor. This was an accepted practice in the city, and had been done for several charitable and religious organizations in the past. It had, however, never been done for a Jewish organization.

Rabbi Pinson asked the Chief Rabbi of Nice to approach the council on his behalf, but the Chief Rabbi explained that he was uncomfortable about making such a bold request. He offered instead to make an appointment with the mayor to speak about a different issue, and take Rabbi Pinson along. Rabbi Pinson could then broach the question about the guarantee.

Seeing no other option, Rabbi Pinson agreed. Before the appointment, he wrote the Rebbe for a blessing, and at the appropriate time met the Chief Rabbi outside the mayor's office.

When they entered, the mayor listened to the Chief Rabbi's request. Although it was a minor matter, the mayor did not offer any assistance. After such an inauspicious response, the Chief Rabbi was hesitant to introduce Rabbi Pinson, but he had made a commitment, and so he made the introduction.

As Rabbi Pinson started to speak, the mayor began to relax. Without any apparent reason, he offered to bring the question to the city council, and to push for its acceptance.

But this was not the end of Rabbi Pinson's trials. Although the city council passed the motion, it still had to be approved by a provincial prefect. The prefect had not heard of either Rabbi Pinson or Lubavitch, and did not understand why the city council had offered to guarantee the mortgage. Without giving the matter a second thought, he vetoed the request.

So Rabbi Pinson found himself calling on the Chief Rabbi again, this time asking him to arrange a meeting with the prefect. The Chief Rabbi agreed to use the same ploy as before; he would approach the prefect on his own business, and take Rabbi Pinson along. The Chief Rabbi would make the introductions, but from that point on, Rabbi Pinson would have to speak for himself.

The earliest appointment the Chief Rabbi could receive was Nissan 11, the Rebbe's birthday. Rabbi Pinson received this news with mixed emotions. He had always spent this day in 770, attending the Rebbe's *farbrengen*. If he were to meet the prefect on this day, he would have to forgo the trip. On the other hand, he understood that the appointment falling on the Rebbe's birthday was an obvious sign of Divine Providence. He told the Chief Rabbi to confirm the meeting, and wrote a letter to the Rebbe asking for a blessing for success.

The prefect greeted the Chief Rabbi and Rabbi Pinson warmly. As Rabbi Pinson explained the nature of Lubavitch activities, the prefect realized that he was dealing with a worldwide organization with a long and proud history of community service. He was prepared to approve the guarantee.

"Just submit your request to the city council again with minor changes," he told Rabbi Pinson. "They will okay it, and this time I will approve it."

Rabbi Pinson asked him if it would be possible for him to simply rescind his previous veto.

"No, that is just not done," the prefect replied. "Once a veto has been issued, it is not overturned. Take the matter back to the city council, and then I will okay it."

Rabbi Pinson realized that his rental contract was running out, and doubted his chances of receiving prompt approval from the city council a second time. "Today is the birthday of our Rebbe, a great spiritual leader recognized by the entire world," he told the prefect. He explained that each year the American Congress would declare Nissan 11 "Education Day."

"You can join in this initiative," he told the prefect. "Yes, it means doing something out of the ordinary, but help us purchase our school! Consider it a birthday present to the Rebbe."

The members of the city council were amazed when Rabbi Pinson brought them the letter from the prefect rescinding his veto; it had never happened before. Nonetheless, they checked their protocols and found that it was acceptable.

With the council as guarantor, he had no trouble obtaining a mortgage. Soon afterwards, holding the sales contract in his hand, Rabbi Pinson watched the children leaving the school.

"Did the Rebbe envision this," he mused, "when he passed this building 40 years ago?"

◈

In the 1960s, the Lubavitch Youth Organization would often organize chassidic *Shabbatons* with synagogues from every part of the religious spectrum. When the congregations were not themselves observant, prayers would be held in the social hall with a *mechitzah,* and afterwards the chassidim and the congregation would join for communal meals.

In May of 5729 (1969), several couples from Crown Heights conducted such a *Shabbaton* in Steubenville, Ohio. The *Shabbos* was beautiful and inspiring; the talks, the singing and dancing, the interpersonal communication — everything exceeded the highest expectations. The couples came back to Crown Heights with wonderful feelings of accomplishment.

That Sunday afternoon, the Rebbe delivered an address as part of the annual convention of the Lubavitch Women's Organization. After the address, the women were given the opportunity to meet with the Rebbe.

One of the women who had traveled to the Steubenville *Shabbaton* took the opportunity to tell the Rebbe about the event. "Everyone was very moved," she related. "The president of the congregation said he was so inspired that he was taking the *mechitzah* home as a souvenir!"

"Instead of taking it home," replied the Rebbe with a smile, "it would have been better if he had decided to leave it in the synagogue!"

◈

Rabbi Yossi Biston and his brother Aaron have developed a slight variation of the traditional Yissachar-Zevulun partnership. Aaron is involved in business, while Yossi dedicates himself to Torah outreach, spreading Torah in and around Broward County, Florida.

At one of the meetings of the *Machne Israel* Development Fund, Aaron told the Rebbe that he was helping Yossi purchase a new facility, but they were encountering problems getting a zoning approval.

The Bistons were completely perplexed by the Rebbe's reply: "In the *sichah* I just delivered, I already said to make *Chabad* centers bigger."

Baffled, they looked at one another... The problem was one of zoning, not size. How could making a building larger convince a city to approve its being rezoned? Moreover, how was it possible to make the building bigger if they couldn't get a permit to use it for commercial purposes? If anything, the current large size and operational scope of the facility appeared to be the problem!

Upon his return to Florida, Rabbi Biston went to the commission meeting in a desperate attempt to resolve the zoning dispute. The mayor greeted him warmly, but explained that the building could not be approved by the zoning commission because it didn't include sufficient parking space for the planned center. The words of the Rebbe, "Make it bigger," echoed in Yossi's mind.

Providentially, a parcel of land at the back of the center came on the market, perfectly suited for the needed parking lot. The sale was consummated the same day.

Having thus fulfilled the Rebbe's directive to "make it bigger," the Bistons were not surprised that the center received the city's approval shortly thereafter.

Chapter 5 —
Digging For Roots

One morning, Reb Dovber, who would become the Mitteler Rebbe, woke up startled at the dream which he had just experienced. Shortly afterwards, he encountered his father, the Alter Rebbe. "Tell me your dream," his father directed him.

Reb Dovber began to relate how he had seen a tall man who limped on his left side, standing on a raft and navigating it through calm, gently flowing waters. Then he had seen his father on another raft, struggling to steer it through turbulent and agitated currents.

"The tall man was my Rebbe, the Maggid," the Alter Rebbe told his son. "His mission was to show *tzaddikim* (righteous people) how to pilot a course in life. Navigating such a passage is a challenge, but a tranquil one. My mission is to direct *baalei-teshuvah*, those who must return to their Jewish core. This is a far more irregular and tumultuous path."

The Alter Rebbe transmitted this mission to his successors. Thus it is no wonder that it was the Rebbe's initiative that sparked the *teshuvah* movement in America and throughout the world. In the 50s, when Rabbis throughout the States were lamenting the inroads that assimilation had made throughout traditional Jewry, Charles Ratner, a secular Jewish historian, asked the Rebbe what place an American Jew who had studied science and has the doors of American society open for him could have within the Jewish tradition. The Rebbe answered that American Jews possessed genuine sincerity, and that this quality would ultimately lead them back to their Jewish heritage.

In the 60s, the Rebbe instructed his chassidim to view the upheaval experienced by American youth, not as a rebellion against authority which should be held in check, but a sincere search for meaning and purpose that should be encouraged. It was in that era that he founded the first *yeshivos* for *baalei teshuvah* and established *Chabad* Houses on university campuses. Not only did the Rebbe encourage others through this endeavor, but as illustrated in the few examples that follow, he played a personal role in guiding many on the path to *teshuvah*.

Digging For Roots

In the early 1970s, a young man from California decided to return to his Jewish roots. He left the university in which he was studying and enrolled in the *Tiferes Bachurim* program for late beginners in Jewish studies in Morristown, N.J.

His parents were less than enthusiastic, considering the decision to be an irresponsible act. After a month in the *yeshivah*, the young man returned home and attempted to smooth things out, but was unsuccessful. His parents remained outspoken in their opposition, declaring that their son was simply trying to avoid taking responsibility for his life. When he saw that nothing he could say would influence them, the young man returned to *yeshivah*.

Now while he had been home, the young man had received a speeding ticket in the family car. For various reasons, he hadn't paid it, and so a copy was sent to his parents' home.

The unpaid ticket provided his parents with added ammunition. "This shows that we are right; see how irresponsible you are," they wrote him. "You break the law, and leave us to pay your fines. Is there anyone in your beloved *yeshivah* who will pay your traffic ticket?!"

The young man, emotionally drained, wrote to the Rebbe asking him for advice. To enable the Rebbe to understand his parents' perspective, he enclosed their letter. A few weeks later, he received a letter from the Rebbe full of support and encouragement, advising him on how to relate to his parents.

Clipped to the letter was a $30 check — the amount required to pay the ticket.

From time to time, Rabbi Chatzkel Kornfeld, one of the *shluchim* in Seattle, would visit Alaska to kindle sparks of Jewish interest there. Over the course of these visits, he met a Jew who had married out of the faith, but still had warm feelings for his Jewish roots.

Rabbi Kornfeld was able to stir this person to heighten his Jewish practice, and he began a gradual but steady growth. As he progressed, he and his wife began to grow apart. Ultimately, they divorced, and the man moved to Seattle to begin a new life.

Rabbi Kornfeld told him that after making such changes, it would be beneficial to write to the Rebbe and ask for his blessings for spiritual and material success.

The ex-Alaskan wrote the Rebbe, describing his personal history, and asking for a blessing. He signed the letter with his name and then added: "a renegade Jew."

When responding to the letter, the Rebbe circled these words and commented in Hebrew: "Immersion is required, as is necessary for an apostate."

When Rabbi Kornfeld saw the response, he asked his friend to own up: had he ever undergone a conversion out of the faith? His friend explained that he had once been baptized. He had never mentioned it, for it had long since ceased to be a factor in his life.

Rabbi Kornfeld explained that Jewish law requires that when a Jew who accepted another faith desires to return to Jewish practice, he must immerse himself in a *mikveh* to wash away all connection to his false beliefs.

The Alaskan performed this immersion, and afterwards continued to progress in Jewish practice. Soon he was ready to build a home according to the chassidic tradition. He met a girl who was studying at Machon Chanah, the Lubavitch school for women who had returned to Jewish practice, and they decided to marry.

The date set for the wedding was two days before Sukkos, because many members of Seattle's Lubavitch community would visit Crown Heights at that time. As is the usual practice in the Lubavitch community, the Rebbe was also sent an invitation.

DIGGING FOR ROOTS 89

The day before the wedding, Rabbi Kornfeld received a call at his in-law's home in Crown Heights; the Rebbe's secretary was urgently looking for him. Although that night was not one on which *farbrengens* were usually held, the Rebbe had decided to hold such a gathering. Nevertheless, since the wedding was being held in Crown Heights, the Rebbe was asking permission of the bride and groom. Would they object to the Rebbe holding a *farbrengen* that night?

Rabbi Kornfeld contacted the couple, who readily consented to the *farbrengen*. When Rabbi Kornfeld relayed the message to the Rebbe's secretary, he was told that the Rebbe invited the couple to come to the *farbrengen* after the celebration and recite the *shevah berachos* (the seven wedding blessings).

And so it was that towards the end of the *farbrengen*, the spirits of the participants were uplifted by a happy group from Seattle.

―

Rabbi Zalman Serebryanski, dean of the Lubavitch Rabbinical College in Melbourne, Australia, once brought a girl to Rabbi Chaim Gutnick. "Please, help this girl convert," he asked.

Rabbi Gutnick listened to the girl's story. She lived in Balaclava, and from her youth had felt a strong attraction to Judaism. Whenever she heard stories of the Holocaust, she was deeply touched. She had been reading and studying about Judaism for a long time, and now wanted to convert.

Rabbi Gutnick was touched by her sincerity. Nevertheless, he did not want to perform the ceremony. The girl was still living at home with her non-Jewish parents. Would she be able to practice Judaism in her parents' home? Would her interest continue as she matured into adulthood? Since he could not answer these questions, he decided to let time take its course. If the girl was still interested when she was older, she could convert then.

Rabbi Gutnick's refusal plunged the girl into deep depression and she had to be confined to a hospital. Reb Zalman, stirred by the depth of her feelings, continued to visit her from time to time.

After several weeks, he called Rabbi Gutnick, telling him of the girl's condition and asking him whether perhaps he would change his mind because of the strength of her feelings.

Rabbi Gutnick answered that the reasons which had dissuaded him from performing the conversion were still valid. Nevertheless, he promised to write to the Rebbe describing the situation. If the Rebbe advised him to facilitate her conversion, he would happily comply.

Reb Zalman told the girl that the Rebbe was being consulted, and her condition improved immediately.

Rabbi Gutnick did not receive an immediate reply to his letter. Afterwards, at the end of a reply to another issue, the Rebbe added: "What's happening with the Jewish girl from Balaclava?"

Rabbi Gutnick was surprised. The girl and Reb Zalman had both made it clear that her family was Anglican!

He and Reb Zalman went to confront the girl's mother. At first, she continued to insist that she was Anglican, but as the sincerity of the two rabbis impressed her, she broke down and told her story. She had been raised in an Orthodox Jewish home in England. As a young girl, she had rebelled against her parents and abandoned Jewish life entirely, marrying a gentile and moving to Australia. She had not given Judaism a thought since. She loved her daughter, however, and would not oppose her if she wished to live a Jewish life.

Once the girl's Judaism was established, Rabbis Serebryanski and Gutnick helped her feel at home in Melbourne's Lubavitch community. She continued to make progress in her Jewish commitment, and today is a teacher in a Lubavitch school.

Digging For Roots

But Rabbi Gutnick still had a question: How did the Rebbe know she was Jewish? At his next *yechidus,* he mustered the *chutzpah* to ask.

The Rebbe replied that, at Reb Zalman's urging, the girl had also written him a letter. "Such a letter," the Rebbe declared, "could only have been written by a Jewish girl!"

Leibl Shifrin is an American *baal-teshuvah* who first came close to Lubavitch in Springfield, MA. But though he felt inspired by chassidic thought, he found study difficult. Discouraged, he wrote the Rebbe for a blessing and advice for success in study.

"Learn about your roots," the Rebbe told him.

(Leibl's grandfather was Reb David Shifrin, one of the chassidim who helped the Previous Rebbe introduce Lubavitch to North America, and his family were Lubavitcher chassidim dating back to the Alter Rebbe.)

"When you know where you come from, your studies will proceed with far greater ease," explained the Rebbe.

Prompted by this advice, Leibl began researching his family's past. As his awareness of his origins increased, he began to feel more at home with Jewish knowledge, and was able to grasp Torah concepts more rapidly.

Chapter 6 —
Jewels in the Streets

Perhaps one of the most common associations people have with the name Lubavitch is the Rebbe's *mitzvah* campaigns. Be it the chassidim who put on *tefillin* with the visitors to the Western Wall in Jerusalem, the self-sacrificing Rabbinical students who man the *mitzvah* tanks that operate in the streets of New York and many other cities, the girls who visit women in hospitals and nursing homes and give them the opportunity to light *Shabbos* candles, or the thousands of *shluchim,* both those employed in that capacity and those who give up their spare time to accept this mantle upon themselves, who tirelessly work to spread Jewish observance,- at one point or another, almost every Jew in the world has met a Lubavitcher who has invited him to perform a *mitzvah.*

Why such an emphasis on observance? Why not spread Jewish ideas, and let the actual observance of the *mitzvos* come totally on the person's own initiative?

First of all, there is a pragmatic dimension. Our Sages teach:[1] One *mitzvah* draws another after it." As

---

1. *Avos* 4:2.

the many thousands whose Torah observance has increased because of casual exposure to one of the Lubavitch *mitzvah* campaigns can attest, this maxim is as true today as it was in *Talmudic* times.

But there is a deeper reason that surpasses even motives of this nature. The word *mitzvah* relates to the Aramaic term *tzavsa,* meaning "connection." Every *mitzvah* is a bond connecting us to G-d's essence. When a Jew performs a *mitzvah* — whoever he is and wherever he is — he is uniting himself with G-d. The bond achieved at that moment reflects the fundamental purpose of creation; there is nothing higher, nothing more perfect.

For the Rebbe, these were not abstract points, but realities that he lived, and encouraged others to live.

Rabbi Shabsi Katz, the Rabbi of Pretoria, the administrative capital of South Africa, and the Jewish Chaplain for the Department of Prisons in that country, maintained a relationship with the Rebbe for many years.

In Kislev 5737 (Dec. 1978), he came to visit the Rebbe for the third time. At *yechidus* a few days before Chanukah, the Rebbe asked Rabbi Katz what was being done for Jewish prisoners in South Africa. Rabbi Katz explained that conditions in South African prisons were much harsher than in New York, but that Jewish prisoners were not obligated to work on Rosh Hashanah, Yom Kippur or Passover, and on Passover, they were given food certified kosher for the holiday by Pretoria's *Chevra Kadisha*.

The Rebbe asked: "And what about Chanukah? Can the inmates light Chanukah candles?" One must appreciate, the Rebbe said, how important it is for a person sitting alone in a cell to light a Chanukah *menorah*. One cannot fathom the warmth and hope this brings, and how this will uplift his spirits in such a dark environment.

Rabbi Katz promised that when he returned to South Africa he would begin working on the project, so that next year the inmates could light Chanukah candles. The Rebbe, however, was not satisfied, and inquired: What about *this* Chanukah?

Rabbi Katz pointed out that Chanukah was only a few days off. Since he was in New York, he doubted it would be possible to do anything. The Rebbe replied that when Rabbi Katz left the *yechidus* he should use the telephones in the outside office to make any calls that were necessary.

Rabbi Katz then reminded the Rebbe that in South Africa it was four o'clock in the morning; at that hour, he dared not wake the general in charge of correctional facilities.

The Rebbe did not accept Rabbi Katz' reply, saying that, on the contrary, when the general saw that the matter was so important that he was called from overseas in the middle of the night, he would be impressed, and would appreciate the need for Jewish prisoners to light this year.

As soon as Rabbi Katz left the Rebbe's office, one of the secretaries led him to the small side office in the front of 770. He showed him the phones and told him to make himself at home.

Rabbi Katz first called his secretary in Pretoria to find the home number of General Sephton, who was a Dominee of the Dutch Reformed Church and Religious Director of Prisons. At the same time, he asked his secretary to call the general and tell him he would soon be receiving a call from overseas. And so, when he called General Sephton a few minutes later, the general was not upset, but instead, inquired how he could help.

Rabbi Katz explained that he had just completed a private meeting with one of the leaders of world Jewry, who had expressed concern about the Jewish inmates in South African prisons. The leader had explained how important it was for the prisoners to light Chanukah menorahs, and how this would bring them warmth, light and hope.

General Sephton was moved. In spite of the fact that his office was due to close that day for their religious celebration, he said that if Rabbi Katz was calling at that time of night from overseas, he could understand how urgent the matter was, and that as soon as he got to his office in the morning he would send a telex to all the prison facilities in South Africa telling them to make it possible for all Jewish prisoners in South Africa to light candles this Chanukah.

Next morning, when the Rebbe came to 770, Rabbi Katz was in the foyer. "*Nu?*" motioned the Rebbe. When he heard that the mission had been accomplished, the Rebbe gave a broad smile and told Rabbi Katz that he wanted see him after *shacharis*.

When Rabbi Katz entered the Rebbe's room, the Rebbe told him that there are 50 states in the US, and all but one allowed Jewish inmates to light Chanukah candles. "Would you believe it," said the Rebbe, "It is only here — in New York State — that prisoners cannot light *menorahs* for Chanukah!"

The Rebbe asked that Rabbi Katz see to it that the inmates of New York State prisons lit Chanukah candles that year. "Tell them what you did, that they should learn from South Africa, and do the same here," he advised.

Rabbi Katz did not know where to start; he told the Rebbe that he did not know whom to contact first.

"Rabbi J. J. Hecht has been working hard on this project, and will know whom to turn to," the Rebbe answered him.

When Rabbi Katz sought out Rabbi Hecht, it was Rabbi Hecht's turn to be astonished. He pointed out that it was Dec. 24, and already past noon; nobody would be at their desks at that time. Could officials be reached at their office parties?!

But after Rabbi Katz told him about his *yechidus* with the Rebbe, and his personal call to General Sephton in South Africa, Rabbi Hecht relaxed. Past experience had told him, he said, that if the Rebbe asked somebody to do something right away, things worked out well even if the timing seemed bad.

After a few calls, Rabbi Hecht was able to locate the director of the New York State Correctional System, and found him in a jovial mood. Rabbi Hecht then introduced Rabbi Katz, who informed the director that Jewish prisoners in South Africa would be lighting Chanukah candles that year, and suggested that if this could happen in South Africa, surely it should happen in New York. The director agreed, remarking that if in South Africa, where Jews are such a minority, the prisons gave them permission to light, there was no reason why it shouldn't happen in New York. He promised to attend to the matter in time for Chanukah.

Rabbi Katz looked at his watch. It was several minutes before three, and the Rebbe would come out for the *minchah* prayers at 3:15. He hurried back to 770 and positioned himself outside the Rebbe's room. When the Rebbe came out for the afternoon prayers, he saw Rabbi Katz and motioned "*Nu?*" Rabbi Katz indicated that the mission had been accomplished. "I want to see you after *minchah*!" the Rebbe smiled.

Rabbi Katz was surprised. What mission would be waiting for him after *minchah*? When he entered the Rebbe's room, however, the Rebbe did not have another project for him. Instead, the Rebbe said that as he had done him a personal favor, he would like to do something in return.

Rabbi Katz was bewildered. He told the Rebbe that it had been a privilege and an honor to do what he had done. He had received so much in blessings and guidance throughout the years that he certainly did not expect anything more.

The Rebbe did not accept this answer, explaining that he didn't want to be indebted to anybody. So Rabbi Katz thought quickly, and asked the Rebbe for a *Tanya* for his son, who would certainly appreciate it. The Rebbe told him that one would be in the outer office shortly. When Rabbi Katz returned to pick it up, he found a Hebrew *Tanya* waiting for Rabbi Katz himself, a leather-bound, deluxe Hebrew/English *Tanya* for his son, "Challenge" for General Sephton in South Africa, and "Woman of Valor" for the general's wife.

When Rabbi Katz returned to South Africa, he called General Sephton. Before he could say anything, the general reassured him that he had sent the telexes the day he had received the call from America, and that the Jewish prisoners had indeed kindled Chanukah candles that year. When Rabbi Katz told the general that the Rebbe had sent gifts for him, the general said he would be right over to pick them up.

Indeed, within an hour, the general was sitting in Rabbi Katz's living room. Asked why he had hurried so, he replied that when a person sitting in New York thinks about somebody living on the other side of the globe — especially somebody imprisoned for wrongdoing — and seeks out someone to bring him light and warmth, he is a genuine leader.

"And if such a leader sends something for me, I want it as soon as possible," exclaimed the general.

It was 9:30 one night in 1943, during the lifetime of the Previous Rebbe. The daily study program at 770 had just concluded, and Rabbi Hershel Fogelman and several of his fellow students were standing in the hallway, discussing the subject which they had been reviewing. Suddenly, a young man burst through the main door. He was not wearing a *yarmulka* and appeared very agitated.

"Where's the Rabbi?" he called out. "I must speak to the Rabbi!"

Rabbi Fogelman went over to the young man and calmed him, while one of the other students went and brought a *yarmulka*.

The stranger's name was Herbert Goldstein. His brothers had just called him from Boston, informing him that one of their relatives was very ill, and asking him to go to the Lubavitcher Rebbe at once to seek a blessing.

Rabbi Fogelman requested him to wait while he asked Rabbi Eliyahu Simpson (the Previous Rebbe's secretary) if it was possible for the Rebbe to receive the young man.

Rabbi Simpson said he would ask the Rebbe shortly, and Rabbi Fogelman returned to Herbert. By this time, the young man had collected himself, and opened up to Rabbi Fogelman. He lived at the Hotel Mayflower in New York, organizing commercial receptions. He and his brothers had seen the Rebbe three years ago. At that time, he had been an alcoholic. The Previous Rebbe had taken his hand in his own, and spoken to him reassuringly, encouraging him to control himself and refrain from drinking.

And it had worked! From that moment onward, Herbert had been able to bridle his desire to drink. Every night, he said, he would kiss the hand which the Previous Rebbe had held.

Rabbi Simpson came back and told Herbert he would be able to see the Rebbe shortly. Herbert continued talking to Rabbi Fogelman until the time came for the *yechidus*.

When Herbert emerged from the Rebbe's room, he was brimming with excitement: The Rebbe had remembered him! He told him exactly where he had stood during their meeting three years earlier, and where Herbert's brothers had stood. He had also given him a blessing for the recovery of his relative, and spoken to him about the importance of putting on *tefillin* every day.

Rabbi Fogelman and Herbert parted warmly. Shortly afterwards, the *Ramash* — that's the way the Chassidim would refer to our Rebbe during the lifetime of the Previous Rebbe — and Rabbi Simpson came over to Rabbi Fogelman and asked about Herbert's story.

There was no hesitation on the part of the *Ramash*. He did not want Herbert's inspiration to remain in the clouds, but rather to be connected to actual deeds. He told Rabbi Fogelman to take a pair of *tefillin* from Rabbi Simpson, go to the Hotel Mayflower the next morning, and put on *tefillin* with Herbert. Rabbi Fogelman was then to give Herbert the *tefillin*, though it would be preferable if he paid for them.

Rabbi Fogelman did as he was told, and Herbert was happy to see him. "It was smart of the Rebbe to send you while I'm still enthused," he smiled, as he willingly donned the *tefillin.*

When Rabbi Fogelman came back to 770, he informed Rabbi Simpson (and the *Ramash,* for the two worked so closely together that by informing Rabbi Simpson, you would automatically be informing the *Ramash*) of the episode. He was told to go back and pay Herbert another visit the following morning.

Herbert was glad to see Rabbi Fogelman again: "You'll never believe what happened this morning," he told him. "When I woke up, I remembered that as a child my parents had told me to say *Modeh Ani* upon arising, and so that's what I did!" He put on the *tefillin* a second time and paid for them, promising to put them on every day.

Rabbi Fogelman was sent to see Herbert a third time, and the young man reiterated his promise to observe the *mitzvah.*

"Today," Rabbi Fogelman explained, "it's hard to appreciate how big a step it was in those days for a non-observant American to begin putting on *tefillin* daily. When the Rebbe saw that such a thing was possible, he refused to let the opportunity pass."

~

In the 1970s, *Mivtza Neshek,* the branch of the Lubavitch Women's Organization dedicated to spreading the practice of kindling *Shabbos* candles, organized a series of radio ads encouraging women and girls to fulfill this *mitzvah*. Because federal law required that every ad have a commercial aspect, the notices mentioned that if the listeners sent one dollar to the Candlelighting Division of the Lubavitch Women's Organization at 770 Eastern Parkway, they would be sent a special set of *Shabbos* candle holders.

Thousands of these holders were distributed. At times, people would err, and instead of addressing their letters to the Lubavitch Women's Organization, they would send them to the Lubavitcher Rebbe.

On one occasion, a woman living on Ocean Avenue in Brooklyn wrote to ask for the *Shabbos* candle holders. She too erred, and addressed her letter to the Rebbe. The Rebbe received the letter in the Friday mail. On Friday afternoon, he had his secretary, Rabbi Binyomin Klein, call Mrs. Esther Sternberg (who ran the *Shabbos* candle campaign) and ask her to see to it that this woman had the opportunity to light *Shabbos* candles *that Friday.*

Mrs. Sternberg is not one to take a request from the Rebbe lightly. With 45 minutes left before *Shabbos* started, she tried to get the woman's phone number, but was told it was unlisted. Then, noting that the woman's address was not far away, she resolved to deliver the candle holders personally. If the woman was not home, she would leave it with a neighbor.

Taking two of her daughters along, Mrs. Sternberg drove (flew!) to the woman's apartment. She rang the bell and knocked several times, but there was no answer. She tried several of the neighbors' apartments, but they too did not answer. Finally, a woman from an apartment down the hall replied that, yes, she knew the woman who had asked for the candle holders. She was an elderly lady, said the neighbor, and hard of hearing. That's probably why she had not answered her bell; she hadn't heard it ringing!

And so Mrs. Sternberg, her two daughters, and the neighbor all knocked hard on the woman's door. Eventually, an elderly Jewish lady answered. She was grateful to see visitors, and even more grateful when she found that she would be able to light *Shabbos* candles that week.

Mrs. Sternberg was happy to give the woman the candle holders, but couldn't help wondering: The woman seemed sincerely committed to the *mitzvah*; why then hadn't she lit candles before? "Don't you have candle holders of your own?" she asked.

"Of course I have *Shabbos* candles," the woman told Mrs. Sternberg, taking her into her kitchen and showing her a large silver candelabra on top of one of the cabinets. "But when my children moved me here," she explained, "they put my candelabra up there. Neither I nor any of my neighbors can reach it! That's why I haven't been able to light." (Apparently, this woman, as do many others, mistakenly felt that *Shabbos* candles had to be lit in a ritual candelabra.)

One of Mrs. Sternberg's daughters climbed up and brought down the woman's candlesticks. And so, thanks to the Rebbe's concern and Mrs. Sternberg's commitment, the woman was able to light candles in her own candelabra that *Shabbos*.

On another occasion, the Rebbe received a letter from a man from Bowie, Maryland, asking that *Shabbos* candle holders be sent to his daughter. Again, the letter arrived on Friday, and again, the Rebbe had his secretary ask Mrs. Sternberg to see to it that the girl lit candles *that* Friday.

This time, it was only 20 minutes before *Shabbos* when Mrs. Sternberg was contacted. She immediately phoned one of the *shluchim* in Maryland and asked if he could deliver candles to the girl. But the *shliach* replied that Bowie was over two hours away; he had no way of delivering the candles in time.

Not seeing any alternative, Mrs. Sternberg located the family's phone number. The mother answered the phone. Yes, her husband had asked for the candleholders. She didn't light candles herself, but thought that it was a good idea for her daughter to light.

Mrs. Sternberg told her that she would be mailing the candle holders, but meantime, she would instruct her on how to make candle holders from aluminum foil so that her daughter would be able to light that *Shabbos*. And with no more than a drop of convincing, the mother agreed to join her daughter and light candles herself.

She listened diligently to Mrs. Sternberg's instructions, and wrote down the transliteration of the blessing word for word.

As they were talking, Mrs. Sternberg asked the woman if her daughter had any other friends who would like candle holders. The woman mentioned that there were several girls in her daughter's Hebrew School class who would probably appreciate such a gift. And in her own *Chavurah* group, she could think of a few women, and she had some other friends....

All in all, when Mrs. Sternberg prepared the package of candle holders to send to Bowie, it contained more than 40!

On the following Friday, Mrs. Sternberg received another call from the Rebbe's office. "The Rebbe wants to know what's happening with the girl in Bowie," the secretary told her.

Mrs. Sternberg again called the woman. Yes, her daughter had lit candles the previous *Shabbos,* and they had received the candle holders in the mail. Everyone was overwhelmed. Women were talking about it all over town.

"Could you send more?" she wanted to know. "My daughter has other friends... and I have other friends...."

And so, the following week, Mrs. Sternberg sent an even larger order of candle holders to Bowie.

The following Friday, Mrs. Sternberg did not wait for a call from the Rebbe's office. Instead, she phoned her new friend in Bowie herself. Yes, the candle holders had arrived and the women were very happy. What's more, the woman's friends and neighbors wanted to meet some of the ladies who had reached out and brought *Shabbos* light into their homes.

A *Shabbaton* was arranged. Women and girls from Crown Heights came and shared a *Shabbos* encounter with the community.

So it was that a few words from the Rebbe snowballed into an ongoing positive Jewish experience.

Chapter 7 —
Opening the Iron Fist

Rav Yosef Caro, author of the *Shulchan Aruch,* had been laboring to understand a certain *Talmudic* passage long into the night. Back and forth he went, checking the conceptual flow of the phrases, the insights of the commentaries, and the ramifications in Torah law. As the light of dawn crept through the windows of his study, he developed an interpretation that satisfied the difficulties he had perceived.

Weary after the night's exertion, he made his way through the winding, hilly streets of Tsfat (Safed). He saw a number of Jews already entering a house of study and decided to join them. There an ordinary Torah scholar was expounding the passage on which he had labored all night — and offering the very same interpretation which he had toiled so long to develop.

Rav Yosef Caro was shaken. Why had he needed to exert himself so to grasp a concept which an ordinary scholar appeared to have mastered without difficulty?

Now Rav Yosef Caro had a medium, an angel who would instruct him in his spiritual development and answer questions for him. At the first opportunity, he asked his angel to explain this phenomenon.

The angel told him that considerable energy was necessary to introduce a spiritual concept into the framework prevailing within our material world. Rav Caro had achieved that through his night of intense effort. Once this was accomplished, the concept became accessible to others, the lesser scholar had thus been able to grasp it.

This pattern can be applied beyond the sphere of intellectual development. Breaking through any new idea, practice or pattern requires unique effort, commitment and sacrifice. Once the breakthrough is accomplished, however, it can — and will — be emulated by others, and will eventually be considered a matter of course.

Today, there are *yeshivos* and Torah schools flourishing throughout the former Soviet Union, hundreds of thousands of Soviet Jews have emigrated to Israel and the US, and many both in and outside that country have demonstrated interest in increasing their Jewish observance.

In the 50s, 60s and 70s, even in the early 80s, this would have been considered a hopeless dream, nothing more than fantasy.

When the Rebbe assumed leadership of the chassidic movement, there was a small hard core of Lubavitcher chassidim left in Russia. The Rebbe labored unceasingly — through directing underground activities in Russia, and by applying influence in both the spheres of international diplomacy and in the spiritual spheres above — for Jewish observance to be maintained and amplified in the Soviet Union, and for all the Jews of Russia to be given permission to emigrate.

In the mid 80s, before Gorbachov's policies had taken form, the Rebbe told his chassidim that these dreams were about to become reality.[1] The full story of the Rebbe's involvement with the Jews in Russia and with those who emigrated to Israel and the US requires a treatment of its own. This chapter merely sheds light on certain personal dimensions of this heroic saga

---

1. See *To Know and To Care*, Vol. I, p. 17-18, which relates this story.

Once in the late 50s, in the middle of *yechidus,* Mrs. Bassie Garelik, wife of the *shliach* in Milan, Italy, mentioned the name of their local supporters, Reb Avraham Tzippel.

The Rebbe interrupted: "He is a very straightforward man."

When Mrs. Garelik returned home, she recounted her *yechidus* in detail to her husband, Rabbi Gershon Mendel Garelik. He felt there was something out of the ordinary in the Rebbe's mention of Reb Avraham Tzippel, and decided to investigate.

He called on the man and asked him about his health and that of his family. How was his business proceeding?

Reb Avraham was puzzled by Rabbi Garelik's queries, and asked the reason for them. Rabbi Garelik told him of his wife's *yechidus.*

"When did the *yechidus* take place?" Reb Avraham wanted to know.

When Rabbi Garelik told him the date, Reb Avraham hesitantly explained the significance of the Rebbe's words.

Reb Avraham was a furrier who had extensive business dealings in the then Soviet Union. He would utilize his trips there to bring Jews *Siddurim, tefillin* and other religious articles, and bring out manuscripts of chassidic thought for the Rebbe. These activities were carried out in absolute secrecy.

Generally, Reb Avraham's trips had proceeded without interference from the authorities. During his most recent visit, however, the authorities had placed him under house arrest for several hours. And then they had freed him, without any explanation for either his arrest or his release.

His release had come shortly after Mrs. Garelik's *yechidus.*

During the 60s, the Rebbe sent several chassidim to Russia as tourists. In some cities, they would have clandestine meetings with members of the chassidic underground. In other places, however, such meetings were too dangerous. Nevertheless, the Rebbe instructed his *shluchim* to pass through these cities and stop at the synagogues and places of Jewish interest.

Years later, after being able to leave Russia, one of the members of the Lubavitch community explained how important those visits were.

"In our city," he explained, "none of us had a chance to speak to the *shliach*. It was not until months later that we knew for sure that it was the Rebbe who had sent him. Nevertheless, his visit had a tremendous effect on us.

"The Russian government had begun a campaign to try to demoralize us. From time to time, it would call in members of the chassidic community and show them headlines from American Jewish newspapers and magazines which spoke of assimilation and intermarriage. 'Your faith is doomed to extinction,' they told us. 'In Europe, your brethren have been wiped out and in America, they have forgotten their heritage. Why must you be so stubborn in your observance?'

"And their words had an effect, not that we believed them totally. But still, when you read an American Yiddish newspaper that speaks of 'the vanishing American Jew,' you become disheartened.

"And suddenly we saw evidence that it was not all that dark in America. There was a young American wearing a *yarmulka* and *tzitzis* and sporting a full beard! It reinforced our faith in the future."

At their first *yechidus* with the Rebbe, in Tishrei 5729 (1968), Rabbi Zalman Leib and Mrs. Raizel Estulin were overcome with emotion. After many years of struggle in the chassidic underground in Russia, they had been able to emigrate to *Eretz Yisrael*, and were finally speaking to the Rebbe face to face!

True to chassidic tradition, Mrs. Estulin's thoughts were not self-centered. Instead, she was worried about her sister and brother-in-law, Rabbi and Mrs. Yaakov Lepkivker. They had applied to the Soviet authorities for emigration visas. Knowing of his involvement with the chassidic underground, the Russian authorities had told Rabbi Lepkivker: "You will rot here. Never will you leave Russia."

On the Estulins' note to the Rebbe, the first item was a request for the Lepkivkers' emigration.

When the Rebbe read their note, he gave a blessing for the Lepkivkers, but Mrs. Estulin felt there was something lacking; she had hoped to hear more powerful words of assurance. Breaking into tears, she told the Rebbe of the Lepkivkers' bitter situation.

The Rebbe listened patiently and answered: "Where would you be today if you had listened to the KGB? G-d performed a miracle and took your family out of Russia. Now a greater miracle is needed. But tell me: Does it make any difference to G-d whether He has to make a great miracle or a small miracle?"

A few months later, Rabbi Yaakov Lipskier went to *yechidus.* Rabbi Lipskier was Rabbi Lepkivker's brother-in-law, so he too would always mention the Lepkivkers before making any requests for his own needs. Each year, the Rebbe would give the Lepkivkers a blessing, but from the way in which he spoke, Rabbi Lipskier understood that the time for their deliverance had not yet come.

That year, before the Rebbe even looked at his note, he told him: "In several months, you will see your brother-in-law."

And indeed, several months afterwards, the Lepkivkers were in *Eretz Yisrael,* thanking G-d for His miraculous providence.

This was not the first time, the Rebbe had been asked to intercede for Reb Yaakov. In 5724 (1954), Reb Yaakov had taken ill. At that time, the health care offered by the government was not very reliable, and private care was prohibitively expensive. Reb Yaakov therefore decided to ignore his ailment. Unfortunately, the ailment did not ignore him, and after several weeks he found himself confined to bed.

His condition was diagnosed as Hepatitis B, a disease which could be life-threatening. At this point, the chassidic brotherhood resolved to locate — and pay for — one of the most capable specialists in the field. But after examining the patient and trying several remedies without success, the specialist refused to continue treatment. "The illness has reached too advanced a stage," he told the chassidim. "Why should I continue to treat the patient? It's only a waste of your money. Nothing any doctor can do will save him now."

By this time, Reb Yaakov was confined to a hospital and had lapsed into a coma. The chassidim met to consider the situation and decided that a telegram must be sent to the Rebbe. Usually, when the chassidim in Russia wanted to get a message to the Rebbe, they would encode it and send it through a chain of people to avoid detection. They realized, however, that in this situation time was of the essence, and so a telegram was drafted to *Zeide* (that's the way the chassidim in Russia addressed their correspondence to the Rebbe) at 770 Eastern Parkway in Brooklyn, telling of Reb Yaakov's condition.

But to what address should the reply be sent? A telegram coming from the Rebbe could certainly arouse the interest of the Soviet authorities. Mrs. Lepkivker volunteered her address and the telegram was sent.

Shortly afterwards Mrs. Lepkivker received a reply from *Zeide* assuring her that the patient would recover. The woman rushed to the hospital, entered her husband's room, and began speaking in his ear. "The Rebbe said you will recover," she told the unconscious man, repeating the message over and over again. At first, there was no response, but soon she began to see signs of life in her husband's face. He woke up, looked at her, and fell asleep with a smile.

The doctors were amazed that Reb Yaakov had regained consciousness. They were even more amazed when, two weeks later, he was well enough to be discharged!

After Reb Yaakov recovered, he felt he should call the specialist who had been consulted originally. When his receptionist told him that Yaakov Lepkivker was calling, the busy physician answered with irate suspicion: "How dare you use a dead man's name to try to get an appointment with me! Don't you have any respect?"

After Reb Yaakov managed to convince the doctor that he was indeed alive, the doctor told him to hire a cab and come to his office at once.

"I'll pay the taxi fare," the specialist assured him. "I just want to see with my own eyes a man who has come back from the dead!"

When Rabbi Nota Barkahan was granted permission to leave the former Soviet Union, he settled in *Eretz Yisrael*. But before setting up house he went to New York for *yechidus* with the Rebbe.

During the meeting the Rebbe told him to encourage all the chassidic immigrants to write descriptions of the *mesirus nefesh* with which they had struggled to observe *Yiddishkeit* throughout the years of Communist oppression.

"There may be some who will hesitate, claiming that their recollections are not exact, and there may even be contradictions between one account and another," the Rebbe told Rabbi Barkahan. "But that is not significant. All the discrepancies can be ironed out for the second printing. What's important is that these messages of self-sacrifice be heard by the world at large."

In the 1980s, during the last years of the Brezhnev regime, the chassidic underground in Russia had yielded a crop of young returnees to Jewish practice. These were Russian youth from secular Jewish homes who had been exposed to the chassidic lifestyle and had adopted it.

To spark their enthusiasm and increase their knowledge, the Rebbe began sending pairs of rabbis to Russia, each one for a stint of several weeks. Through the work of these emissaries, the *Chabad* activities expanded even further. Moscow, the city which boasted Russia's largest Jewish population, was one of the centers of Lubavitch activity.

At that time there was only one *mikveh* in the Russian capital, in the main *shul* known as the Choral Synagogue on Archipova St.

For this and other reasons, in 5746 (1986) the chassidim decided to build a *mikveh* in Moscow's chassidic *shul*, Marina Roscha. One of the chassidim, Sasha Lukatsky, took charge of the project, hiring black-market builders who secretly borrowed building supplies from the nearby regional headquarters of the KGB. This enabled them to complete the *mikveh* in an attractive fashion.

But a *mikveh* requires more than just builders and materials. Rabbinical supervision is necessary. Rabbi Gershon Grossbaum of S. Paul, Minnesota, had built many *mikvaos* in outlying cities, and was contacted with regard to the *mikveh* in Moscow. Upon the Rebbe's direction, Rabbi Meir Posen, a London-based Rabbinical expert who had built many *mikvaos*, was also contacted. Because of a freak accident, Rabbi Posen was prevented from going to Moscow. He drew up the plans for the *mikveh* and gave directions for Rabbi Grossbaum, who went to Moscow to complete the project.

Rabbi Grossbaum arrived in Moscow in the summer of that year, just before the Hebrew month of Av. According to Jewish law, the first nine days of Av are days of mourning, commemorating the destruction of the First and Second Temples in Jerusalem. There are certain restrictions against building during these days. For this reason, the Moscow chassidim were surprised to receive a message from the Rebbe telling them to hurry and try to complete the *mikveh* during this period.

Later they realized the reason. The KGB had learned of the plans to build the *mikveh*, and had established a lookout across from the *shul* to check if any suspicious activity was going on. But all those agents were given a week-long summer holiday, precisely during these nine days!

When the *mikveh* was completed, pictures were smuggled out and brought to the Rebbe. At the time, there were certain chassidim who wanted to publicize this evidence of observance by the Jews in Russia. The Rebbe, however, advised against doing so, maintaining that this would have negative consequences.

Directly after the *mikveh* was opened, the Russian government learned of its existence and threatened to demolish it. The Lubavitch women tried to prevent this by promising to lie down in front of the entrance and blocking the bulldozers with their bodies.

Their achievement, though heroic, was short-lived. The KGB was intent on destroying the *mikveh*. Ultimately, agents broke into the *shul* at night, smashed the pipes, filled the *mikveh* with rubble and paved its top with cement. As a finishing touch, they covered it with a decorative parquet flooring.

When Rabbi Berl Levy and other chassidim in New York heard what had happened, they asked the Rebbe whether they should now publicize the pictures of the *mikveh* and inform the world of its destruction. The Rebbe counseled against this course of action. "The *mikveh* was destroyed by underlings," he told the chassidim. "When the higher ups learn what happened, they will volunteer to rebuild the *mikveh* themselves. If this is made a point of international controversy, however, the *mikveh* will not be rebuilt."

The Rebbe did, however, agree to have the story told to several Congressmen and Senators who were involved in the struggle for human rights in the Soviet Union. Simultaneously, Sasha and other members of the Lubavitch community in Moscow put pressure on the local authorities to permit the *mikveh* to re-open.

In the spring of the following year, the Russian Minister of Religion made an international tour, trying to demonstrate that there was freedom of religion in the Soviet Union. Wherever he held a press conference, Lubavitch arranged that someone in the audience would ask about the *mikveh* in the Marina Roscha *shul.*

After a year these efforts bore fruit, and the Russian authorities agreed to reopen the *mikveh.* To save face, they announced that they were closing the *mikveh* in the Choral Synagogue. So as not to leave an entire city without a *mikveh,* they announced, they would allow one to be opened in the Marina Roscha *Shul.*

The authorities called Sasha and told him he could rebuild the *mikveh.* Sasha told them adamantly that he would not; the KGB would have to rebuild it! They were the ones who destroyed it, and they would be the ones to rebuild it.

Two weeks later, a group of Russian builders arrived at the *shul* with the necessary equipment. They dug out the cement and rubble and repaired the pipes. Within a short while, the *mikveh* was open. The decorative parquet floor was also preserved, and now graces the platform where the Torah is read!

Reb Moshe Katzenellenbogen had studied diligently in the underground Lubavitch *yeshivos* in Stalinist Russia. Arrested together with his mother, the legendary *Muma Sarah*, for obtaining forged Polish passports that enabled hundreds of chassidim to leave Russia, he was sentenced to many years in hard labor camps. After being freed, he rejoined the Lubavitch underground and shouldered many responsibilities in spreading observance of the Torah and its *mitzvos* through the Soviet Union.

When he was allowed to leave Russia he settled in England. At his first opportunity, he flew to New York to see the Rebbe.

At *yechidus,* the Rebbe instructed him to participate in a conference scheduled by *Aggudas HaRabbonim,* a prominent Rabbinical organization dedicated to clarifying *halachic* issues.

Reb Moshe protested. What place did he have at such a high-level conference?

"Don't display false modesty," the Rebbe told him: "I have heard that you have a thorough knowledge of the four portions of the *Shulchan Aruch.*"

Reb Moshe shrugged as if to disclaim the Rebbe's statement.

"I was told so in this room," the Rebbe declared with a smile. "And at this table, words that are not true are not spoken."

The Rebbe then reiterated his instructions, and emphasized that Reb Moshe should participate in the conference with no false modesty.

Then the Rebbe asked Reb Moshe if he had brought his *tallis* and *tefillin* with him from Russia. Reb Moshe answered that he had taken his *tefillin,* but not his *tallis.*

"Why didn't you leave your *tefillin* there as well?" the Rebbe exclaimed. "Outside Russia, it is easy to get new *tefillin,* while in Russia, no new *tefillin* are being produced, and it is difficult to bring them in from outside."

Reb Moshe answered that there were many pairs of old *tefillin* in Russia. The problem was that there were not enough people who wanted to wear them. *Talleisim*, by contrast, were also used for burial, so there was always a shortage.

Things soon changed. Within a few short years, the snowballing *teshuvah* movement in Russia created a need to smuggle in large numbers of new *tefillin*.

~

Mrs. Shoshana Cardin, past-president of the National Conference for Soviet Jewry, has a long-standing relationship with the Rebbe and with Rabbi Shmuel Kaplan, the Rebbe's *shliach* in Maryland. This notwithstanding, there are times when she has taken positions different from those of the Rebbe.

At one point, she wrote a letter to the Rebbe concerning the stand he had taken on a particular issue, explaining the perspective of those who shared opposing views. The Rebbe did not respond.

Several years later, Mrs. Cardin attended one of the conferences of the *Machne Israel* Development Fund. Each of the participants was given a chance for a brief private meeting with the Rebbe.

When Mrs. Cardin approached, but before she had a chance to speak, the Rebbe told her: "I know I owe you a letter."

Her amazement at the Rebbe's memory did not keep Mrs. Cardin from asking the question that had been on her mind. In light of the *perestroika* introduced by Mikhael Gorbachov, there were forces in the American Congress pushing for the repeal of the Jackson-Vanik amendment instituted to protect human rights — and largely Jewish rights — in the Soviet Union. "Should the National Conference for Soviet Jewry support this move?" she asked.

"Must the decision be made immediately?" the Rebbe replied.

"No," Mrs. Cardin conceded.

"Then wait," the Rebbe responded. "Although there has just been an election, it is not clear in whose hands the power rests. Wait until the time a decision must be made, and then get the most information you can from both inside and outside the Soviet Union. May G-d help you make the right decision."

At the time, the Rebbe's words were difficult to fathom; Gorbachov was at the height of his power. But in the subsequent years, with the abortive Red Army Coup, the collapse of the Soviet Union, and Gorbachov's loss of status, Mrs. Cardin was able to appreciate the visionary nature of the Rebbe's words.

In the late 1960s, the Russian government began letting out a trickle of Jewish emigrants. Some of these found their way to the United States. Of those who settled in New York, several families chose to live in Crown Heights. Most of these Jews weren't observant at all, let alone chassidic. They were drawn to the neighborhood because of the relatively cheap housing, and the lively relief agencies which the Lubavitch community had set up to help them.

One of those who settled in Crown Heights was a doctor in his 30s. He had been very successful in Russia, but had left for the States to maximize his opportunities. Unfortunately, his dreams had not been fulfilled. On the contrary, he was having difficulty receiving a license to practice in the States, and adjusting to the new environment presented challenge after challenge.

At one point, close to despair, he took a stroll along Eastern Parkway, his thoughts on suicide.

How would he do it? Should he step in front of a car as it was speeding down the parkway? Or should he walk to Prospect Park, where he was likely to be mugged?

As he wandered with these dark ideas in mind, a car pulled up to the curb in front of him. The passenger rolled down the window and looked at him with warm, penetrating eyes. Not a word was said, but something inside the doctor changed; he felt recharged, ready to take on life's challenges again. And soon his fortunes also changed. He received his license, began to practice, and was able to build his life anew.

Without saying a word, the Rebbe had saved a life.

Chapter 8 —
Shepherding His Flock

One of the chassidim in Moscow had been wealthy before the revolution, but had been reduced to poverty by the Communist regime. Once during the 1920s, when the Previous Rebbe visited that city, this chassid did not have the money to pay the trolley fare, and so he walked from one end of the city to the other to see him at *yechidus*.

At *yechidus*, he asked only about his divine service.

"And what about your material concerns?" the Rebbe asked.

"My material concerns don't interest me," the chassid replied.

"But they interest me," the Rebbe responded.

Unquestionably, the Rebbe thinks of every Jew. That said, there is undeniably a unique degree of closeness and care shown for *Anash,* the members of the chassidic brotherhood. A chassid regards the Rebbe as his father, sharing with him his inner conflicts, appealing to him for help in times of need.

And the Rebbe responds — sometimes with advice, sometimes with words of blessing, and sometimes with a blessing that is not expressed in words.

A chassid's relationship to the Rebbe is not one of give and take. His commitment is based on the genuineness of the Rebbe's message and the truth of his principles.

And indeed, the relationship goes deeper than that. As the Alter Rebbe writes in *Tanya*,[1] there are certain comprehensive souls who serve as a conduit for the spiritual nurture of others. A chassid feels that the Rebbe is the source of his spiritual vitality, and therefore he is willing to devote that energy to the Rebbe's objectives without reservation.

Such wholehearted devotion calls forth a reciprocal commitment to the chassid on the part of the Rebbe. The Rebbe will keep him in mind and invest energy in seeking out his material and spiritual welfare.

---

1. Ch. 2.

Every parent is concerned with his children's future. This is particularly true with *shluchim*. They want their children to grow up with the same dynamic attachment to the Rebbe that they themselves feel. They understand, however, that these feelings do not sprout spontaneously, but must be carefully nurtured over time.

A *shlichus* environment provides both advantages and disadvantages for such a process. The exposure to — and participation in — outreach efforts certainly has a effect on the *shluchim's* children, producing a heightened sense of commitment to the goals and values that Lubavitch endeavors to spread. On the other hand, growing up in a city far from observant Jewish communities does not have the greenhouse effect that growing up near Crown Heights does.

With these thoughts in mind, whenever Rabbi and Mrs. Heschel Greenberg, *shluchim* in Buffalo, NY, went to the Rebbe to receive a dollar on Sunday morning, they always thought of asking for a blessing for their children's education. But they always refrained. They didn't want to make any extra demands on the Rebbe's time, and felt that from a certain perspective, such a request was unnecessary. By the very fact that the Rebbe had appointed them as *shluchim*, he had certainly granted them all the blessings necessary both for themselves and for their families. On the other hand, they felt that although the Rebbe would grant them the blessings anyway, they should nonetheless ask for them themselves.

For several years, Rabbi and Mrs. Greenberg thought and spoke about the matter. Once, when Mrs. Greenberg was preparing for a trip to Crown Heights, she decided that this time, when she appeared before the Rebbe to receive a dollar, she would ask for a blessing for her children.

As she was preparing to leave Buffalo, her telephone rang. A relative of one of the members of the *Chabad* community had become ill. Mrs. Greenberg naturally responded that when she approached the Rebbe that Sunday, she would ask for a blessing for the person's recovery.

Inside, however, she felt a twinge of regret. She didn't want to hold the Rebbe back by asking for two blessings. Asking for the sick person would prevent her from asking for her own children.

But *shluchim* are trained to put the needs of others before their own. She therefore did not give the matter a second thought, and when she approached the Rebbe, she wholeheartedly asked for a blessing for the sick person.

The Rebbe responded with a blessing. And as Mrs. Greenberg prepared to walk away, he continued with a fatherly smile: "May you have satisfaction from them."

Once a *shluchah* left for a foreign country shortly after marriage, and while in the first months of pregnancy. She did not know the local language, felt difficulty adjusting to the culture in her new country, and was overwhelmed by the estrangement from Judaism which prevailed there.

These factors, combined with the natural feelings of depression and melancholy which occasionally accompany pregnancy, made her feel even more despondent. These feelings multiplied as the woman considered her position: here she was, she was the representative of the Rebbe in this country. And what was she doing? Absolutely nothing! No outreach, little teaching; all she did was feel sorry for herself.

Rather than let herself be overwhelmed by these feelings, she decided to write the Rebbe and ask for a blessing. The Rebbe replied that such feelings are natural during pregnancy. She should talk to other woman, he said, and see that they also experience such emotional states.

The Rebbe did not content himself with these words of reassurance. Shortly afterwards, he addressed the annual convention of Lubavitch women. The *shluchah*'s sister was one of the organizers. Each of the delegates was able to enter the Rebbe's room for a short *yechidus*. The Rebbe told Rabbi

Chodakov, his personal secretary, to see to it that the *shluchah*'s sister entered last.

At *yechidus*, the Rebbe told her of her sister's letter, and advised her to have a woman-to-woman talk with her. "Tell her," the Rebbe explained, "that these feelings are natural, that she shouldn't be weighed down by them. This will help her regain her equilibrium and return to a productive life."

※

Rabbi Shlomo Matusof, a *shliach* in Morocco, visited the Rebbe for the first time during Sukkos, 5715 (1954). At *yechidus* the Rebbe inquired into many details of the *shlichus*, and asked how Rabbi Matusof and his family had adjusted to life in that country.

"Do you have pictures of your children?" he asked.

Rabbi Matusof had several photos in his wallet. The Rebbe looked them over intently, but instead of returning them, he left them on his table. Although somewhat surprised, Rabbi Matusof did not ask for them back.

Now, a few years earlier, while living in Poking — the camp for displaced persons which housed many *Chabad* families after World War II — Rabbi Matusof had become acquainted with the Rebbe's mother, Rebbitzin Chanah.

A day or so after the Sukkos *yechidus*, Rabbi Binyamin Gorodetsky, the Rebbe's chief representative in Europe and North Africa, asked Rabbi Matusof if he would like to visit Rebbitzin Chanah. Rabbi Matusof happily consented.

Rebbitzin Chanah greeted Rabbi Matusof warmly. "You have charming children," she told him, explaining that the Rebbe had shown her the pictures that Rabbi Matusof had left with him at *yechidus*.

※

One of the Rebbe's *shluchim* took his wife to the hospital for the delivery of their fourth child. Before leaving home he called the Rebbe's office, asking the secretary to request a blessing for an easy and successful birth.

The delivery took longer than usual, so it was several hours before the *shliach* was able to inform the Rebbe's office that both mother and child were well. When the secretary heard the news, he remarked: "A short while ago, the Rebbe asked 'What is happening with...'?"

※

Once a Lubavitcher chassid teaching in an out-of-town *yeshivah* came to *yechidus* with a question: The school at which he had been working was several months late in paying his salary. This situation had been recurring for several years. A member of the community in which he worked had seen his difficulties, and had offered to help set him up in business. Should he accept the offer?

As soon as the Rebbe read the letter, he made a wry face. He paused for a second and asked the chassid: "How much do you need to tide you over your immediate difficulties?"

The chassid named a figure. The Rebbe told him to go to Rabbi Chodakov the following day, and that Rabbi Chodakov would give him a loan for that amount.

The chassid remained a teacher, educating thousands of students throughout his lifetime.

※

Once at *yechidus*, Rabbi Yaakov Gluckowsky had a question: He was teaching at the *Beis Yehudah* school in Detroit. He took his job seriously, spending many hours preparing classes and organizing activities for the students. Nevertheless, he also saw that the Jewish community at large needed attention.

Would it be considered a conflict of interest for him to involve himself in such matters?

The Rebbe replied that when a school hires a teacher, the intent is that in addition to teaching, he perform a certain measure of community service. Every teacher should look for one or two matters outside the school that require attention, and devote himself to them. This is not in conflict with his job; it is *part* of his job!

This message stayed with Reb Yaakov all his life. In his later years, he was teaching a *Bar Mitzvah* program for Israeli youth in Toronto. Besides the classes, he would spend Sunday mornings with the boys, arranging a *minyan* and a breakfast.

The director of the program, Rabbi Landau, wanted to pay him extra for the Sunday morning hours, but Reb Yaakov refused to take the money.

He told Rabbi Landau the above story and concluded: "The situation with these Israeli boys is one of the matters in the community that require attention. I have decided to devote myself to it, and so the extra time is already included in the check I receive for teaching."

As a member of the Lubavitch underground in Russia, Reb Aharon Chazan had often risked his life to preserve Jewish tradition and observance for the coming generations. When he left Russia for *Eretz Yisrael,* Reb Aharon was an elderly man, and it was several years before he made his first trip to the Rebbe. Finally, in 5733 (1973), he came to spend *Yud* Shvat at 770. That year *Yud* Shvat fell on *Shabbos,* so the Rebbe held two *farbrengens:* one during the day, and a second after nightfall, which was broadcast by telephone to Lubavitch centers around the world.

The first *farbrengen* ended shortly before sunset. After reciting the afternoon prayers, Reb Aharon hurried to his hosts to partake of the *Shabbos* meal. The meal extended past nightfall, after which Reb Aharon recited the evening prayers and hurried back to 770 to find a place for the second *farbrengen*.

Now Reb Aharon had always been very careful about observing the custom of partaking of the *Melaveh Malkah* ("accompanying the [Sabbath] queen") meal. He wondered when he would be able to observe his custom that night. As he was waiting for the *farbrengen* to begin, he had an idea. He had completed the *Shabbos* meal after nightfall. Could that also be considered a *Melaveh Malkah*, despite the fact that the *Havdalah* prayer had not yet been recited?

He began discussing the matter with a *rav* sitting next to him, noting that the Machanovka Rebbe would partake of bread for the *Shalosh Seudos* (third *Shabbos*) meal, and then before reciting the grace after meals, partake of another portion after nightfall. Thus the same meal served him as both *Shalosh Seudos* and *Melaveh Malkah*.

As the two were discussing the matter, the Rebbe entered and their dialogue ceased. In the middle of one of his talks, however, the Rebbe began a tangential discussion about the uniqueness of the hours after *Shabbos*.

"All the matters involving *Motzaei Shabbos* must be carried out after *Havdalah*. A meal which is eaten before *Havdalah* (i.e., by prolonging the *Shalosh Seudos*) is not considered a *Melaveh Malkah*," said the Rebbe.

When he heard those words Reb Aharon was transfixed. He had always felt connected to the Rebbe, but now, on his first visit to 770, he comprehended just how powerful this bond could be. It was as if the Rebbe had read his mind!

A girl from a prominent Lubavitch family was finishing high school and considering her future. She wanted to go to college, and indeed had qualified for a Regents scholarship. Her parents, however, did not view that option favorably. After months of discussion, they reached a compromise: she would go to seminary for a year, and afterwards, if she still wanted to attend college, her parents would allow it.

When it came to choosing a seminary, she thought of places that would enable her to transfer credits to university. She narrowed her options down to one school in *Eretz Yisrael*, and wrote to the Rebbe telling him of her plans. For the first time in her life, she bared her heart to the Rebbe, writing a letter several pages long that spoke of her desire to attend college, her discussions with her parents, and their ultimate decision. She promised to follow the Rebbe's advice, but wanted his assurance that the decision would ultimately bring her happiness.

The Rebbe did not answer immediately. Indeed, for many weeks, the girl did not receive a reply. Several months later, Rabbi Klein called her with the Rebbe's response.

Rabbi Klein told her that the Rebbe had kept her letter, choosing to respond only to her question about the particular school she had chosen.

The Rebbe's answer was written several days after Chanukah, and referred to the theme of that holiday, saying: "We are now coming from the holiday of Chanukah, which is connected with the concept: 'Ascend higher with regard to holy matters; do not descend.' You should apply this maxim to your life. The school which you attend should be one which raises you to a higher level of fear of G-d and observance of His *mitzvos*. At the very least, it should not be at a lower level."

Taking the Rebbe's words to heart, the girl realized that the school she had chosen did not meet the Rebbe's criteria. She changed her plans and decided to spend the next year in the *Beis Rivkah* Seminary in Kfar Chabad. It proved to be a year of personal transformation, as chassidic thought and many other aspects of her Jewish heritage took on a new relevance. Although she still had the option of using the Regents scholarship, that alternative no longer held any attraction. She continued in the seminary and received her diploma.

It was a choice that helped shape her future. Twenty years later, she reflects on the path her life has taken. "Going to *Beis Rivkah* allowed me to discover who I really was and where I wanted to go. It was a decision that brought me great happiness."

It was one of those moments when a person unburdens himself. Two old *yeshivah* friends were speaking, and one was telling the other of his difficulties. He had been married for a little over a year. He'd tried several jobs, but had not been able to find anything satisfying. Neither his parents nor his in-laws were able to help him financially or establish him in business. Ultimately, he was forced to resort to driving a truck in order to support his family. But even so, his income was insufficient; every month, he was sinking deeper and deeper into debt.

But that wasn't the only thing that bothered him about truck driving. The main problem was that he felt himself growing coarser; after a day behind the wheel, he had no patience to study, and was losing touch with spiritual refinement. This had also affected his relationship with his wife.

He wanted to change, but had seen no way to do so until one of his clients — an older man who ran a book bindery — told him he was planning to retire and wanted to sell the business. Now the bindery was not so prosperous, but the young man felt that if he invested enough energy, he could make a go of it. True, he would have to borrow money to purchase the business, but he had taken and repaid loans before.

In truth, he didn't want to run a bindery, but he was desperate for a change, and this seemed to be the best opportunity available. Should he take it?

His friend didn't know how to answer him. "From a business perspective, anyone would say No. So why are you thinking of trying it? To reverse the downward trend in your

Shepherding His Flock

life? That isn't a question for me. Write to the Rebbe," he told the trucker.

Now the trucker hadn't written to the Rebbe for years; ever since he had left *yeshivah,* he had been too embarrassed. It was hard for him to write the letter, but he put his heart into it, telling the Rebbe about his dissatisfaction with the direction his life had taken, his difficulty in making a change, and his hope that this opportunity might allow him to do that.

He delivered his letter to the Rebbe's office and waited.

And waited.

After two weeks, he sent in another copy, but still there was no answer. Nonetheless, he began to notice a change in his business. He found several new customers, and one offered him a part-time job selling. His debts began to evaporate and his tension lifted. He suddenly found time to study, and his relationship with his wife improved.

He never did receive a written reply from the Rebbe, but he knew that he had been answered.

In 1965, Prof. Yitzchak Block, an expert on Plato and a full-fledged Lubavitcher chassid, was serving in the philosophy department of the University of Western Ontario.

One of the professor's colleagues, the head of the philosophy department at Brown University, invited Prof. Block to read a paper at a conference on Plato. But there was a difficulty: Prof. Block would be expected to speak on *Shabbos* morning.

There was no question in Prof. Block's mind; he would not violate the *Shabbos.* On the other hand, the Rebbe had always encouraged Prof. Block to speak at conferences. In certain instances, the Rebbe had urged Prof. Block to participate even when a conference had been held on *Shabbos.*

But Prof. Block made a distinction between those conferences and this one. They had been held in small conference rooms in hotels. He had been able to bring his notes to the room before *Shabbos,* and there had been no need for a microphone. At Brown University, he did not know where he would be able to put his notes beforehand, and he would probably be asked to use a mike.

He called Rabbi Chodakov, the Rebbe's personal secretary, and explained his dilemma. Rabbi Chodakov promised that he would bring the matter to the Rebbe's attention.

After a few months, Prof. Block called Rabbi Chodakov again. Rabbi Chodakov told him that he had informed the Rebbe about the professor's problem, but the Rebbe hadn't replied. He promised to bring the matter up again.

Two weeks later, Prof. Block called back. Rabbi Chodakov answered that he had mentioned the matter to the Rebbe, but again had received no answer. Prof. Block told him that it was now only two weeks to the conference and he needed a reply. "Could Rabbi Chodakov please communicate this to the Rebbe?"

This time, Rabbi Chodakov called Prof. Block back with an answer. The Rebbe had said to call the professor organizing the conference and tell him that an emergency had arisen requiring that Prof. Block be in New York that Friday evening, but that he would be happy to deliver his paper on Friday morning instead.

Professor Block was very uncomfortable, because this type of bartering for time is frowned upon in academic circles; conference schedules are set well in advance, and speakers cannot be shuffled around at will. Nevertheless, having asked and been given this answer, he saw no alternative.

Prof. Block's colleague at Brown received his call happily. "Block," he said, before the professor could speak, "I was just going to call you. One of the professors at Yale was supposed to deliver a paper on Friday morning, but he just called and said that he has a throat infection and won't be able to make it.

I have no one else who can speak at that time. Would it be possible to shift you from Saturday to Friday?"

Prof. Block explained that Friday morning presented no problem, but that an emergency would require him to be in New York Friday evening. Would that be a difficulty?

Happy to have solved his main problem, the Brown department head told Prof. Block that he would be able to leave directly after delivering his paper. There was a bus leaving Providence in the early afternoon, so the professor could be in New York by Friday evening.

Prof. Block delivered his paper, received favorable comments, and was able to catch the bus. Despite a difficult journey, he arrived at Crown Heights for *Shabbos*. On *Shabbos* afternoon, the Rebbe held a *farbrengen*. Spotting Prof. Block in the crowd, he asked him to fill his cup of wine and say *LeChaim*.

"What's with Yankel Friedman's *Tehillim?*" the Rebbe asked his secretary, Rabbi Leibl Groner, one morning in the winter of 5713 (1953).

Rabbi Groner didn't understand the Rebbe's question, but promised to speak to Rabbi Friedman and get an answer.

Rabbi Friedman reacted with surprise when informed of the Rebbe's inquiry, and asked Rabbi Groner to tell the Rebbe that the matter would be rectified.

Later Rabbi Friedman explained the story. He worked in the office of the Central Lubavitcher *Yeshivah*, then located at Bedford and Dean. At that time, the *yeshivah* was always short of funds, and therefore perpetually short-staffed. In his devotion to his duties, Rabbi Friedman found himself continually taking on new responsibilities.

The municipal authorities in New York City paid for *yeshivah* students who lived beyond walking distance to be bussed to school. But there was a difference of opinion between the *yeshivah* administration and the city authorities as to just how far "walking distance" was, and so there were many students for whom the *yeshivah* felt it necessary to provide bussing without being reimbursed. To relieve some of this pressure, Rabbi Friedman received a bus driver's license, and every morning would pick up those students who lived in the area surrounding the *yeshivah*.

Now, the Previous Rebbe had instituted the practice of reciting a portion from *Tehillim* each day after the morning service, so that the recitation of the entire book would be completed once a month.

Rabbi Friedman was not known to hurry his prayers, but children must not be late for school, and so, as a compromise with the clock, he would sometimes postpone his recitation of the daily portion of *Tehillim* until after he had completed his bus route. He understood the Rebbe's question to be an affirmation that yes, what he was doing was important, but that it should not come at the expense of *Tehillim*.

From that time on, he somehow managed to complete the daily portion of *Tehillim* and also get the children to school on time.

Chapter 9 —
Unveiling Hidden Treasures

The wife of one of New York's distinguished Rabbis came to the Rebbe one Sunday to receive a dollar for charity. The Rebbe greeted her warmly, saying: "It's so nice to see you. You have not been here for a while. But that's the way it is with really precious things. You see them only from time to time."

The Torah relates that when G-d sought out Moshe our teacher, He appeared to him in a burning bush. When Moshe saw the bush, he said:[1] "I will turn aside now, and see this great sight."

There are commentators who explain that this was a test of Moshe's leadership ability. A leader must be sensitive to a great sight. When he sees it, rather than continue his ordinary routine, he should turn aside to give it the attention it deserves.

Others take issue, explaining that the uniqueness of Moshe, and similarly his spiritual heirs, the Jewish leaders of subsequent generations, is not merely the ability to respond to

---

1. *Shmos* 3:3.

obvious greatness. What distinguishes a Jewish leader is his appreciation that every Jew possesses innate greatness, and his care and sensitivity in nurturing that potential and enabling it to flourish.

On the weekend after Shavuos 5745, the Aleph Institute organized a two-week Torah Study Retreat in Crown Heights for Jews in federal prisons.

The 18 participants were involved in lectures, study programs and hands-on workshops about their Jewish roots. Included in the program was participation in the Rebbe's *farbrengen* on *Shabbos* afternoon.

Shortly before the *farbrengen*, Rabbi Leibl Groner, the Rebbe's secretary, came looking for the institute's director, Rabbi Sholom Ber Lipskar. "The Rebbe has asked," Rabbi Groner told him, "that the prisoners not be seated together at the *farbrengen*, but be interspersed among the crowd."

Rabbi Lipskar looked at him quizzically; he had reserved seating in one area, and re-seating the participants would involve considerable adjustments. Rabbi Groner, however, proceeded to explain the Rebbe's reason. If they are seated together, the Rebbe had said, people will ask who they are. It will be said that they are prisoners, and this will be embarrassing to them. To prevent this from happening, they should be seated separately.

The Rebbe also explained that although at the end of the *farbrengen* he would be distributing bottles of *mashkeh*, he would not give a bottle to this group, although they were most deserving of this extra concern. This would attract attention, and their identity would be revealed. Rather than risk causing them embarrassment, the Rebbe preferred not to give them *mashkeh*. Instead, the Rebbe raised their spirits by including in that *farbrengen* an extraordinarily forward-looking dissertation concerning prisoners.

A woman from France who had begun the journey back to her Jewish roots once went to the Rebbe for *yechidus*. Her parents had never given her a Jewish name, and one of her requests was that the Rebbe choose a name for her.

The Rebbe responded: "Your French name is Jacqueline. That is the feminine form of Jacque. Jacque resembles the Hebrew Yaakov. You should choose the name Yaakovah."

The woman thanked the Rebbe, but he sensed a certain apprehension. "You don't understand Hebrew," he continued. "Don't worry, I will write it down for you so that you will not forget." And the Rebbe wrote the name Yaakovah on a small piece of paper and gave it to the woman.

She appreciated the gift, had it encased, and wore it as a pendant.

※

When Miriam Rosenblum (née Wolosow) was nine years old, she and her family were living in Dublin, Ireland. In that city, there were relatively few Jewish families with girls her age, so she was happy to find a friend by the name of Lila Zolondik. The friendship also had a spiritual dimension, since Miriam encouraged Lila to observe the *mitzvos* with warmth and care.

Shortly afterwards, tragedy struck the Zolondik family and Lila's father passed away. Miriam wrote the Rebbe about her friend and asked for a blessing.

Two years later — during which the Rebbe received countless other letters and requests for blessings — Miriam went to New York for her first *yechidus*. The Rebbe's first questions were: "How is Lila Zolondik? Are you still in contact with her?"

※

The widow of renowned sculptor Jacques Lifchitz came for a private audience with the Rebbe shortly after her husband's sudden passing.

In the course of the meeting, she mentioned that her husband had been working on a massive sculpture of a phoenix (a mythical bird) for the Hadassah Hospital on Mt. Scopus.

A sculptor in her own right, Mrs. Lifchitz had considered completing her husband's work, but had been advised that the phoenix is a non-Jewish symbol.

How could she complete such a sculpture and have it brought to Jerusalem?

The Rebbe called for his secretary, Rabbi Yehuda Krinsky, and asked him for the book of *Job*. When he received the sacred text, the Rebbe opened it to chapter 29, verse 18, which reads: "and I shall multiply my days like the *chol*."

The Rebbe proceeded to explain the *Midrashic* commentary[2] to the verse, which describes the *chol* as a bird that lives for 1,000 years, dies, and then is resurrected from its ashes.

Clearly, the phoenix *was* a Jewish symbol!

Mrs. Lifchitz was delighted at the explanation, and dedicated herself to the project, which she completed shortly thereafter.

The Rebbe had given her a gift of personal rejuvenation that enabled her to complete a symbol of rejuvenation for others.

※

Shortly after the Rebbe assumed the *nesius,* several young American men from secular backgrounds began studying in the Lubavitcher *yeshivah.* One of them, a student from Chicago, received his draft notice a few short months after he had begun studying.

He was very upset. "While I was not observant," he explained to his friends, "I had all the time in the world and

---

2. *Bereishis Rabbah* 19:5, *Yalkut Shimoni,* Vol. II, sec. 917, cited by *Rashi* in his commentary to the verse.

misused it, and yet I was not drafted. Now suddenly, when I've started to appreciate the importance of time, and have begun using it wisely, I am no longer my own master. How could G-d do this to me?"

With complaints of this nature, and with some practical questions such as "Should I claim to be a conscientious objector, or should I flee to Canada and begin studying in the Lubavitcher *yeshivah* in Montreal?", he approached the Rebbe at *yechidus.*

The Rebbe told him to enter the army and not to worry about the lost time. "It is a descent," the Rebbe explained, "for the purpose of an ascent."

And then the Rebbe stood up to illustrate what he meant. "Standing next to the chair like this," he told the student, "I would never be able to jump over it. But if I were to take a few steps back" — and the Rebbe did so — "and get a running start, I could jump over it."

The student spent two years in the army, serving in different posts in Western Europe. Throughout this period, he fastidiously observed the *mitzvos,* finding time to pray and study in even the most difficult of circumstances.

When he completed his tour of duty, he returned to New York and prepared to enter *yechidus.* He had several serious questions concerning his future: Should he return to *yeshivah,* or should he begin contemplating a career? Should he start considering marriage? And he had some questions regarding religious observance. Should he begin growing a beard, for example.

All in all, he had 10 major questions, each with several minor inquiries associated with it. For example, if the Rebbe told him to grow a beard, how should he deal with his mother's objections? If the Rebbe told to think about a career, in which area should he start looking?

He wrote down his 10 major questions, but instead of handing the list to the Rebbe, he held it in his own hand and asked the questions verbally. To each of his major questions, the Rebbe answered in great detail, anticipating all the minor questions that were in his mind.

As the young man asked question after question, he began to grow more amazed at the Rebbe's answers. Obviously, he was reading his mind! On every point which he wanted clarified, the Rebbe answered in precise detail, foreseeing all the secondary issues he had thought of bringing up.

After having five questions answered in this fashion, he froze in amazement, unable to continue. The Rebbe, however, continued for him, stating both the questions and the answers, until in this fashion he had dealt with all 10 issues that the young man had wished to resolve.

※

This story must be appreciated within the context of the unique harmony which prevails in Pittsburgh's religious community. There have always been close feelings between the city's Lubavitcher chassidim and other traditional Orthodox communities. At one point, the Lubavitch *Yeshivah* and the Orthodox Hillel Day School shared the same property. On a personal level, the families were so close that in many ways they comprised a single homogenous entity.

For this reason, it was not surprising that Yale Butler, son of one of the leading Orthodox families, became an active member of Lubavitch's *Mesibos Shabbos* youth program and developed a personal relationship with Rabbi Yossi Shpielman, its director. Not that Yale was becoming a Lubavitcher. On the contrary, he was an active member of *Bnei Akiva* and was comfortable with that ideology. But he saw no contradiction between that and absorbing the vibrancy which Lubavitch infused into Jewish life.

Yale has always been an individualist, and a creative one. In 1960, when he was a seventh-grader, he became editor of the Hillel newspaper. He wanted his first edition to attract attention throughout Pittsburgh's Jewish community, so he thought of a spoof.

One of the more active figures in Pittsburgh's Jewish community was a Lubavitcher who often wore an army hat and jacket. This and his untrimmed beard reminded many of Fidel Castro. In fact, the association was so common that he was nicknamed "Castro" throughout the community.

(This was almost 40 years ago, and Castro's dictatorial, anti-American policies were not widely known at the time. On the contrary, to many Americans, he was a flashy underdog fighting Cuba's despotic leader, Batista.)

Yale decided to expand on the association. He wrote a fictional account about an invasion of Cuba in which Castro's troops were in danger of being wiped out. In desperation, Castro called to his brethren in 770. They contacted the Rebbe and the order was given: chassidim were to march on the Brooklyn Navy Yard, commandeer several submarines, and sail to Castro's rescue.

Yale's story did attract attention, but not the kind he desired. Many in Pittsburgh's Jewish community read his article, but few approved. Even as a jest, it was simply out of place.

Leaders of the traditional Orthodox community reprimanded the 12 year old for his lack of sensitivity, as did his parents. He was encouraged to apologize to Rabbi Sholom Posner, the head of the Lubavitch community. In the end, this first issue of the paper was also its final edition.

Rabbi Shpielman, with whom Yale shared a developing relationship, did not think of reprimanding him. Instead, he wanted to introduce Yale to the chassid-*Rebbe* relationship.

"You have to meet the Rebbe," he told Yale. "Once you discover who he is, you will see how inappropriate your piece was."

Yale was not unwilling, and Rabbi Shpielman began to speak to him about *yechidus*. Shortly afterwards, Yale's *Bnei*

Akiva chapter had a *Shabbaton* in Crown Heights, and this appeared to be a perfect opportunity. On the Sunday after the *Shabbaton*, he would do some shopping, in Judaica stores on the East Side, and that evening he would meet the Rebbe.

Rabbi Shpielman had promised to meet him at 770 and enter *yechidus* with him, so Yale felt comfortable when he arrived that evening. He did not have to wait long for *yechidus*, and soon he and Rabbi Shpielman entered the Rebbe's room.

The Rebbe motioned for Yale to sit down. As he did, he noticed Rabbi Shpielman leaving. At this point, he began to feel a little daunted. After all, he was only a seventh-grader and was sitting alone with the Rebbe!

The Rebbe spoke to Yale warmly, telling him that he knew of his family and its work on behalf of the *mikveh* and Jewish education in Pittsburgh. Yale was moved by the cordial words. The Rebbe continued, complimenting Yale for his talent as a writer.

Up until this point, Yale had been mesmerized by the Rebbe's eyes, but then he noticed a copy of his article on the Rebbe's desk! The Rebbe, however, made no mention of the article at all. Instead, he spoke of a person's obligation to appreciate that his talents are a trust that he should use for the benefit of others. In particular, the Rebbe emphasized, a writer should use his abilities to promote Jewish unity and the love of one Jew for another.

Instead of the sheer terror Yale felt when he saw his article on the Rebbe's table, his feelings turned to relaxation and then empowerment. The Rebbe had recognized his potential and given him encouragement with regard to its expression.

Years passed. In 1979, after receiving his Rabbinic ordination and working as a Rabbi in Vancouver, Yale moved to Los Angeles, where, among his other responsibilities, he wrote a weekly column for the B'nai Brith *Messenger*. After several months, Joe Cummins, its publisher, asked him to write an additional column on the weekly Torah reading.

Rabbi Butler explained that he was already over-committed, and could not do the column himself. "If you want a good piece on the weekly portion," he told Mr. Cummins, "why don't you use the talks of the Lubavitcher Rebbe? They come out every week, they're articulate, and a wide range of people would be interested in reading them." Mr. Cummins accepted the idea, and the Rebbe's *sichos* began to appear weekly in the *Messenger*.

In 1982, Yale became the publisher of the paper. One of the programs he introduced was lifetime subscriptions. One night, as he sat reviewing the list of people who had purchased these subscriptions, he came across the name, M.M. Schneerson. The Rebbe had answered the ad personally, and had enclosed his own check in payment.

Rabbi Butler had been sending the Rebbe a paper each week without charge; after all, the Rebbe's column appeared in it. The Rebbe, however, had felt the need to pay for a subscription.

From time to time, the Rebbe would ask Rabbi Butler to publicize his perspective with regard to certain issues such as Israel's right to Judah and Samaria, the *halachic* perspective with regard to the Law of Return, and other concerns facing the American Jewish community.

It appears that the Rebbe never forgot the "Castro" article, once telling Rabbi Shimon Raichik of L.A. that Yale had shown skill as a writer "since childhood."

A noted Rabbi had come to the Rebbe for *yechidus* before his eldest daughter was to be married. "Forgive me for mixing into your personal life," the Rebbe told him at the conclusion of their meeting, "but I have a request of you. Let your beard grow. It's appropriate for a man of your position.

"And," the Rebbe added with a smile, "it's appropriate for the new phase that will begin in your personal life. After all, soon you're going to become a *zeide* (a grandfather), and you should *look* like a *zeide*!"

The Rabbi happily agreed to the Rebbe's request, and asked: "Perhaps I should also change my style of hat (the Rabbi would wear a round hat) to that worn by the Rebbe?"

"No," the Rebbe replied with a wave of his hand, "that's a superficial matter. I have followers who think that by putting on the same hat I do, and having it dented exactly as I do, they'll establish a connection with me. That isn't the way.

"The way to establish a connection is to invest energy in the same areas in which I invest my energy."

Once a Rabbi who was active in various educational programs in the Orthodox community came to consult the Rebbe about them at *yechidus*. At the end of the *yechidus,* he requested a blessing for his son, Moshe, who was suffering from pneumonia.

The Rebbe asked for the name of the child's mother. The Rabbi answered: "Fruma." The Rebbe then gave his blessing. Shortly afterwards, Moshe recovered.

Fifteen years later, this same Rabbi came to see the Rebbe at *yechidus* regarding another communal matter. As he entered the Rebbe's room, the Rebbe greeted him: "How is your son doing?"

"I have three sons," the Rabbi answered. "About which son is the Rebbe asking?"

"Moshe ben Fruma," the Rebbe replied.

"Letters to the Rebbe," explains Rabbi Yisrael Deren, "are not always answered on paper." To illustrate his point, Rabbi Deren tells the following story.

When he moved to Stamford to open the regional office of Lubavitch, he noticed that a men's *mikveh* was being built in the city, and was curious as to whose initiative this was. He was told that it was being built by an Israeli who was not well known in the Jewish community.

Shortly thereafter, he received a fax from Mr. Dov Parshan, who had been vacationing in Miami. Mr. Parshan reported that he had met an Israeli who was living in Stamford and was interested in advancing his Jewish involvement.

Shortly afterwards, Rabbi Deren received a call from a woman who wanted to register her child in his pre-school. As they were talking, the woman mentioned that her husband was Israeli and that they had just returned from a vacation in Miami. She was amazed when Rabbi Deren addressed her by name and conveyed regards from Mr. Parshan!

The woman had not realized Rabbi Deren was associated with Lubavitch; she had heard about the high educational standards of his school, and that was what had attracted her attention. When he explained that he was the local Lubavitch representative, she told him that her husband would like to speak to him.

Rabbi Deren was agreeable, and shortly afterwards, the husband called. He said he wanted to speak to Rabbi Deren at length, and so they arranged an appointment for eight that evening. Rabbi Deren was puzzled when the man said he would see him at eight, and that his wife would come over at nine.

As soon as the man began to speak, Rabbi Deren understood why he and his wife were coming separately; there was a certain distance between them.

The husband began to tell his story. He used to live in Queens, and operated a business there. Each Friday, students from the Central Lubavitch *yeshivah* would come by to put on *tefillin* with him. He was not receptive at first, but the students' friendliness gradually won him over, and he began to look forward to their visits. Once, a few weeks passed without them stopping by, and he realized that he genuinely missed them.

One *mitzvah* led to another, and slowly but surely, he began to advance in Jewish practice. He purchased his own *tefillin*, began observing *Shabbos,* and started eating kosher.

His wife, however, was less than interested. When they moved to Connecticut, their differences had been aggravated. The husband wanted to identify with the more observant community. He was also anxious to take other steps which reflected his increased commitment, but his wife, by contrast, wanted the *status quo.*

Rabbi Deren tried to smooth things out, talking to them until 3 a.m.. He was able to convince the husband to relax the pressure on his wife. "It took time before you reached this level of commitment," Rabbi Deren reminded him. "Give your wife a chance to do the same. Let her Jewish involvement grow at her own pace."

And he explained to the wife the need to respect her husband's spiritual development. Even if she did not share his interest in Jewish practice, she should at least show appreciation for his efforts to advance himself spiritually.

Their discussion took place Tuesday night. On Wednesday, the Israeli called and reported that the domestic friction had not abated. On Thursday, he came to Rabbi Deren's office and poured his heart out in frustration.

Rabbi Deren did not know what more to do; he had said everything he had to say. He had only one suggestion: write to the Rebbe.

The man composed a letter to the Rebbe and Rabbi Deren faxed it to the Rebbe's office. That weekend, Rabbi Deren had to attend a *Bar-Mitzvah* in England, so he hurried off to the airport.

On Sunday, Rabbi Deren called his wife, and she told him that it was imperative for him to call the Israeli; the man had called several times with urgent messages.

So Rabbi Deren called him from England, and was surprised by his happy tone. His wife had begun to show a positive interest in Jewish practice!

What had happened? That Thursday night, the couple had gone to a vegetarian restaurant with several non-Jewish friends. There they were joined by a non-Jew who worked as a butler for a Jewish multi-millionaire. The table talk turned to religious observance, and the butler explained how his employer, the magnate, put on a *tallis* and *tefillin*, and prayed every day.

The Israeli's wife was shocked. She had always made fun of her husband's *tefillin*, and now she was hearing a gentile speak of the practice with a respect that bordered on reverence. And the idea that a contemporary multi-millionaire was steadfast in his Jewish observance was also an eye opener; so religious practice *wasn't* only for the ghetto!

That Friday, the man lit *Shabbos* candles. Shortly afterwards, he heard his wife pull up in the driveway. Was it too late? she wanted to know, could she still light the candles?

And as they talked over *Shabbos*, she showed a new-found respect for her husband's Jewish practice. Thursday afternoon, the letter had been sent to the Rebbe, and Thursday night, her attitude had begun to change.

Yechidus, a personal meeting with the Rebbe, has always been regarded as a special experience. For the Rabbinical students in 770, however, the event was treated with a uniqueness all its own. Well before the day of *yechidus*, and certainly on the day itself, the student would occupy himself in earnest preparation. As he waited outside the Rebbe's door, he would recite *Tehillim* (Psalms) with devotion. He would write out his requests beforehand and, when his turn came, would enter the Rebbe's room with awe and trepidation. He would not dare shake the Rebbe's hand, or sit. Instead, he would stand at rigid attention, straining to concentrate on every word the Rebbe said.

Just as the student strove to focus his spiritual energies, so too the Rebbe responded with intense concentration. He would read the student's letter carefully and responded with short, pointed answers.

There was a student from a non-Lubavitcher *yeshivah* who came to many leading Rabbis seeking blessings and advice. Before he visited the Rebbe, he asked several of the students at the Lubavitcher *Yeshivah* students how they conducted themselves during *yechidus,* and tried to imitate their behavior. For several years, he went to *yechidus* once a year. He was inspired by these meetings, but would have liked to relax and exchange ideas.

After four years of visiting the Rebbe, and before leaving to study in *Eretz Yisrael,* he decided to change his approach. "I don't have the advantage of being a Lubavitcher, so why should I have the disadvantage?" he asked himself. "I don't have the intense, ongoing relationship with the Rebbe that the other students have, so why should I be limited by the restrictions associated with it?"

He decided that this time, he would talk freely, and air several issues of concern.

With this thought in mind, he entered the Rebbe's room. As if he had read his mind, the Rebbe welcomed him with a warm *Shalom Aleichem,* and extended his hand in greeting!

Elimelech Seidman was a US army chaplain who in the fall of '91 was serving in Frankfurt, Germany. He had been visiting the States, and was due to return to Germany from New York. Before leaving, he called one of his fellow chaplains, Rabbi Yaakov Goldstein, partly to talk army business, and partly because they were old friends.

"Now that you're in New York," Rabbi Goldstein said, "you've got to come to the Rebbe to receive a dollar."

Elimelech had other plans, but it was impossible to say No to Rabbi Goldstein. And so, a few hours later, the two met in uniform outside 770.

Rabbi Goldstein instructed Elimelech to write a short note asking for a blessing, to put that note on the Rebbe's table, and tell him his name, rank and posting.

Elimelech did exactly as Rabbi Goldstein told him. When he approached the Rebbe, he placed the note on the table and told the Rebbe his name and rank.

"You've written to me before, haven't you?" the Rebbe asked.

"Well, I wrote a note just now," Elimelech answered.

"I mean a while ago," the Rebbe continued.

"I don't remember," Elimelech responded.

Rabbi Goldstein said something tactful to smooth things over, and the two departed. Afterwards, Elimelech heard that a friend, Rabbi Yossi Shemtov, the *shliach* in Tuscon, Arizona, whom he had shared a relationship while serving as a chaplain in that area, was visiting in Crown Heights that day and stopped by to pay him a call.

He told Rabbi Shemtov about his meeting with the Rebbe, and Rabbi Shemtov reminded him that, five years before, Elimelech and his wife had been childless. They had seen many doctors, but none had been able to help. When he had mentioned the matter to Rabbi Shemtov, he was advised to write the Rebbe. "You may not receive a written answer," Rabbi Shemtov had told him, "but I can assure you that the Rebbe takes note of every letter written to him. And he will pray for anyone who needs a blessing."

Elimelech had thought to himself: "We have been seeing so many doctors, why not give this approach a chance?" He wrote the letter, and did not receive a written answer.

But now, he was certain that the Rebbe indeed kept all letters in mind. He had forgotten about the letter, but the Rebbe — who had received so many thousands of letters in the interim — had remembered.

Elimelech was also a little remorseful; he had missed an opportunity. In those five years, he and his wife had been blessed with two children. Just as he had asked the Rebbe for a blessing, he should have shared the good news that his wish had been granted.

※

Morrie Steiman is one of San Diego's leading Jewish philanthropists. Through his father and uncle, his family shared a connection to the Lubavitcher Rebbeim and, encouraged by Rabbi Moshe Bogomilsky, he sought to renew the relationship.

He had met the Rebbe several times, and had begun to develop a bond with him. "Do chassidim give *shalom* to the Rebbe?" he asked Rabbi Bogomilsky, referring to a custom among Polish chassidim, but not practiced within Lubavitch, to greet one's Rebbe and shake his hand.

"Everyone has their own relationship with the Rebbe," Rabbi Bogomilsky answered. "What I do and what other chassidim do does not have to affect the way you relate to him."

And so Mr. Steiman asked for an opportunity to give *shalom* to the Rebbe. In those years, the Rebbe would recite his morning prayers alone, but every Monday and Thursday he would hear the Torah reading at the service conducted by the *yeshivah* students in the small *shul* upstairs at 770. It was arranged that Mr. Steiman would attend a Monday morning Torah reading. After being honored with *Hagbah,* he hurried to stand in the small foyer between the Rebbe's room and the *shul,* intending to stop the Rebbe as he passed and shake his hand.

But plans do not always go as expected. That day, there were many visitors to 770. The Rebbe walked briskly out to his office, and Mr. Steiman was not able to catch his attention.

Mr. Steiman was slightly surprised. On previous occasions, he had received much personal encouragement from the Rebbe, and yet now the Rebbe had walked past without even a sign of recognition. Needless to say, Mr. Steiman was disappointed; he was certain that the Rebbe had not recognized him.

Several weeks later, he received his first and only letter from the Rebbe. The Rebbe began by thanking him for his visit to 770, and apologizing for the fact that although he had noticed him, circumstances had not allowed for a proper exchange of greetings.

Once at *yechidus,* the Rebbe asked Prof. Paul Rosenbloom where he was sending his son to school.

Prof. Rosenbloom answered that the boy was attending the Manhattan Hebrew Day School.

"Oh, Rabbi Sholom Rephun is the principal there," the Rebbe responded. "He used to work in Release Time for us."

When the Rosenblooms described the encounter to Rabbi Rephun, he was amazed. "I never met the Rebbe, or even wrote to him," he exclaimed. "Yes, I worked for Release Time, but so did over 200 other rabbinical students, and that was 19 years ago. The only way the Rebbe could have known about my involvement was from the reports that Rabbi Hecht's office submitted. This means that the Rebbe had minor details of reports that were 19 years old at his fingertips!"

If you go through the Boro Park section of Brooklyn, you'll find many *shuls* named for European towns or chassidic courts: Bobov, Gur, Munkatch, Belz, and many others. One of the smaller *shuls* on 49th Street is named Foltichen, after a Rumanian city that was home to the chassidim of the Foltichener Rebbe.

Today, his grandson, Rabbi Yisrael Meir Twersky, continues the family tradition. From morning to night, the young Foltichener Rebbe is involved in helping others.

One day, a young Lubavitcher family visited from Providence, RI. The Foltichener Rebbe had met them several years earlier when he had visited New England. Now they stopped in after visiting Crown Heights.

As is customary with some chassidic Rebbeim, the guests do most of the talking. In this case, one of the children mentioned that they had just stood in line for hours to receive a *berachah* and a dollar from the Lubavitcher Rebbe.

The Foltichener smiled and said proudly: "I too received a blessing and a dollar from the Rebbe. Only I didn't stand in line. In fact, I didn't even ask for it!"

He was immediately pressed for the story. "A poor widow approached me for *tzedakah*. Rather than just give her a donation, I helped her set up a business. She purchased some items to resell, and I let her use the women's section of our *shul* as her store. Every day, people from around the neighborhood would come and buy things.

"Once, she decided to go to the Lubavitcher Rebbe for a *berachah* for *parnosah*. After standing in line, the Rebbe gave his *berachah* and a dollar. Then he gave her another dollar. Before the young woman could ask for an explanation, the Rebbe smiled and said: 'Give this to the one who helps you!'

Rabbi Eli Kaplan has many Lubavitch relatives, and so found many occasions to ask for the Rebbe's blessings. One Sunday, when the Rebbe was distributing dollars for charity, he came to seek a blessing for a daughter who had just become pregnant.

The Rebbe asked for his daughter's Hebrew name and her mother's name, and gave a blessing for a successful pregnancy and a healthy child.

Rabbi Kaplan then continued, telling the Rebbe that since he was a *kohen*, he would like to give the Rebbe a blessing. The Rebbe agreed, and so Rabbi Kaplan said: "May G-d enable you to continue with your holy work and be successful."

"Thank you," the Rebbe answered, "but I cannot do this alone; I need your help."

As Rabbi Kaplan was turning to leave, the Rebbe asked him: "Are you ready to recite the Priestly Blessings in the *Beis HaMikdash?*"

Chapter 10 —
Precious Souls

In pre-war Poland, the chassidim of R. Avraham Mordechai of Gur would boast that their Rebbe had tens of thousands of chassidim who did not put on *tefillin,* nor did they fast on Yom Kippur. If a listener questioned this statement, they would take him to any local *cheder* teeming with happy, young faces, adding: "These are some of the Rebbe's most ardent followers."

It is common to compare the relationship between a chassid and a Rebbe to that between a father and a son. True as this is in general, it has a unique meaning when applied to the relationship which children share with the Rebbe. The energy and intensity the Rebbe would show at a children's rally or at Lag BaOmer parades was singular. When he would speak to children at *yechidus* or while distributing dollars for charity, he was focused on them entirely; it was as if there was nothing else in his world at that time. The stories that follow try to capture something of that relationship.

A Lubavitch woman took two of her children to the Rebbe for *yechidus*. Her son was seven and her daughter was five-and-a-half. At *yechidus,* the Rebbe asked the boy if he could recite the *Shema*. The son answered that he could, and at the Rebbe's prompting, proceeded to recite it word for word. The Rebbe smiled in appreciation, reached into his drawer, took out a shiny silver dollar and gave it to him.

He then turned to the daughter. "Can you say the *Shema?*"

Perhaps because of shyness or perhaps because she was simply awe-struck, the girl remained tongue-tied. The Rebbe reached into his drawer, took out another silver dollar, and gave it to the girl's mother. "This is for your daughter," he told her. "Tonight, before she goes to sleep, she will recite the *Shema.* Give it to her then."

***

"My most memorable encounter with the Rebbe took place at my first *yechidus*," a *shliach* in a Mid-Western city recalls. "I was eight years old. My family had taken great strides in increasing their Jewish practice due to the influence of the local *shliach,* and because of a unique relationship my father had established with the Rebbe.

"At home, we had been told much about how great the Rebbe was, and now I was encountering him first hand. After speaking to my father and mother, the Rebbe turned to my sister and myself, and asked for our Hebrew names.

"My sister answered at once, but I was too overcome with awe to speak. My father pushed me: 'Dovid, tell the Rebbe your name,' but I was just too nervous to get a word out.

"The Rebbe diverted the conversation, and shortly afterwards, the *yechidus* ended.

"On the following day, I was playing on the lawn outside 770 with some of the children of the family that was hosting us. Suddenly, it was announced that the Rebbe was leaving for home. I rushed to the walkway and stood at attention as the Rebbe strode down the stairs.

"He stopped and stood still right in front of me. '*Now,* can you tell me your Hebrew name?' he asked.

"'Sure, it's Dovid,' I replied. The Rebbe smiled and walked on.

"Over 20 years have passed, and yet I still marvel at how deeply that encounter touched me."

Every year, on the day before Pesach, the Rebbe would personally distribute *matzos* to the chassidim. Young Yosef Yitzchak was very excited. This year, he was *Bar Mitzvah*. Because of his father's Rabbinic responsibilities in a New Jersey suburb, he was unable to go himself, and so Yosef Yitzchak would be bringing a *matzah* from the Rebbe for the entire family.

Yosef Yitzchak felt very proud about having been entrusted with this responsibility. When he approached the Rebbe and received a piece of *matzah,* he had a thought, and without thinking much farther, he asked: "Can I have a special piece for my father?"

The Rebbe gave one at once. Seeing the Rebbe's willingness, Yosef Yitzchak asked again: "Can I have a piece for my mother?" And when the Rebbe gave him another piece, he asked again: "And for my *zeide,* for my *bubbe,...* for my brother...and for my sister?" With a subtle smile, the Rebbe gave him pieces of *matzah* for each one.

Yosef Yitzchak made the trip home in high spirits. The Rebbe had given him so many pieces of *matzah* for his family!

But Yosef Yitzchak's happiness was cut short when he presented the pieces to his father. Instead of responding with joy, his father gave him a short, stern lesson on how precious the Rebbe's time was, and how chassidim did whatever they could to prevent that time from being wasted. "It is not important how much of the Rebbe's *matzah* you have," his father told him. "Even the tiniest piece is enough. We could have all broken off pieces from the piece you received for yourself.

"And what did you do? You asked for a piece for me, for your mother, for your *zeide* etc. etc., causing the Rebbe to wait unnecessarily."

Yosef Yitzchak understood, and now regretted what he had done.

A year later, the lad again went to receive *matzah* from the Rebbe for his family. He had taken his father's reprimand to heart, and resolved to say absolutely nothing when receiving his piece. He approached the Rebbe, received his *matzah*, and began to move away. The Rebbe looked at him with a warm, gentle smile and called him back: "What about your father? Your mother? Your *zeide*?" the Rebbe asked him, giving him another large piece.

⁐

Menachem always looked forward to the Rebbe's Shavuos *farbrengen*. Beyond the excitement every chassid feels at such gatherings, this one had special significance for Menachem. The day after Shavuos was his birthday, and he would consider the *kos shel berachah* — the wine which the Rebbe distributed at the conclusion of the *farbrengen* — as the Rebbe's birthday present.

One year, as was his custom, Menachem did not hasten to get in line for *kos shel berachah*. Although there were some who hurried to approach the Rebbe, the *yeshivah* students generally chose to wait, sing joyous chassidic melodies, and watch the Rebbe while he distributed the wine.

Menachem reviewed the subjects expounded at the *farbrengen* with some friends, and then joined them in singing and watching the Rebbe. He would, he thought, approach the Rebbe after the lines thinned out.

Watching the Rebbe can be very absorbing, and Menachem did not realize that the number of people in line was dwindling. Suddenly, he realized that a song had ended, a few last people approached the Rebbe for wine, and then the Rebbe reached for his *siddur* to recite a final blessing. *Kos shel berachah* had ended; Menachem had missed his opportunity!

If it had been another *farbrengen,* Menachem might have resigned himself to the loss, but this was his "birthday" *farbrengen!* The following day, he wrote the Rebbe that he had unwillingly missed receiving *kos shel berachah* the night before. Was there any way to receive it now?

A short while afterwards, the Rebbe's secretary, Rabbi Binyomin Klein, entered the *yeshivah*'s study hall and called Menachem out. He did not want the others to know, he told Menachem, but he had something for him from the Rebbe.

The Rebbe had sent him wine from *kos shel berachah!*

When he was eight or nine, Levi Markel would often go to receive a dollar from the Rebbe on Sundays. One Sunday, after receiving a dollar for himself, he told the Rebbe that the day was his brother's birthday. The Rebbe gave him a second dollar and told him: "This is for Moshie."

At the time, Levi did not think this was anything special, but afterwards it struck him. That the Rebbe remembered Moshie's name without being reminded was out of the ordinary, yet understandable. But Levi had two other brothers besides Moshie. How did the Rebbe know it was Moshie's birthday?

Chapter 11 —
"The Language of the Wise is Healing" (Proverbs 12:18)

A poor family once came to the Maggid of Mezritch asking for a cure for their lame son.

Departing from his ordinary selfless practice, the Maggid told the family: "Bring me 50 gold rubles and your son will be healed."

"Fifty gold rubles!" the woman said in shock. "That is far beyond our means. Would the Rebbe be satisfied with a little less?"

"Not a *kopke* less," answered the Maggid.

And so the family set about selling their meager possessions and taking loans, trying to amass the sum the Maggid had mentioned.

When they had scraped together 30 gold rubles, they again approached the Maggid.

"Would this sum suffice?" they asked, for they saw little hope of gathering more.

With unexpected severity, the Maggid refused. So once again, they went out to knock on doors, begging and borrowing to try to accumulate the full sum.

When they reached 40 rubles, they came to the Maggid a third time.

"This is all we can raise," the mother pleaded. "Please take it and bless our son."

"I said 50 gold rubles," the Maggid replied. "I will not accept a penny less."

In exasperation, the mother threw the money out the window. "G-d will help us without the Maggid," she told her husband.

"That's what I was waiting for," the Maggid exclaimed. "Moshe," he said turning to the lame boy, "Go out and collect those coins. Your mother will need them."

And as the parents looked on, their son walked out the door!

The Maggid explained: "As long as you put your faith in me personally, your prayers could not be answered. Once you put your trust in G-d, there was a chance for your son's recovery."

We all know what infirmity is. We have all seen friends or relatives stricken — or perhaps have been afflicted ourselves — with various physical, psychological or spiritual infirmities.

We often feel helpless in the face of such ailments. For regardless of the great strides man has made in medicine, there are still sicknesses and conditions which mortals cannot remedy. These feelings of helplessness, however, are our greatest enemies, perhaps more debilitating than the sicknesses themselves.

What is the key to recovery? A positive outlook.

This does not involve naive euphoria, for a person must look reality squarely in the face. But having said that, a person who is ill should never consider himself beyond help. On the contrary, such negativity will only reinforce the infirmity, and restrict any potential for recovery.

In this vein, the Rebbe would frequently reiterate the popular *Yiddish* maxim: *Tracht gut, vet zein gut,* "Think positively, and the outcome will be positive." For example, the Hebrew term for hospital is *Beis Cholim,* literally meaning: "A home for the sick." "Call it a *Beis Refuah,* 'a house of healing,'" the Rebbe would say.

And when doctors told patients that there was no hope, he would criticize them harshly. "The Torah tells us," he would repeat, "that a doctor is given permission to heal. That is his expertise. When he gives a prognosis of doom, he has exceeded his authority."

We must understand that healing is in G-d's hands, and therefore is always possible. He is the absolute Master of our lives, and we cannot put any limits on what He can do.

And this also applies with regard to the G-dly potential invested in each of us. Every one of us has a soul which is an actual part of G-d. This is the core of our being, our true selves. Therefore there is always the possibility within ourselves for healing and recovery.

One Friday, a package of X-rays arrived at the office of Rabbi Moshe Feller, the Rebbe's *shliach* in Minneapolis-S. Paul. Together with it came a letter from Rabbi Groner asking Rabbi Feller to take the X-rays to Dr. John Moe, a professor at the University of Minnesota Medical Center.

A chassid had sustained a back injury in the plant at which he was employed. All the doctors he had seen had recommended surgery, but before undergoing the operation, the chassid wanted the Rebbe's advice and blessing. The Rebbe, however, had hesitated. He wanted, Rabbi Groner's note explained, to hear the opinion of Dr. Moe, an internationally renowned expert on the spine.

Rabbi Feller had heard of Dr. Moe. Indeed, most people in Minneapolis had; his reputation had attracted patients from around the world. How could one get in touch with such a sought-after physician?

But a chassid does not ask too many questions. Rabbi Feller drove to the University of Minnesota campus and tried to see Dr. Moe. "There is a world-famous Rabbi in New York who respects Dr. Moe's opinion," Rabbi Feller told the receptionist. "Although he has recommendations from other doctors, this Rabbi wants Dr. Moe's advice. Can I show him these X-rays?"

Rabbi Feller's insistence got him past the receptionist, but not beyond Dr. Moe's personal secretary. "The doctor isn't in right now," she told him, "but even if he was, I couldn't schedule an appointment; he's booked for weeks."

Rabbi Feller tried to explain who the Rebbe was, and that the future of a man with a serious back injury was involved.

"Look at all this mail," she replied, pointing to her desk, "and look at my appointment book. What do you want me to do?"

After discussing the options, she asked Rabbi Feller to leave the X-rays with her. She would mention the matter to the doctor and get back to Rabbi Feller when she could.

It was Friday afternoon — and a short Friday at that. Rabbi Feller did not see any alternative and so agreed to her suggestion, putting the matter out of his mind After all, he had a busy *Shabbos* coming up, and did not know when — if ever — he would receive an answer.

It *was* a busy *Shabbos,* and the *melaveh malkah* with his students Saturday night kept Rabbi Feller up late. So he was somewhat dazed when his phone rang at 6 a.m. Sunday morning.

"Hello. This is John Moe," said the voice at the other end.

"John who?" mumbled Rabbi Feller, wondering why a non-Jewish person would be calling him so early on Sunday morning. Was it a prank?

"John Moe."

"Who?"

"Dr. John Moe. You left X-rays for me, and a message from a Rabbi in New York."

Rabbi Feller was stunned. Dr. Moe himself! He quickly apologized and shook himself awake. Dr. Moe explained that he could not render an opinion merely by looking at X-rays; he would have to see the patient for himself.

"When could that be?" Rabbi Feller asked.

"Well, if you get him here at the end of next week," the doctor responded, "I can get him a bed at the hospital, and we'll take it from there."

The injured chassid flew to Minnesota, and Dr. Moe gave him a thorough examination. Instead of surgery, the doctor recommended a diet to lose weight, whirlpool baths and a brace. Nine weeks later, the chassid left Minnesota walking erect, and within months, there was no sign of his injury.

"In 85% of the cases with such an injury, I too would have recommended surgery," Dr. Moe wrote in his report. "In this instance, however, I saw a way of avoiding it."

"So what's so unique about this story?" Rabbi Feller was asked when he related the incident to a group of chassidim.

"First of all," he answered, "I think it's important for everyone to know that the Rebbe never wants people to rush into surgery. Even if they had already consulted several doctors, he would suggest seeing others — particularly those known to hesitate before using the knife.

"And yet, it is quite an uncommon story. Dr. Moe was at the top of his field, consulted by doctors from every part of the world. Normally, even getting to speak to him took weeks, and waiting for an examination was a matter of months. And here, on his own initiative, he hurried the case through all the red tape and showed a personal interest in the patient's rehabilitation.

"Ask Dr. Moe's secretary whether or not this was unique!"

∽

Late one evening in 5714 (1954), a Lubavitch woman arrived in the obstetrics ward of an out-of-town hospital. There had been complications throughout her pregnancy, and now her contractions had started.

After examining her, the obstetrician called in her husband. "I did not want to alarm your wife," he told him, "but the situation is very grave. The fetus is being carried breech, and birth could endanger the life of either the mother or the child. I might not be able to save both. Give me permission to choose which life to save. For legal reasons, it is customary that the husband sign a waiver, freeing the doctor of liability in the event of death."

The husband was shocked. He told the doctor that he would have to consult his Rabbi, and rushed to call 770. He described the situation to Rabbi Chodakov, the Rebbe's personal secretary, who brought the matter to the Rebbe's attention.

The Rebbe told Rabbi Chodakov to tell the husband not to sign any waiver, and to insist that the doctor try to save both the mother and the child. He concluded with a blessing.

When the husband conveyed this message to the doctor, the doctor reiterated his warning, adding that he had not explained the full seriousness of the situation. If he tried to save the mother *and* the child, he said, he might lose them both. "It is best," he said, "if you sign the waiver."

The husband called Rabbi Chodakov again to relay the new information. Rabbi Chodakov informed the Rebbe, but the Rebbe's answer remained the same: Insist that he save both the mother and the child.

The husband informed the doctor that the Rebbe had instructed him to save both the mother and the child. The doctor then explained that the delivery was very complicated and the process could be lengthy. Since it was already late, he advised the husband to go home, and he would inform him as soon as there was any news.

The husband returned home, said several chapters of *Tehillim* in earnest prayer, and lay down to rest. Despite his weariness, he could not sleep, and lay in bed waiting for the doctor's call.

Shortly after four in the morning, the phone rang. "*Mazel tov*," the doctor told him, "at four o'clock your wife gave birth to a healthy girl. Both your wife and the baby are safe."

Unable to contain his excitement, the chassid called Rabbi Groner, one of the Rebbe's secretaries, and asked him to inform the Rebbe.

At 7 a.m., the phone rang again. It was Rabbi Chodakov. He told the husband that the Rebbe wanted to know whether his wife had in fact given birth at four, or whether the birth had taken place at 3:30.

The husband went to the hospital to see his wife shortly afterwards. When he asked to see the doctor, the nurse told

"THE LANGUAGE OF THE WISE IS HEALING" 169

him that the doctor had been up all night and would not return until 11 o'clock. The chassid went home and returned at 11.

He thanked the doctor profusely for his efforts, and then asked when the birth had taken place. Was it 4, or 3:30? The doctor explained that the delivery had been very trying, and that he had not noticed the exact time. On the baby's crib, however, it clearly said 4 AM.

The husband called the nurse over. "Four o'clock," the nurse explained, "was when the baby was brought into the nursery. If we consider the time it took to wash the baby, give it its initial tests and the like, it is quite possible that the actual birth took place at 3:30."

The doctor was curious. "Your wife and daughter are both healthy," he reminded the chassid, "so what difference does it make what time the birth took place?"

The husband explained that the Rebbe had asked. The doctor repeated his question: "What difference does it make?"

When the chassid conveyed the information to Rabbi Chodakov, he respectfully added that the doctor was curious as to why the time was so important.

"Out of concern," Rabbi Chodakov replied in the name of the Rebbe, "the Rebbe did not go to sleep the entire night. At 3:30 in the morning, when he knew that both the mother and daughter were safe, he finally laid down to rest."

Rabbi Nissan Mangel heard this story from the husband. To him, Rabbi Chodakov's closing remarks suggest an allegory:

The Rebbe will not lie down to rest until the mother (in *Kabbalah,* an analogy for the source of the Jewish people in the spiritual realms) and the daughter (the Jews in this material world) are both safe. If the Rebbe could not sleep when one mother and one child were in danger, surely he will not rest until the people as a whole are secure.

The above story has a sequel:

Coming back to yourself physically after childbirth can be trying for any woman. In addition to the difficulties most women face, one Lubavitch woman had problems with bleeding. It wasn't a heavy flow, but it caused worry, and concern that perhaps there was a more serious problem.

She consulted medical authorities, who declared that the spotting indicated a malignant tumor.

The doctor who had delivered the baby in the previous story was a renowned obstetrician, and the woman approached him for consultation. After an examination, he also diagnosed the difficulty as cancer. Somberly, he told the woman that there were several options, but that the situation was very serious.

The couple hurried to New York to seek the Rebbe's advice and blessing. After hearing the couple out, the Rebbe told the woman: "No, it is not cancer. After the birth, the doctors erred and did not complete the process necessary at that time. There is a simple medical procedure which they can perform — the Rebbe outlined this to the couple — and the staining will stop."

The couple returned to the doctor and asked him to perform this procedure.

The doctor was dumbfounded. "From a medical perspective," he told them, "it is absolutely absurd to think that this is the problem. Moreover, taking this step could be very dangerous. If the problem *is* cancer, such a procedure could prove fatal."

When the couple insisted, the doctor asked on what basis were they requesting such treatment; they were not physicians, and should not insist on treatment that ran contrary to medical norms. The couple replied that they had received this advice from their rabbi, and that this is what they wanted to do.

On hearing this, the doctor relaxed. "Is your rabbi, by any chance, Rabbi Schneerson of Lubavitch?" he asked. The couple replied that he was. The doctor told them that he had already had experience with Rabbi Schneerson, and therefore would be willing to follow his suggestion. Had the suggestion come from any another person, he explained, he would have refused; the danger was simply too great.

The doctor performed the procedure, and shortly afterwards, the woman stopped spotting. Afterwards, she gave birth to several other children with no complications.

Reb Peretz Chein was an elderly chassid who ran the *mikveh* on Eastern Parkway across from 770. When he was in his late seventies, he developed a throat condition which the doctors feared might be cancer. His doctors told him the situation was serious, and that the only way he could prevent the illness from spreading was to refrain from speaking.

When Reb Peretz informed the Rebbe of his infirmity and the doctors' advice, the Rebbe gave him totally different advice. "Relate chassidic teachings in *shul* on *Shabbos* afternoons," he told him.

Reb Peretz followed the Rebbe's advice and lived for another 15 years.

In the late 1950s, a two-year-old boy in a Lubavitch family became very sick. His family took him from doctor to doctor in hope of finding a remedy. Ultimately, the doctors took an X-ray and diagnosed TB. They wanted to send the baby to a sanitarium.

"He's not going anywhere until we write the Rebbe," the mother replied.

The Rebbe's answer was unequivocal. "The baby doesn't have TB. He should not be sent to a sanitarium because the disease is very contagious, and he could contract it there. Instead, the family should get another opinion."

This last instruction presented a problem. Since the baby's illness had been protracted, his concerned parents had already consulted all the doctors they knew. When the doctors diagnosed TB, they had asked their friends for the names of specialists, and consulted them as well. At this point, they were pretty much out of names to ask for another opinion.

A Lubavitcher doctor in the area had just taken in a young associate, and the family decided to consult him. After looking at the X-ray, the doctor said: "It looks like TB, but if the Rebbe says it's not, then it is worth considering other alternatives. It is possible that the problem is merely a stomach infection, but because of constant coughing, some of the fluids have come up into the chest. We'll put the boy on antibiotics. If it *is* a stomach infection, this will clear it up."

The boy began taking the antibiotics as the young doctor prescribed. Two weeks later, he was well on his way to recovery.

⁂

"It all began 11 years ago," Charlie Zablotsky related. "At the time, I lived in Norwich, Connecticut, and often traveled to New York. One time when I was in the city, a Lubavitcher friend asked me if I wanted to *daven* at the Rebbe's *shul*.

"Even though I wasn't observant at the time, I agreed. We went to 770 and davened in the *shul* upstairs. This was my first exposure to the Rebbe. Afterwards, we repeated the experience several times.

"One day in the middle of summer, my wife found a growth on my neck. I immediately went to a doctor friend of mine, who took a biopsy and sent it to the lab. As soon as the results came back, my friend called me. His words were brief and to the point. 'It's no good. Malignant melanoma.'

"To help determine the best course of treatment, my friend sent me to Yale Hospital in New Haven. After looking at the X-rays and doing their own tests, the specialists recommended

"THE LANGUAGE OF THE WISE IS HEALING" 173

radical neck surgery. They wanted to remove all the tissue on the right side of my neck, including the muscles that hold my head up. When the doctor and I heard their suggestion, we decided to get a second opinion, and so I traveled to Columbia Presbyterian in New York. After another series of tests, Columbia's doctors recommended the same thing — radical neck surgery.

"While I was staying in New York, I visited 770 with my chassidic friend. 'Before you do anything,' he told me, 'write to the Rebbe.' So I told him the facts and he wrote them down and mailed the letter. By the time I got back to my hotel in Manhattan, there was an answer. The Rebbe said: 'Let a friend who is a doctor decide.'

"I was a little surprised. First of all, I never told the Rebbe that I had a doctor who was my friend. Second of all, I had just been to some of the biggest specialists I could find. Still, when the Rebbe says something, you listen.

"I asked my family doctor. He said: 'In my opinion, you don't need that kind of surgery.' He performed the operation himself, removing the entire growth. My cancer was gone.

"Unfortunately, my good health didn't last. A year later, I got sick again. This time, I was diagnosed with Crohn's Disease — an illness that causes perforations and bleeding in the intestines. Soon, I was receiving blood transfusions three times a week to replace the blood I was losing. I was so weak that I couldn't even drive.

"To save my life, the doctors scheduled surgery to remove the destroyed intestines. During the pre-surgery testing, they had performed a coloscopy, an MRI and a CAT scan. The tests revealed massive scarring, and showed that even the scar tissue had holes in it. To make matters worse, they found a large black mass that looked suspiciously like a tumor.

"During the week in which I was scheduled for surgery, my wife and I decided to ask the Rebbe for a blessing. With the help of my Lubavitch friend, we got in line with one of my sons, who was then 12.

"My son went first. The Rebbe looked at him and said: 'Here's a dollar for you and a dollar for your father, *refuah shelaimah* ("May he have a complete recovery").'

"No one had told the Rebbe who my son was.

"My Lubavitch friend was next in line. He told the Rebbe: 'My friend is sick, he's going through surgery.' A moment later, I was standing before the Rebbe. I had been to him for dollars before, but had never experienced anything like what happened next. The Rebbe looked at me and gave me a dollar, along with a blessing for a *refuah shelaimah*. Then he added, almost as an order: 'It should be a fast and complete one.' While saying this, he made a fist with his right hand, raised it and drew it down.

"The whole episode was very startling, even to the chassidim around me. But that's not all. As the Rebbe moved his hand, I felt a burning sensation from my esophagus down to my stomach. I almost collapsed right there.

"Several days later, I went to surgery. My brother is a doctor, and as soon as the surgery was over, he asked for a lab report. Everyone expected the surgeons to remove yards of destroyed intestine, but they only took out 18 inches!

"'There must be some mistake!' my brother protested, but the doctors assured him that there was no mistake; they could only find 18 inches of damaged tissue! What's more, the dark object they thought was a tumor turned out to be only a mass of dried blood.

"After surgery, they wheeled me back to my room. When I woke up from the anesthesia, the doctors came in and told me the results. Then they asked: 'What do you want to do?' I said that I wanted to walk. The nurse helped me get to my feet, and I walked from the bed to the bathroom. The doctors were incredulous.

"Three days after the surgery, I wanted to wash my own feet. The doctor who was in the room laughed and said:

'Whenever you're ready.' After all, I had an incision several inches long down my belly.

"The doctor watched in absolute amazement as I stood and lifted my feet up to the sink and proceeded to wash them. He shook his head. 'This is unbelievable.'

"But I knew it wasn't. It was the Rebbe's blessing."

※

In 5750 [1990], several weeks before the wedding of their son, Rabbi and Mrs. Yosef Cohen, Slonimer chassidim from Jerusalem, traveled to New York to visit relatives.

But two weeks before the wedding, Mrs. Cohen suffered a severe heart attack, and the family's joy turned to sorrow. The doctors who examined her told the family that it was only a matter of time. Their question was only whether or not the wedding celebrations would be marred by mourning.

Rabbi Cohen went to the Rebbe that Sunday morning to receive a dollar and a blessing for his wife. After hearing Rabbi Cohen's request, the Rebbe gave him an explicit promise that his wife would attend their son's wedding.

To everyone's amazement, in less than a week, Mrs. Cohen's condition improved — so rapidly that the doctors allowed her to return to Jerusalem and participate in the wedding.

※

Once an active member of the Lubavitch community fell ill and was admitted to hospital to await surgery. His ailment was painful, but he was even more uncomfortable at the thought of the operation, and uneasy with his confinement.

The Rebbe asked Rabbi Groner several times to ask the family how the man was doing. The Rebbe's concern was directed more to the patient's state of mind than his physical condition.

A few weeks after he had been confined, the man's daughter had *yechidus*. The Rebbe asked about her father.

"I hear that he is depressed," said the Rebbe. "Where is his *bitachon* (faith)? Here are two dollars, one for him and one for him to give another Jew in the hospital. When he sets out to teach another Jew about *Yiddishkeit* and raise the other man's spirits, this will automatically have a positive effect on him."

***

A 16-year-old boy in Italy was diagnosed as having cancer in the groin. The doctors proposed an operation, but told his parents they had little hope. When the family turned to Rabbi Gershon Mendel Garelik for solace, he told them to ask the Rebbe for a blessing.

The boy's brother-in-law went to the Rebbe for *yechidus* and asked for his blessing, which he received. The brother-in-law responded that he wanted not only a blessing, but a *promise*.

The Rebbe promised that the boy would be healthy, his parents would lead him to the wedding canopy, and he would have children of his own.

When the brother-in-law returned to Italy and told the family of the Rebbe's promise, his news was met with mixed reactions. Some believed in the Rebbe's words, and were able to proceed with uplifted spirits. Others were more skeptical. One uncle was very upset. "Why does the Rebbe nurture hope," he complained to Rabbi Garelik, "when there is no hope?"

The boy underwent the operation successfully. A few months later, he traveled to New York to thank the Rebbe for his blessings.

When the Rebbe saw the youth, he asked him: "Are you the one who was operated on?" When the youth answered that he was, the Rebbe gave him a series of instructions regarding his spiritual development, including reading the Torah every Monday and Thursday.

The youth followed the instructions carefully. Today he is married with children of his own.

At one point, three sons of a Crown Heights chassid had medical problems. Two of the boys had small hernias and one had a large birthmark on his face that had begun to expand. The concerned parents consulted two doctors, and both recommended surgery for all three boys.

The family decided that they would like the surgery to be performed by Dr. Mestel, a world-famous pediatric surgeon who was also an observant Jew. They made an appointment with the doctor, who concurred with the other doctors' diagnoses. With regard to the hernias, an operation was clearly necessary. With regard to the birthmark, however, the doctor said as follows: "Even if it does not expand any further, such a growth will never disappear. If surgery is performed now, only a small scar will be left; it will probably not even be noticeable. But if the surgery is postponed, a larger scar will be made. Moreover," he said, turning to the chassid, "you'll probably want your son to have a beard just like yours. If the surgery is done later, his beard will never cover that part of his face."

The doctor then volunteered to arrange for surgery for all three boys on the same day, and for them to share a room together. While he was making the calls necessary for these arrangements, the husband told the wife that since this was the third doctor to make the same recommendations, he was willing to accept the plan, but that they could agree to nothing without the consent of the Rebbe. Needless to say, the wife agreed.

When the doctor returned, the husband told him that he personally agreed to the operation, but would not make any binding commitment until he consulted the Lubavitcher Rebbe.

Dr. Mestel immediately expressed his respect for the Rebbe and added: "Go ahead and call the Rebbe. I know what he will tell you. He will tell you to consult with another doctor before agreeing. I have no difficulty with that."

The chassid informed the Rebbe that he had consulted three doctors, and that all three were of the opinion that surgery was necessary for each of the boys.

Within half an hour, the Rebbe answered. With regard to the two hernias, he agreed to the surgery. But about the birthmark, the Rebbe asked: "Why is that necessary?"

Needless to say, the chassid did not allow the third operation. Within four weeks, the boy's birthmark began to change color, and shortly afterwards it disappeared.

It must be emphasized that there are times when the Rebbe, through his *ruach hakodesh* (divine inspiration), sees that a request cannot be granted.

Once the sister-in-law of a Lubavitch woman became ill with cancer. When she heard the diagnosis, the Lubavitch lady immediately thought of seeking the Rebbe's blessing. Although she lived in South America, she flew to New York for *yechidus,* anxious to hear words of reassurance.

Because she was so emotionally involved, she asked her brother to enter *yechidus* with her. Her brother prepared a short note telling the Rebbe that his sister would like to speak about her sister-in-law, but not mentioning the medical condition. Rather than have her request written out, his sister preferred to describe her sister-in-law's condition orally.

When the woman and her brother entered *yechidus,* she gave the Rebbe the note her brother had written. The Rebbe looked at it and began speaking warmly to the woman about her own family in South America, her husband's business, and several issues of personal concern, without making any mention of the sister-in-law! After speaking for several minutes, the Rebbe looked down at his desk, a sign that the *yechidus* was over.

The woman's face turned white, and she sat frozen in her chair, unable to move or speak. From the Rebbe's avoidance of the issue, she understood that pressing the point would be of no benefit. Struggling to maintain her composure, she mustered up the strength to leave the room. As soon as she was outside, she burst into tears.

Her sister-in-law passed away approximately a month later.

～

The first two children born to a Lubavitch couple had Down's Syndrome. Many doctors advised the two to forget about having children of their own; the risks against having an ordinary child were obviously too high. But the couple wanted children very much, and against the doctors' recommendations, the woman entered her third pregnancy.

One of the natural steps for a Lubavitch couple expecting a child is to seek the Rebbe's blessing for a successful pregnancy and a healthy child. Needless to say, this couple felt a particular need for the Rebbe's blessing.

But their letter remained unanswered. This troubled them greatly, because they had not received an answer from the Rebbe after notifying him with regard to the woman's first two pregnancies either. This third silence filled them with foreboding.

Anxious and distraught, the man went to the office of the Rebbe's secretariat. "Please, you must get us an answer," he implored.

The secretary promised to bring the matter to the Rebbe's attention, and to tell the Rebbe of the stress the husband and wife were experiencing.

Several hours later, the secretary called the husband. The Rebbe had given his blessing, but had also advised the couple to observe the laws of *kashrus, behiddur* (in a careful and punctilious manner).

The couple weren't sure what the Rebbe meant; they already kept strict standards, they ate only *glatt kosher* meat and *cholov yisrael* dairy products (i.e. from dairies owned and operated by Jews). What more were they supposed to do?

So they began to study and seek advice from Rabbis and friends. As a result, they became aware of a level of observance even more stringent than their own. Anxious to be worthy of the Rebbe's blessings, they adopted these practices.

After a full-term pregnancy, the woman gave birth to a healthy girl, and the couple proceeded to have other healthy children.

Rabbi Hirsh Altein suffered from a painful physical condition. Though all the doctors he consulted recommended surgery, his son, Rabbi Mordechai Altein, asked the Rebbe if his father should undergo the operation.

The Rebbe suggested he consult a specific physician who had treated the Rebbe, but implied that surgery was unnecessary and that the ailment could be treated with the application of an ointment.

Yet the doctor the Rebbe recommended also felt Rabbi Altein's problem could be remedied only through surgery.

Rabbi Avraham Seligson, the Rebbe's personal physician, heard about the matter and volunteered to offer an opinion. After conducting an examination, he agreed that the proper course according to conventional medicine would involve surgery. He reported this in a letter to the Rebbe, but stated that if the Rebbe advised that an ointment be applied, he would have a salve prepared.

The Rebbe advised Dr. Seligson to have the ointment prepared. Dr. Seligson did so, and Rabbi Altein's problem vanished.

～

On Sunday *Chol HaMoed* Sukkos, Rabbi Shmuel Lew and his in-laws, Rabbi and Mrs. Zalman Jaffe, were visiting Crown Heights. The Lews' son, Shalom Ber, was running a high fever that day — his temperature had risen to 105.

Mrs. Jaffe was disturbed at the Lews' apparent lack of concern. "You mean you haven't made an appointment with a doctor?!" she told her son-in-law. "Do so immediately!"

Unable to argue with his mother-in-law, Rabbi Lew made an appointment with a local physician. He and his in-laws then hurried to get in line to receive a dollar from the Rebbe.

As they were waiting in line, who came to join them but young Shalom Ber, temperature and all! This was too much for Rabbi Jaffe. He had few inhibitions when it came to speaking to the Rebbe, and so, when he approached, he complained about his grandson and his high temperature.

"A fantasy," the Rebbe replied. "He's a healthy chassid!"

Needless to say, the Lews canceled the appointment with the doctor, and within a few hours, Shalom Ber's temperature fell.

That same Sunday, Rabbi Lew's son-in-law, Menachem Junik, went to the Rebbe with his infant son. When the Rebbe gave the man a dollar he said: "*Refuah shelaimah* (May he have a complete recovery)."

Rabbi Junik was surprised; as far as he knew, the boy was healthy! Several months later, he understood. His son's health was affected by an unusual childhood ailment and required sustained treatment.

※

In the early 1970s, Rabbi Sholom Ber Lipskar entered a hospital for tests that required general anesthesia. With G-d's help, the tests went well. Rabbi Lipskar awoke from the anesthesia, and was to be discharged the following day.

The next morning, Rabbi Lipskar's wife called. Her husband was sharing a double room, so she was not surprised when his roommate answered. But when his roommate tried to wake him and he did not respond, she became alarmed and hurried to the hospital. When she arrived, she found a team of doctors and nurses surrounding her husband. He had experienced a delayed reaction to the anesthetic, and could not be roused.

Mrs. Lipskar's immediate response was to call the Rebbe's office. She spoke to Rabbi Klein, the Rebbe's secretary, and asked that a message be given to the Rebbe right away. Rabbi Klein transferred her to Rabbi Chodakov, the Rebbe's personal secretary, who told her to wait on the line.

After a few minutes, he returned and told Mrs. Lipskar that he had a message from the Rebbe ... for her husband! Mrs. Lipskar was bewildered. Hadn't she just told Rabbi Chodakov that her husband was unconscious? Rabbi Chodakov continued, explaining that when he had spoken to the Rebbe, the Rebbe had given him a message for Rabbi Lipskar, and had insisted that it be communicated to him directly.

Without questioning, Mrs. Lipskar told the doctors around her husband's bed that there was an urgent telephone message for him. To humor her, the doctors paused in their treatment and allowed her to put the phone next to her husband's ear.

"Reb Sholom Ber!" Rabbi Chodakov called.

"Yes," murmured Rabbi Lipskar.

"The Language of the Wise is Healing" 183

"You sound a little weak," Rabbi Chodakov commented. "I have a message from the Rebbe for you." Rabbi Chodakov proceeded to tell Rabbi Lipskar that Dr. Yirmeyahu Branover, who had just been released from Russia, was scheduled to speak in Winnipeg, Canada. Since Rabbi Lipskar originally came from Toronto, he probably had some contacts in Winnipeg. "Can you help make Dr. Branover's visit more successful?"

Rabbi Lipskar promised to do what he could and hung up. He then looked around, startled to find doctors and nurses all around his bed.

Why were they all staring at him that way?

❦

Rabbi Zalman Gurary had a friend who had married late in life. The friend had four children, and his entire life revolved around them. Unfortunately, one of his daughters developed a dangerously swelling cyst. The doctors advised an operation to remove it, but the man was reluctant to subject the young girl to surgery. Instead, he asked Rabbi Gurary to arrange *yechidus* so that he could consult the Rebbe. If the Rebbe advised surgery, he would go ahead without compunction.

When the *yechidus* was arranged, the man asked Rabbi Gurary to accompany him.

At *yechidus,* the concerned father asked the Rebbe if the surgery should go ahead. The Rebbe answered that it was already the last days of Kislev, and he doubted the procedure could be performed immediately. It would be unwise, the Rebbe continued, for the cyst to be removed in the months of Teves or Shvat. They should wait, he concluded, and have the surgery scheduled for Adar, a month associated with happiness and well-being.

Then the Rebbe inquired about the school the girl was attending. The man named a neighborhood Jewish day school which, though orthodox, was more modern and leaning toward compromise.

"It would be better for her to study in *Beis Yaakov*," the Rebbe said. He continued: "In previous generations, there was less emphasis on the *chinuch* girls received at school. Today, that is no longer true. Therefore, I am speaking to you about this matter."

The man replied that he thought his daughter was receiving an excellent education at the school she was attending.

The Rebbe responded sternly: "*Chinuch* is my field, and medicine is not. Why do you ask me about medicine and not about *chinuch?*

The man looked at the Rebbe without replying, then thanked him for his advice. He did postpone the surgery, but didn't enroll his daughter in *Beis Yaakov*.

About a month later, Rabbi Gurary was walking down Eastern Parkway when he happened to meet an acquaintance who was also a friend of the man whose daughter had the cyst. Rabbi Gurary was bound for Manhattan and knew this man worked there, so he asked if he could ride with him.

Rabbi Gurary's acquaintance consented, adding: "I'm really happy I ran into you. Do you know why I am in Crown Heights?"

Rabbi Gurary did not, and so his acquaintance continued: "It's about so and so's daughter. The cyst became so badly infected, the girl developed a high fever and had to be hospitalized. Moreover, because of the infection, it's impossible to perform the surgery now.

"Why did the Rebbe mix into a medical matter? It's none of his business. I was here consulting with another Rabbi in the community."

Rabbi Gurary was very disturbed that following the Rebbe's advice appeared to have had negative consequences. When he returned from Manhattan, he asked for a meeting to tell the Rebbe what had happened.

Permission was granted and Rabbi Gurary told the Rebbe of the girl's turn for the worse. "Did the father enroll her in *Beis Yaakov?*" the Rebbe asked.

Rabbi Gurary did not know for sure, but assumed that the father had not, and so remained silent.

"Tell him to enroll her in *Beis Yaakov*," the Rebbe said, bringing the *yechidus* to an end.

Rabbi Gurary felt uncomfortable. His acquaintance had implied that the father currently had less than positive feelings toward the Rebbe, and there was no way the girl could attend school now anyway; she was in the hospital. And the man had said that he was happy with his daughter's school. How could he call him now and tell him to enroll her in *Beis Yaakov?*

But Rabbi Gurary was a *chassid*; there was no question but that he would do what the Rebbe told him. And he also knew that the Rebbe appreciated all the factors involved and if, despite this, he still wanted him to communicate the message, it must be vital to the girl's health. Under the circumstances, he could not let himself be deterred by what others might take to be proper social graces.

He called the father and communicated the Rebbe's message, stressing how important it was that the man hear him out. When the father heard Rabbi Gurary's sincerity, he began to think differently. Although the girl was unable to attend school, he called *Beis Yaakov* to enroll her.

A few days later, the cyst burst. All the pus drained, and the girl was discharged from hospital shortly thereafter. She became an eager pupil at *Beis Yaakov*, participating in every aspect of the school's activities.

Rabbi Gurary related the story to the Rebbe, and told him that everyone was marveling at the miracle.

The Rebbe responded: "The greatest miracle is that you went ahead and conveyed the message at the right time."

Heshy Sternberg is a Belzer chassid who worked in the public relations office of 47th Street Photo. He shares a friendship with Rabbi Yehoshua Metzger, whose Chai Foundation is responsible for placing the attractive ads Lubavitch runs in the *New York Times* to heighten public awareness of the Jewish holidays.

Before one holiday, Rabbi Metzger was having difficulty securing ad space. At that time, 47th Street Photo was a major advertiser with the *Times*, and so he called Heshy for help. After a few well-placed calls, Heshy was able to assure Rabbi Metzger that the ad would run.

Rabbi Metzger was very appreciative, asking Heshy if he would like to bring his family to the Rebbe one Sunday for dollars. Rabbi Metzger promised to introduce them, and said they would have a chance to ask for a personal blessing.

Heshy jumped at the opportunity, for he felt very much in need of a *tzaddik's* blessings. He had a daughter who was 18 months old but who was unable to walk or even stand. The family pediatrician had been observing her for several months, and feared the possibility of cerebral palsy. On his recommendation, the Sternbergs had already made an appointment with a noted neurologist.

When the Sternbergs met the Rebbe, Heshy's wife told him of their daughter's problem. The Rebbe answered: "She will walk. Your husband will walk her to the *chuppah*."

Six days later, on *Shabbos* morning, the Sternberg's little girl was playing on the living room floor. Suddenly, she stood up and began walking! She did not take hesitant baby steps, but walked confidently, like a child who had been walking for several months. When Heshy returned from *shul*, he was overwhelmed to see his daughter walking toward him!

The Sternberg's appointment with the neurologist had been scheduled for Monday. Needless to say, they canceled it. What could the doctor tell them?

~

Rabbi Naftoli Estulin's first child was delivered by Cesarean section. When his wife became pregnant again shortly afterwards, she was inclined to try bearing the child naturally, but several doctors advised another Cesarean.

In the middle of the pregnancy, Rabbi Estulin was in New York and met with the Rebbe at *yechidus*. He asked the Rebbe whether they should try for a natural birth or have another Cesarean.

The Rebbe answered that doctors held different views regarding this question — some recommended natural birth, while others thought the risk was too great. Mrs. Estulin, the Rebbe advised, should follow whichever course her doctor thought appropriate. "But whatever he decides," the Rebbe counseled, "he should postpone the delivery for as long as possible."

Mrs. Estulin's doctor favored performing a Cesarean, and proposed a date. Mindful of the Rebbe's answer, the Estulins asked him to wait a month. The doctor argued that doing so would be dangerous for the mother, but when the Estulins pressed him to listen to the Rebbe, the physician eventually agreed to postpone the operation for two weeks.

After the delivery, the doctor said it was a miracle that they had listened to the Rebbe. The pregnancy had begun a month later than the doctor and the Estulins had calculated. As it was, the child was born prematurely. Had the operation taken place on the day the doctor had suggested, the child might not have survived.

~

Reb Aharon Wohlberg is a Polish chassid who met Lubavitcher chassidim in Samarkand, Russia while fleeing from the Germans in World War II. When the war ended, and the Rebbe visited France to expedite his mother's immigration to the US, Reb Aharon had the opportunity to hear him speak on several occasions.

After settling in Cleveland, Reb Aharon felt the need for a connection with a rebbe. And so, although he did not consider himself a Lubavitcher *per se,* he attached himself to the Rebbe, and would visit New York from time to time for *yechidus* or to attend a *farbrengen.*

As Reb Aharon grew older, he developed a condition known as "trigger finger" — his index finger became bent, and could not be straightened. He went to several doctors, and their response was less than encouraging. "Surgery is necessary," they told him, "but even then, we are not sure that the problem will be solved."

Even before the affliction arose, Reb Aharon had scheduled a *yechidus* with the Rebbe, so he delayed his decision as to whether to schedule surgery until after he consulted with the Rebbe.

When Reb Aharon broached the subject, the Rebbe responded: "There is no need for surgery. A cortisone injection will solve the problem."

When Reb Aharon relayed this suggestion to his doctor, the physician was incredulous. "Cortisone! That will never work!"

But Reb Aharon insisted that the doctor follow the Rebbe's advice. After receiving the injection, he was able to move his finger and the problem did not recur.

Reb Aharon's recovery was talked about throughout Cleveland's Jewish community. Shortly afterwards, a friend developed the same condition. "Give me the same injection you gave Rabbi Wohlberg," he told his doctor. The doctor complied, but the condition was not alleviated.

Reb Aharon wasn't surprised. He understood that the cortisone was just an intermediary; it was the Rebbe's blessings that had brought about his recovery.

Rabbi Yechiel Michel Charlop, author of the famous *Halachic* works *Chof Yamim,* was one of the leading Orthodox rabbis in America in the previous generation. In 1957, on *Tishah BeAv,* the fast commemorating the destruction of the *Beis HaMikdash,* he was on the West Coast, and his son, Rabbi Zevulun Charlop, a rabbi in the Bronx, was visiting his in-laws in Buffalo. Thus the wife of the elder Rabbi Charlop was home alone in New York for the fast.

Ordinarily, being alone for the fast would not be a matter of concern for Mrs. Charlop. Herself, the daughter of a leading rabbinical family in Jerusalem, she was used to spending the day in private, lamenting the tragedies which had occurred on this date.

That year, the strenuous fast and the recitation of the *Kinos* prayers with intense concentration took its toll. At nightfall, Mrs. Charlop's vision suddenly became blurred, and then she could not see at all. At the same time, she felt piercing pain in her temple. Stunned at this strange course of events, she desperately groped her way to the phone and called the Katz family, friends who lived not far away and whose son — Dr. Sheldon Katz — was chief resident neurosurgeon at the Montefiore Hospital.

Dr. Katz hurried to the Charlop home and, after a brief examination, he called in the chief of neurology at the Albert Einstein College of Medicine, to come to see Mrs. Charlop at home. His diagnosis was that Mrs. Charlop had suffered an aneurysm in one of the major blood vessels in her head. The doctor felt that her only chance — slim though it was — would be an operation to stem the blood leakage in the head. In those days, doctors were just learning how to perform this operation, and the chances for survival were not bright. But the doctor felt there was no alternative.

Upon Rabbi Zevulun Charlop's insistence, Dr. Katz called in Dr. David Seecof, a noted pathologist, who was especially close to the elderly Rabbi Charlop. In turn, Dr. Seecof was able to persuade Dr. Morris Bender, a world renowned neurologist, to come up to the Bronx near midnight and examine Mrs. Charlop. After his examination, Dr. Bender was convinced that rushing Mrs. Charlop to surgery was mortally dangerous.

He arranged to have Mrs. Charlop brought to Mount Sinai Hospital, where he practiced, so that he could evaluate her condition more thoroughly and determine what course to pursue. Both Rabbi Yechiel Michel Charlop and Rabbi Zevulun Charlop rushed home.

After several days, Dr. Bender met with the Charlops. He explained to them that in order for him to definitively ascertain Mrs. Charlop's problem and possibly avert impending catastrophe, she would have to undergo an encephalogram — an angiogram of the head. While today, this is a more or less routine procedure, at that time, it was a much more complicated matter. "The angiogram itself," Dr. Bender acknowledged, "involves some danger to the patient." Nonetheless, he felt they had little choice. For this reason, he was consulting with the Charlops, before carrying out the procedure.

The Charlops told Dr. Bender that they would like to think about the matter before giving their consent. Mrs. Charlop asked Rabbi Baruch Putterman, a family friend who was a distinguished rabbi in the Bronx and a noted Lubavitcher chassid, to ask the Rebbe whether or not they should go ahead with the encephalogram.

The Rebbe advised the Charlops: "Find a doctor who would say no to the procedure!" Thereupon, the Charlops asked Dr. Bender to help them get a second opinion. "Who would Dr. Bender recommend?"

The doctor was livid. He must have felt that the Charlops were a bit ungrateful, after he had extended himself, and to such effect, in Mrs. Charlop's behalf.

Dr. Bender was at the top of his field. There were few doctors whose opinion he would consider at all worth reckoning with. He gave the Charlops two names: Dr. Houston Merritt, President Eisenhower's doctor, and Dr. Samuel B. Wortis, Dean of the New York University Medical School. He was sure they would agree with his opinion.

The Charlops contacted Dr. Merritt. He was in Colorado then attending to President Eisenhower, who had suffered a stroke. Understandably, he could not leave the President's bedside. "Consult with Dr. Wortis," he told the Charlops. "He'll be able to evaluate whether the angiogram is necessary or not, although I doubt he or I would override Dr. Bender."

Dr. Wortis was called, and after examining the patient and closely studying the medical notations, he told the Charlops, "It's hard to disagree with Dr. Bender. Nevertheless, in this situation, I'm convinced that an angiogram is not called for. It's not worth even the small risk."

Rabbi Charlop wanted to pay Dr. Wortis for his time, but the doctor refused. The rabbi insisted, and so Dr. Wortis mentioned a minimal fee.

"And to whom should I make out the check?" Rabbi Charlop asked. "Shmuel Ber Wortis, thank you," the doctor replied, explaining that he had come from an Orthodox background and contact with the rabbi and his wife had reminded him of his strong Jewish roots.

Although Dr. Bender was surprised when he heard the recommendation of Dr. Wortis, he did not press the point, and Mrs. Charlop did not undergo the angiogram.

She asked her son to bring her *siddur* to the hospital and place it at her bedside, so that if her sight returned, she would be able to use it again for holy matters. Her faith was wondrously rewarded. Several days later, she was able to see again, and except for occasional weakness in her left foot, she fully recovered. The cause of her blindness and pain was never diagnosed.

Rabbi Leibl Baumgarten was an elderly man when the Rebbe assumed the *nesius.* He was bothered by cataracts, and asked the Rebbe's advice about surgery. At first, the Rebbe counseled him to postpone the operation and have someone read to him if reading had become difficult.

When the problem became more severe, Rabbi Baumgarten consulted the Rebbe again. This time, the Rebbe told him to go to Dr. Rosenhort, a noted eye-surgeon who had performed cataract operations on the Viznitzer Rebbe, the Kapitznitzer Rebbe, and other Jewish leaders.

Dr. Rosenhort explained that the removal of a cataract was a routine operation. "If the patient remains still," he explained, "there is almost no danger whatsoever."

Those last words lit a red light in Rabbi Baumgarten's mind. He had a chronic cough. What would happen if he coughed in the middle of the operation? So the matter was delayed.

As time passed, however, the cataracts continued to worsen, and Rabbi Baumgarten eventually consented to the operation. While Dr. Rosenhort was speaking to him before the procedure began, he showed him pictures of the Rebbeim he had treated. Mendel Baumgarten, Rabbi Baumgarten's grandson and then a *yeshivah* student, in turn showed Dr. Rosenhort a picture of the Rebbe.

"Can I keep the picture?" the doctor asked. Mendel of course agreed.

The operation was successful, but on the following day a blood clot formed. Since Rabbi Baumgarten was in his 80s, this was a dangerous development. Mendel and his brother Berel hurried to 770 to inform the Rebbe. But the Rebbe passed the matter off. "It's nothing," he said, waving his hand.

The Baumgarten brothers took note of the exact time the Rebbe had spoken, and returned to the hospital to convey the news to the family.

When they arrived, they found everyone in good spirits. The blood clot had dissolved! They asked the doctors when this had happened, and the time they were told was the exact hour at which the brothers had spoken to the Rebbe.

When Dr. Rosenhort heard the story, he told everyone in the hospital of the miracle the Rebbe had performed. The Baumgartens informed the Rebbe that Dr. Rosenhort was praising him as a miracle worker.

The Rebbe responded: "May it be G-d's will that miracles be used for healthy things."

Chapter 12 —
"Rejoice O Barren One"
(*Isaiah* 54:1)

It is a well-known story.[1] Chanah the prophetess had been childless for many years. Each year, she and her husband Elkanah would journey to the Sanctuary at Shiloh. One year, embittered by her barrenness, Chanah left the sacrificial feast, entered the Sanctuary and opened her heart in prayer for a son:[2]

"She prayed at length before G-d... only her lips moved, but her voice was not heard. And Eli [the High Priest] thought her to be drunk.

And Eli said to her, 'How long will you be drunk? Put away your wine.'

'No, my lord,' replied Chanah. 'I am a woman of sorrowful spirit. I have not drunk wine or strong drink; I have poured out my soul before G-d...'

And Eli answered, 'Go in peace. May the G-d of Israel grant your request....'"

---

1. See *I Shmuel*, ch. 1; see also *Timeless Patterns in Time*, p. 13ff., where this concept is developed.
2. *Ibid.* 1:12-17.

A few words of explanation by the Rebbe enable us to peer beneath the surface of this familiar narrative. Eli never regarded Chanah as literally drunk; otherwise, he would have had her removed from the Sanctuary. On the contrary, he heard Chanah's prayer and perceived her sincerity. When he accused her of drunkenness, he was speaking figuratively. He could not understand how Chanah — standing before G-d, in the holy Sanctuary — could think of herself and ask for a son. He considered her to be intoxicated by her personal desires, immoderately given to self-concern.

To this, Chanah replied, "I am not drunk." (I.e., "I did not want anything for myself.") Rather, "I poured out my soul before G-d." (I.e., "My desire came from the very depths of my being.")

Chanah was not at all motivated by self-concern. This may be seen from her vow to dedicate her son "to G-d all the days of his life."[3] In "pour[ing] out her soul before G-d," she expressed the inner motivation of her soul. For at the core of each of our beings lies the desire for posterity. This desire is not self-oriented, but instead relates to G-d's desire for a dwelling in the lower worlds.

As soon as Eli heard Chanah's explanation, he responded with a blessing, asking that Chanah be granted the opportunity to bring the innermost desire of her soul to fruition.

Throughout the years, *tzaddikim* have been sensitive to the prayers of men and women who like Chanah desire a posterity. And like the blessing giving by Eli, their blessings have borne fruit.

---

3. *Ibid.* 1:11.

David and Gail Goldberg were married in 1965. By 1969, Gail had delivered two stillborn babies, and had been warned by her doctors not to consider another pregnancy.

She and her husband desired children, however, and began to consider the possibility of adoption. Gail's brother had been in contact with Rabbi Shlomo Zalman Hecht of Chicago. Although at that time he was not observant, David wanted to know whether the Jewish tradition included any restrictions with regard to adoption, and what the pertinent laws were. Before contacting the adoption authorities, he decided to sit down with Rabbi Hecht.

Rabbi Hecht was friendly, and provided a great deal of relevant information. But then he asked why David was thinking about adopting children when there was a chance to have his own? As David looked at him incredulously, Rabbi Hecht told him that many childless couples had been helped by the Rebbe's blessings.

The Goldbergs didn't understand: "Who is the Rebbe?" they wanted to know. What were they to do? Rabbi Hecht promised to arrange a personal meeting with the Rebbe, at which they should request a blessing for children.

The Goldbergs were willing to try. At *yechidus,* the Rebbe told them: "You shall have a boy and a girl. Conceive them in love, raise them in *Yiddishkeit,* and come back in a year with good news."

Within a year, their first son was born. A few years later, they were blessed with a girl.

※

In the '50s and '60s, the orthodox community in Detroit had few chassidim. Nevertheless, Rabbi Meir Avtzon was respected by all for his self-sacrifice in Russia, his Torah knowledge, and his strict adherence to Jewish law. His growing family (ultimately to include 15 children) also attracted the attention of everyone.

A respected teacher from a "Litvishe" background once approached Rabbi Avtzon and asked to study *Talmud* and *Tanya* with him twice a week. As their relationship developed, the teacher and Rabbi Avtzon became close friends.

After the teacher had been married for two years without having children, he and his wife began seeking medical advice. Two doctors told them they would never have children. When the teacher told Rabbi Avtzon about his problems, Rabbi Avtzon suggested that he see the Rebbe at *yechidus* and ask for his blessing.

At *yechidus,* the Rebbe questioned the teacher concerning the medical tests he had undergone. It was clear that the Rebbe was not pleased with the doctors' approach.

Suddenly, without being prompted, the Rebbe asked: "Before your marriage, were you ever engaged to anyone else?" And before waiting for an answer, he continued: "You gave your fiancée a present."

Shocked, the teacher nodded, and the Rebbe continued: "Did you ask her forgiveness when you broke the engagement?"

"No," the teacher answered, explaining that he had merely told her the reasons, and that she had understood.

"That's not enough," the Rebbe replied. "You must ask her forgiveness. When you do, your personal difficulty will be solved."

The teacher asked the Rebbe if he should ask the woman directly. The Rebbe replied that it would be better to do so through a third party, and that another person should be present.

The teacher asked: "Since forgiveness is dependent on a person's feelings, how do I know that she will forgive me with a full heart?"

The Rebbe responded: "Tell her — through a third party — in my name, that if she forgives you with a full heart, I promise that she will soon find her intended, marry, and establish a Jewish home."

The teacher was amazed. "Do you really mean that?" he blurted out.

"A promise is a promise," the Rebbe answered.

The *yechidus* took place on Thursday night. On Friday, the teacher returned home and located the phone number of his former fiancée's brother. On Saturday night, he called, telling him the entire story and asking him to approach his sister on his behalf.

At first the brother refused to believe the story, so the teacher told him that he could verify the particulars by writing to the Rebbe's secretariat.

This appeared to satisfy the brother. He asked the teacher if his wife could serve as the other person present when his sister gave her forgiveness, and the teacher agreed. The brother then revealed that his sister had been visiting that *Shabbos,* and if he would wait on the line, the entire matter could be concluded then and there.

The woman willingly gave her forgiveness. Three weeks afterwards, she became engaged and a month after that the marriage took place. Within days of his former fiancée's engagement, the teacher's wife entered her first pregnancy.

When one of Rabbi Avtzon's children retold this story at a chassidic *farbrengen,* one of the participants remembered a similar story that had taken place in Manchester, England.

One of the members of the Lubavitch community who had been childless for many years wrote the Rebbe for a blessing. The Rebbe replied that he should try to recall whether he had insulted anyone on his wedding day. If he had, he should ask forgiveness.

As he recalled the day of his wedding, he remembered the incident involving the *badchan.*

In many Eastern European communities, it was common for a *badchan* to perform at weddings, singing comical rhymes to lift the spirits of the celebrants. In many parts of England's Jewish community, this custom is still practiced.

At this young man's wedding, a *badchan* had performed. Now there are different types of *badchanim.* The humor of some borders on — or goes beyond — satire, and after a few *LeChaims,* can even be perceived as biting. And so it was at this wedding. Moreover, the *badchan* chose the groom and his family as the subject of his barbs. Rightly or wrongly, the groom could not appreciate the jest, and as the performance continued, he exploded and chased the *badchan* off the stage.

Was the *badchan* the person he had shamed? Could he have stopped the performance without embarrassing him?

The young man looked up the *badchan* and asked his forgiveness. The *badchan* said he had long forgotten the matter, and gave his forgiveness willingly.

Shortly afterwards, the young man and his wife were blessed with the first of many children.

Phil and Elaine Brown were married for many years but had no children, even though they had visited several doctors and tried many kinds of treatment. One of the doctors told Elaine bluntly: "There is absolutely no chance that you will ever conceive naturally."

Hearing this, they decided to adopt, and went to a social service organization to fill out the papers. The case worker looked at their forms and said: "It's difficult to find Jewish children. The wait may be anywhere from a year to two or three or more." Still, the Browns decided to go ahead.

The agency examined their financial background, their education, their friends, their attitudes to children, their friends' attitude toward children, their attitude towards their friends' children, and dozens of other factors. After 13 months of questions, the agency finally asked for references.

At the time, Phil and Elaine lived across the street from Rabbi and Rebbetzin Zalmen Kazen, Lubavitch *shluchim* in Cleveland. Every time Rabbi Kazen would see Phil, he would say "hello" and invite the couple over for *Shabbos* dinner. Now, although Phil didn't know what to make of a Rabbi with a beard, the adoption agency wanted references, and so Phil thought that maybe he could combine business with pleasure. He could get a reference for the social service agency — after all, what could be better than a reference from a Rabbi? — and fulfill his obligation to the Kazens once and for all.

During dinner, Phil and Elaine told the Kazens that they were looking to adopt children. The Kazens told them that many couples had been blessed with children after receiving a blessing from the Rebbe, and suggested that the Browns try this route as well.

The Browns politely declined; they were not observant and did not want to make any commitments. Mrs. Kazen, however, is a very persistent lady. Ultimately, she persuaded the couple to send in a letter.

Several weeks later, the Browns received a reply. The Rebbe suggested they observe the mitzvah of *taharas hamishpachah*.

While they appreciated the Rebbe's concern and his suggestion, Phil and Elaine didn't feel ready for formal observance of any sort, and so they put the letter away. By this time, all their references had been checked, their personal character had been analyzed, and their bank statements reviewed. Still there was no child for adoption.

One day, a representative of the social service agency came for a visit; as part of the decision-making process, the agency wanted to inspect the home. The Browns graciously let the representative in, but it wasn't long before their attitude changed. The representative pulled open drawers, looked through closets, peered under beds and behind bookshelves.

After going over every inch of their home, the representative departed. By that time, Elaine had made up her mind.

"Let's try the *mikveh*," she told her husband.

They did, and that month she became pregnant with the first of their many children. Shortly afterwards, the agency called and told them it had a child for adoption. The Browns, however, replied that they were no longer interested.

One day as Phil was cleaning out some drawers, he noticed the Rebbe's letter. He read it again and saw that the Rebbe had told him that in the month of ___ , they would hear good news. That was the month in which their first son Mordechai was born.

Several months afterwards, Phil's mother Sadie became so ill that she was hospitalized and lost consciousness. The doctor solemnly told the family to call all her children together. "She probably has only several hours to live," he said. "It is highly unlikely that she will regain consciousness. If she survives beyond morning, it will be as a vegetable."

Phil sat with his brother and two sisters. It was as if they had already started mourning.

And then Mrs. Kazen arrived. "Did you write the Rebbe yet?" she asked the Browns. "You'll see! He will give his blessing and everything will be all right!"

The family were amazed, and even upset. Their mother was on the verge of death, and here this lady was treating it in what seemed a cavalier fashion.

Phil's brother Burt was piqued enough to usher Mrs. Kazen out of the room, but not before she had secured Mrs. Brown's Hebrew name and that of her mother.

"I'll write the Rebbe for you," she promised as she was being pushed out.

A few hours later she came back. The Brown family were deep in sorrow, and hardly listened as she told them: "I spoke to Rabbi Chodakov, who caught the Rebbe as he was leaving

770. 'Tell the family there is no need to worry,' the Rebbe said. 'Let the doctors repeat the tests; they'll see they made a mistake. In the morning, everything will be fine.'"

The Rebbe's answer did not make the Browns feel any better. They could not understand how a Rabbi in New York could know their mother's condition more accurately than the doctors who were treating her. But in the morning, their attitude changed. Mrs. Brown woke up, demanded a cup of coffee, and read the morning newspaper. Her answers to questions were sharp and to the point. This lady was no vegetable.

At that point, Phil's brother Burt decided to adopt a chassidic lifestyle. "The Rebbe didn't just give a blessing," he explained. "He set a time. That's putting yourself on the line. When he proved right, I felt I had to make a commitment."

※

To be one of the Rebbe's *shluchim*, you don't have to be officially employed in that capacity. On the contrary, the Rebbe gives everyone the opportunity to take such an initiative.

Mordechai Baron is one individual who takes this invitation seriously. An Israeli jack-of-all-trades, with the outgoing assertiveness that characterizes his countrymen, he always carries an extra pair of *tefillin* with him, and often puts them on with others.

One summer, as he drove from his home in Kfar Chabad, he would often pass a new housing development in Ramat Gan. Apartments were being constructed, as well as a commercial center, but not a synagogue. Each time Mordechai passed the project, it became more and more obvious that the complex must contain a *shul*.

One day, he pulled over at the development, put his *tefillin* in his briefcase, and went to speak to the owner about the importance of adding a synagogue.

"May I speak to the owner?" he inquired at the rental office.

"Who shall I say is calling?" answered the receptionist.

"Mr. Baron," Mordechai answered. "I have an important offer regarding the development of this property."

And so Mordechai went from secretary to secretary until he reached the project manager.

"I need to speak to the owner," Mordechai told the manager.

"That's impossible," the manager said. "He's overseas. Listen, tell me about your offer. If it's attractive, I'll tell the owner."

"I want to build a synagogue here," Mordechai replied.

"You must be a Lubavitcher," the manager smiled.

"That's right," responded Mordechai. "How can you tell?"

"That's not important," the manager told him. "Come to my office. I have to ask you about writing a letter to the Rebbe."

As Mordechai entered the manager's office, he reached into his briefcase for his *tefillin*. The manager could not protest; after all, he had invited Mordechai in!

After performing the *mitzvah*, he told Mordechai his story. He and his wife had been childless for 12 years, and had gone to the most renowned fertility specialists in *Eretz Yisrael,* but to no avail. After hearing that with the Rebbe's blessings, many childless couples were able to conceive, he and his wife had decided several months earlier to write the Rebbe, but did not know any Lubavitchers.

"You came at the right time," he told Mordechai. "We had almost despaired of getting the message to him."

"I'll gladly help you write the Rebbe," Mordechai replied. "But if you want something from him, you have to give something in return."

"How much?" asked the manager, reaching for his checkbook.

"No. I'm not speaking about money. What the Rebbe is most interested in," explained Mordechai, "is *mitzvos*. Make a commitment to observe a *mitzvah*. Tell the Rebbe that, and ask for a blessing."

"Which *mitzvah* should I chose?" asked the manager.

"Have you ever kept a *Shabbos?*" asked Mordechai. "Tell the Rebbe that you will observe one *Shabbos:* no driving, no cooking, no electricity, you'll go to *shul.* And then ask for your blessing. Put in your name, your mother's name, your wife's name and her mother's name. That's all you have to do.

"Write the letter now. I'll wait here and mail it for you."

The manager wrote the letter, and within two months his wife was pregnant. He invited Mordechai to the *bris,* and there, among all the leading real estate figures in Tel Aviv, he told the story.

Mordechai and his *tefillin* were very busy that afternoon.

In 5752, several weeks before the Rebbe suffered his first stroke, a middle-aged woman from Jerusalem joined the thousands of men and women waiting to receive a dollar and a blessing. A childless descendant of a long line of distinguished Rabbis, she asked for the Rebbe's blessing that she be granted children.

The Rebbe responded with a smile and gave her three dollars: one for herself and two for the children to be born. Her joy could not be contained.

She returned home, put the dollars in a safe place, and waited.

She waited almost five years. In the interim, she shared the grief over the events of 27 Adar and 3 Tammuz. And she had her own private grief, for the Rebbe's blessing had not been fulfilled.

Then, when she was nearly 50, the woman gave birth to twins, a boy and a girl. At the *bris,* her husband told the story of the dollars the Rebbe had given for his children, and promised that they would receive them when they came of age.

Chapter 13 —
Beyond Nature's Limits

In the 1950s, a group of Jewish university students met with the Rebbe to speak about the questions and difficulties they experienced maintaining their faith despite the challenges which scientific knowledge and the demands of secular American society appeared to present. In the course of the discussion, one of the students bluntly asked the Rebbe: "It has been said that the Rebbe can perform miracles. Is this true?"

The Rebbe answered: Every Jew possesses a soul which is an actual part of G-d. Like G-d, the Jew's soul is not limited by the constraints of the natural order. The Torah is the medium which connects a Jew to his G-dly source. When a Jew attaches himself to the Torah, his G-dly potential is revealed, and he is not bound by the natural order.

At the conclusion of the meeting, the Rebbe turned to the students and said: Let us all work miracles. We entered this room with limited spiritual horizons. Let's all make a commitment to expand them immeasurably, to advance in our devotion to the Torah and its *mitzvos* in a manner which could truly be considered miraculous.

The Rebbe's words recall an old chassidic adage with regard to miracles: "Our Sages say:[1] 'A *tzaddik* decrees, and G-d carries out his will.' It is, however, far more instructive to watch a *tzaddik* carry out G-d's will, than to watch G-d carry out a *tzaddik's* will."

We see, nevertheless, that chassidim have always told stories of the miracles their Rebbeim performed. Indeed, those stories have a unique attraction, sometimes luring our attention far more persuasively than an instructive story of how to advance our divine service.

The Baal Shem Tov, founder of the chassidic movement, has been identified with miracles, so much so that Yiddish speakers use the expression "a *Baal Shem'ske maaseh*" (a story like those of the Baal Shem Tov) to refer to a miracle.

It is popularly explained that Baal Shem Tov performed miracles out of necessity. A Jew was in dire need, and out of concern, he worked a miracle to extricate him from his situation.

But there is a deeper motif. The Baal Shem Tov performed miracles not merely to help the person, but to reveal a dimension of G-dliness which transcends the natural order. A miracle expands our perspective and enables us to appreciate the inner G-dliness that permeates every dimension of our existence.

Nature and its limitations are not the sum total of our frame of reference. On the contrary, there is a higher reality which is not confined by these limitations. As our Sages said:[2] "He who ordained that oil should burn [can] ordain that vinegar shall burn."

Seeing one miracle makes it possible for us to understand that our lives and the world we live in is

---

1. 1. Cf. *Taanis* 23a.
2. *Ibid.*, 25a.

one continuous series of miracles. Hearing of the miracles performed by the Baal Shem Tov and his spiritual heirs lifts us beyond the day-to-day details of material existence and sensitizes us to the spiritual reality which lies at the core of our lives.

Beyond Nature's Limits

Pinchas Krinsky had developed a relationship with the Rebbe during the lifetime of the Rebbe Rayatz. As a student in the Lubavitcher *Yeshivah,* he would volunteer to help with various tasks that came up in the organizations — *Kehot* Publications, *Merkos* (the Central Organization for Jewish Education), and *Machne Israel*— which the Rebbe directed.

Pinchas returned to Boston before the Rebbe Rayatz passed away. On 14 MarCheshvan, 5711 (1950), three months before the Rebbe formally accepted the *nesius,* the mother of one of Pinchas's friends called him with somber news. Her son, A.S., who had been a student in the Lubavitcher *Yeshivah* in New York, had been found unconscious in the street. Evidently, he had been hit by a car. He was brought to the hospital, where he remained in a coma.

Pinchas called New York and spoke to Rabbi Chodakov, asking him to inform the Rebbe of A.S.'s condition and request a blessing.

Rabbi Chodakov called back with the following message from the Rebbe: Pinchas should immerse himself in a *mikveh* before going to the hospital. He should approach the patient directly and speak the following words: "A., the Rebbe, Rabbi Joseph Isaac, son of the Rebbe, Sholom DovBer, has been notified. Therefore you will be well." The Rebbe also asked that Pinchas apprise him of any positive developments.

When Pinchas got to the hospital, A. was unconscious and attached to various life-sustaining machines. After the nurses allowed him to approach the patient, Pinchas followed the Rebbe's instructions to the letter.

Despite his absolute faith in the Rebbe, he was dumbfounded at what took place. Within moments, A. regained consciousness, looked at Pinchas, and said: "Hi, Pinny." He then asked to have the feeding tube in his nose removed because it was uncomfortable. Pinchas went into the hall and relayed his friend's request to the doctors. Without waiting to hear that it was A.S. himself who had asked that the tube be removed, they said: "It can't be removed. He will be lucky if he comes to in a week or ten days." They were shocked to find that he had regained consciousness. Pinchas then called New York to inform the Rebbe of what had happened.

The next time Pinchas went to New York, the Rebbe asked him: "Were there other people on the ward?"

"Yes," Krinsky answered.

"Did you go to them as well?" the Rebbe asked.

"No," Krinsky answered, suddenly aware of the Rebbe's intent. Here the gift of life had been in his hands, and he had not used it fully!

When the story was told, the Rebbe said that his father-in-law was still performing miracles. The chassidim thought otherwise.

In the summer of 5719 (1959), two brothers arrived at the *shul* of Rabbi Moshe Aharon Geisinsky. They were wearing black *shivah* ribbons and recited *Kaddish*. Over the coming weeks they continued to attend services, and Rabbi Geisinsky was able to develop a relationship with them. The brothers, Louis and Max Hozinsky, prided themselves on being direct descendants of the great *tzaddik*, R. Levi Yitzchok of Berditchev.

Louis bore the *tzaddik's* Hebrew name. Perhaps for that reason, he showed a greater interest in Jewish practice. He began to put on *tefillin* every day, invited Rabbi Geisinsky to his home to put up *mezuzos*, and took on certain aspects of *Shabbos* observance.

After he had been putting on *tefillin* consistently, Rabbi Geisinsky encouraged him to write a letter to the Rebbe informing him of his commitment and asking for a blessing. Louis did so, and received a warm reply.

One weekday evening, Rabbi Geisinsky took Louis to join the Rebbe for the evening service. Louis emerged awe-struck. "It must be that he's too holy for me," he told Rabbi Geisinsky. "Never have I felt such fear! I've met Roosevelt, Truman and Eisenhower, but none of them made me feel like this! It's too much for me! I don't want to see him again!" Rabbi Geisinsky did not press the issue, and their relationship continued.

In 1959, Yom Kippur began on Sunday evening. At 10 PM on Saturday night, less than 24 hours before the beginning of that holy day, Rabbi Geisinsky was startled to hear his door bell ring. Though it was later than usual for guests to call, Rabbi Geisinsky answered the door. He was surprised to see a very worried Louis Hozinsky. Louis explained that his younger brother Max was waiting in the car, too embarrassed to speak to the Rabbi. Rabbi Geisinsky approached Max and invited him in.

Max began to tell his story. A week earlier, he had been examined at a hospital and the doctors had diagnosed cancer. They had wanted to operate immediately, and only sent him home because there were no empty beds. He had gone from doctor to doctor for another opinion, and all had concurred with the previous diagnosis.

Earlier that day, he continued, he had seen a great specialist, who told him that the diagnosis was probably correct, and that an operation would be necessary in the near future. Nevertheless, he was not as emphatic about the time factor and felt that Max could wait a while for the operation. When Max returned home, the doctors from the first hospital had called, saying they now had an open bed and that Mr. Hozinsky should come immediately.

"Give me a blessing and advice," Max asked Rabbi Geisinsky, "What should I do?"

Rabbi Geisinsky tried to explain that such matters were beyond his ability, but the brothers pressed him for an answer.

"This is a matter with which only the Rebbe can deal," Rabbi Geisinsky told them. He then instructed them to speak to

Rabbi Chodakov, the Rebbe's personal secretary, and ask to see the Rebbe immediately. If Rabbi Chodakov would not agree, Rabbi Geisinsky advised them to wait for an opportunity to approach the Rebbe and speak to him directly.

The brothers immediately proceeded to 770, arriving at approximately 11:00 p.m. Rabbi Chodakov explained that it was impossible to see the Rebbe at this time, and suggested they write a letter. (In general, the custom among the *Rebbeim* was to remain awake the entire night before Yom Kippur and not to receive any callers whatsoever.)

The brothers waited outside the Rebbe's office until about midnight, when the Rebbe emerged and locked the door.

Louis introduced himself and told the Rebbe that he had an urgent matter to discuss. The Rebbe re-opened the door to his room and invited the brothers in. "I was expecting you," he told them.

After hearing the details of his condition, the Rebbe told Max: "I have a medicine for you. Begin putting on *tefillin*, starting tomorrow. There is no need for an operation. All you need is a diet. I will prescribe one for you. After three weeks, visit Dr. Seligson (the Rebbe's personal doctor and *chassid*) and take his advice."

As they were about to leave, the Rebbe reiterated: "I was expecting that you would come tonight for medicine, and your medicine is to put on *tefillin.*" Three times, the Rebbe repeated "Your medicine is to put on *tefillin.*"

The brothers called Rabbi Geisinsky at 12:45 and told him of their meeting.

The next day, as was his custom every year on the day before Yom Kippur, the Rebbe distributed *lekach* (honey cake) to his chassidim. Rabbi Geisinsky joined the long line of followers. When his turn came, the Rebbe told him: "The Hozinsky brothers were here last night."

Rabbi Geisinsky replied that he knew of their visit.

"Did he put on *tefillin?*" the Rebbe asked.

"I don't know," Rabbi Geisinsky answered, "I assume he did."

"Make sure he puts on *tefillin*," the Rebbe said.

Afterwards, Rabbi Geisinsky called and found out that Max had indeed put on *tefillin*. He told the two brothers about the importance of fasting on Yom Kippur, and Louis agreed to fast for the first time in his life. Because of Max's physical condition, Rabbi Geisinsky consulted with other rabbis, and they agreed that he should eat small amounts at spaced intervals, as prescribed in the *Shulchan Aruch*.

Max was too concerned about his condition to wait three weeks before consulting Dr. Seligson. Instead, he called him directly after Yom Kippur and arranged an examination.

When Max entered, he told Dr. Seligson that the Rebbe had sent him. "What did the Rebbe say?" the doctor asked.

"Are you a chassid or a doctor?" Max replied.

Dr. Seligson performed an examination and saw that a severe problem existed. He also advised an operation. It was only then that Max told him the Rebbe's advice.

"Wait until I consult the Rebbe," Dr. Seligson told him.

Late that night, Dr. Seligson called Max and told him that he no longer advised an operation. Instead, Max should follow the Rebbe's instructions carefully.

Max immediately called Rabbi Geisinsky — it was then Tuesday night — and told him all the particulars, adding that since Saturday night he had already gained three pounds, which, for a cancer patient, is more than surprising.

Several days later, Max called Rabbi Geisinsky again. His sister was pressing him, he explained, to have X-rays taken and to consult a well-known specialist. Would doing so be going against the Rebbe's wishes? Could Rabbi Geisinsky ask the Rebbe for him?

Rabbi Geisinsky submitted the request. The Rebbe replied that if Max *himself* wanted the examination, he should go.

Max scheduled the examination, but the X-rays were inconclusive. The doctor scheduled another visit in six weeks.

During the next three weeks, Max gained 12 pounds. After taking the second set of X-rays, the specialist declared that there was no trace of cancer. Indeed, he called the hospital and demanded to know why they had thought of operating! The hospital doctors couldn't understand; the growth was obvious in the original X-rays. Why had it disappeared?

∗

On *Yud-Beis* Tammuz (Tammuz 12), 5687 (1927), the Previous Rebbe, R. Yosef Yitzchak Schneersohn, was released from prison in Stalinist Russia. Ever since then, the date is celebrated as a major holiday among Lubavitcher chassidim.

Rabbi Berel Baumgarten, the Rebbe's *shliach* in Argentina, cherished this occasion, and often spent the day at 770, taking in the Rebbe's *farbrengen.* At other times, he used the holiday as an opportunity to spread awareness of chassidism to others.

One year, however, he was forced to travel from Argentina to Brazil, and realized that on *Yud-Beis* Tammuz, he would be in the middle of his journey. Disturbed at the prospect of spending this auspicious date far from anyone with whom he could share his feelings, he sent the Rebbe a telegram before he left home, asking to be remembered on that date.

In order to reach Brazil, Rabbi Baumgarten had to cross the Iguacu River by ferry — a boat with an open deck covered by an awning, with several heavy-duty rafts tied together to carry cars and cargo.

Together with several others, Rabbi Baumgarten followed instructions and drove his car onto the raft. As soon as the cars were parked, he and the others left their vehicles and enjoyed the fresh air beneath the awning. At first, Rabbi Baumgarten was happy to find that two of his fellow passengers were Jews. But his joy turned to consternation when he discovered that they were totally alienated from their heritage, and had no desire to hear about Jewish practice or ideas. One of them brazenly flaunted a ham sandwich before him, making it clear how little Judaism meant to him. Feeling that further conversation would be futile, and offended by their actions, Rabbi Baumgarten returned to his car and opened his books to study.

Suddenly, there was a powerful jolt — a banana boat had slammed into the raft! Huge beams that had been piled in a corner of the raft began tumbling down, pushing cars off the raft and into the Iguacu River. To his shock, Rabbi Baumgarten's car also began to move. He slammed his foot on the brake, but was powerless to stop the car's forward motion. It too crashed into the waves and started to sink!

Now Rabbi Baumgarten was a big man, over six feet tall and more than 250 pounds. Yet, as big and strong as he was, he couldn't open the car door; the water pressure was simply too great. What happened next, he never knew, but suddenly his door opened, and he found himself out of the car and in the water, being pulled upward.

His troubles, however, were far from over. Yes, he had escaped the sinking vehicle, but Rabbi Baumgarten had never learned to swim. Frantically kicking and flailing his arms for what seemed like hours, he was at the end of his strength when his head suddenly broke through the water. Exhausted, Rabbi Baumgarten could only bob helplessly up and down; he had no idea what was keeping him afloat. Between waves, he could see the raft close by, but was powerless to move towards it.

To make matters even worse, he could hear a rumbling thunder in the distance, and realized with horror that the river's powerful current was beginning to pull him away from the raft, and towards a waterfall! As the white water crashed over him, Rabbi Baumgarten looked up to see a man heaving a life-preserver toward him. It splashed into the river just within reach.

Rabbi Baumgarten grabbed the life-preserver and drew it close. He tried to put it over his body, but he was simply too big. Though his strength was giving out, there was no alternative; he would have to hold on by hand. While in the water, he pictured the Rebbe's face before him.

After he had been hauled into the raft and was able to regain his composure, the two Jews whom he had met previously approached him, overcome with remorse. They realized that it was because of them that Rabbi Baumgarten had returned to his car, and apologized for their previous conduct. The man who had flaunted the sandwich even promised to keep kosher from that time onward.

After Rabbi Baumgarten reached the far shore, he began to contemplate his situation. He had no explanation for the miracle that had occurred. Days later, he understood. When he called the Rebbe's office and asked that the Rebbe be told what had happened, one of the secretaries told him when his telegram had been delivered. Calculating the difference in time-zones, he realized that the Rebbe must have been reading the telegram at precisely the time that his car had been dislodged from the raft!

All these calculations, however, came later; at the moment, he had more immediate concerns. His personal belongings had all been lost with the car, and he was far from any Jewish community. Where would he find a *tallis* and *tefillin* with which to pray?

Now in Brazil, Tammuz falls in the winter and the days are short. Rabbi Baumgarten found that there was a small airport nearby, but no flights were scheduled until late afternoon; he would not be able to reach another city before sunset. He did not know what to do, being unable to conceive of letting the day pass without putting on *tefillin*.

He inquired about hiring a private plane. Although the cost was exorbitant, he was able to find a pilot who could fly him to another city before sunset. He sent a telegram to the leaders of

Beyond Nature's Limits

the Jewish community there, asking them to meet him at the airport with *tefillin*.

There was a mix-up in communications, however, and no one greeted Rabbi Baumgarten at the airport. With less than an hour left before nightfall, Rabbi Baumgarten grabbed a cab and told him to hurry to the nearest synagogue. Unfortunately, night fell before he could get there. Broken-hearted, he stopped the cab and sat down on a nearby park bench and cried.

At his next *yechidus,* he asked the Rebbe how he could atone for not putting on *tefillin* that day.

Before answering his question, the Rebbe looked up at him and asked: "Well, did I think about you? Yes or no?"

He then instructed Rabbi Baumgarten to study the laws of *tefillin* in the Alter Rebbe's *Shulchan Aruch,* and the discourses in chassidic thought that speak about the subjugation of heart and mind — the spiritual message associated with the *mitzvah* of *tefillin.*

Rabbi Baumgarten lamented that a pocket-sized *Siddur* and *Tanya* which he had been given by the Rebbe were now at the bottom of the Iguacu River. "Could the Rebbe please replace them?" he asked.

"Why? Is it my fault?" replied the Rebbe with a smile. He did, however, give Rabbi Baumgarten another *Siddur* and *Tanya.*

In 5732 (1972), Yocheved Chanah Ratner married Avraham David Stauber. It was a gilt-edged wedding. Both came from wealthy, well-connected Californian Jewish families. They seemed to be riding the peak of good fortune.

But the wheel of fortune has been known to turn. Two years later, when David graduated from law school, the Ratner-Staubers took a long-awaited European vacation. While driving through Greece, their sportscar veered off a mountain road and plunged into a deep ravine. Avraham David escaped with minor injuries, but his young wife was stuck in the wreck for hours. When she was finally extricated she was bleeding all over, and partially paralyzed. By helicopter, she was flown to a hospital in Athens.

The extent of Yocheved Chanah's injuries was beyond the expertise of the Greek doctors. Fearing damage to her spine, they inserted a metal plate in her back. The surgery was unsuccessful; indeed, it increased the extent of her paralysis. Gangrene and hepatitis set in. Out of fear and frustration, the doctors advised the Ratner-Staubers to have her transferred to an American facility.

Resolving to provide their daughter with the finest medical care, her parents had her brought to a hospital in California. After an initial examination, the doctors were very pessimistic. They doubted Yocheved Chanah would ever be able to sit up again.

Shortly after her arrival at the hospital, Rabbi Shlomo Cunin, West Coast Director of *Chabad*-Lubavitch, visited Mrs. Ratner-Stauber. Yocheved Chanah's father had been one of *Chabad*'s initial supporters in Los Angeles, and for several months before leaving for Europe, the Ratner-Staubers had attended *Shabbos* services at the *Chabad* House. Indeed, a week before they departed, they had been *Shabbos* guests at the Cunin home.

Rabbi Cunin was direct and to the point: Many seriously ill people had been helped by the Rebbe. Yocheved Chanah should write to ask for a blessing.

Yocheved Chanah had never written to the Rebbe before, but the thought that his blessing might help filled her with hope. As she composed the letter, she felt a spiritual connection and a sense of inner peace.

The Rebbe replied immediately, sending a response in duplicate by special delivery, one copy to the hospital where Yocheved Chanah was convalescing and another to Rabbi

Cunin. Moreover, he had one of his secretaries call Rabbi Cunin and convey the essence of his message verbally, to make sure that Yocheved Chanah received an answer before *Shabbos*.

The Rebbe instructed Yocheved Chanah to light *Shabbos* candles,[1] preferably by kindling the lights herself. He also emphasized the importance of *bitachon* (trust in G-d's ability to heal), and concluded with a blessing.

Yocheved Chanah was partially paralyzed, and had been given instructions not to move, for any movement could further damage the nerves in her spine. For her to light candles meant that her husband had to place one in her hand and move it so that she could light. This he did for several months.

Yocheved Chanah's condition began to improve, and she was moved from the hospital to a rehab center. One Friday her husband was visiting and her parents were supposed to come and bring the *Shabbos* candles. The Ratners became stuck in traffic, however, and arrived after *Shabbos* had begun. Yocheved Chanah knew that she should not light candles after *Shabbos* had started, and so did not have the opportunity to fulfill the *mitzvah*.

Later that night, she began hemorrhaging. The doctors did not know what to do. At one point, they thought she had only moments to live.

After the *Shabbos* ended, her husband called Rabbi Cunin and told him the story. Rabbi Cunin had him promise never to allow such a situation to repeat itself and called the Rebbe's secretariat. Shortly afterwards, the hemorrhages stopped.

From that point onward, Yocheved Chanah made marked improvements, and within four months she was discharged from the rehab center. Although she remained confined to a wheelchair, she returned home and began to resume ordinary

---

1. This was before the Rebbe began *Mivtza Neshek*, the widespread campaign to encourage women and girls to light *Shabbos* candles.

life. So complete was her recovery that she would — and still does — swim for several hours a day.

When she was discharged, the doctors warned her not to enter pregnancy for at least two years. She did not heed their warning, and entered her first pregnancy shortly thereafter. It goes without saying that one of the first things she did after conceiving was to write to the Rebbe telling of the doctors' concern and asking for his blessings.

The Rebbe replied, promising her an easy pregnancy and an easy birth, that both she and the baby would be healthy, and that she would deliver a happy and healthy child at an auspicious hour.

When Yocheved Chanah told her doctor about the pregnancy, he advised her to abort. Having a child would be too risky, he told her.

When he saw she was adamant, he changed his tone. "We'll schedule a Cesarean delivery," he told her. In his mind, a natural childbirth was absolutely out of the question.

Yocheved Chanah was resolute. She switched doctors, explaining: "My Rabbi promised me an easy birth. Why shouldn't it be natural?"

She chose the same obstetrician who had delivered Rabbi Cunin's children. He respected the Rebbe, and was willing to attempt a natural birth. He made one condition. "If at any moment, I decide a Cesarean is necessary, you must agree without argument," he told Yocheved Chanah.

True to the Rebbe's words, the pregnancy was easy. The birth was natural and the baby was delivered without complications.

And the baby was born "in an auspicious hour." The Ratner-Staubers had planned to name the child Aliyahu Simcha Adom after Yocheved Chanah's grandfather, and Adom was born on his namesake's *yahrzeit*.

Beyond Nature's Limits 223

A little less than two years after Adom was born, Yocheved Chanah entered a second pregnancy. Again, she wrote to the Rebbe for a blessing and received a warm reply.

Several months later, she was surprised to receive an unsolicited letter: "I am reiterating my blessings for your child. May you raise him to Torah, marriage and good deeds."

The family's curiosity was further piqued when, at the Rebbe's *Yud-Alef* Nissan *farbrengen,* Yocheved Chanah's father approached him and asked for a blessing. The Rebbe covered the microphone and told him: "Your grandson will be fine."

Several days later, the Ratner-Staubers understood the Rebbe's intent. On the morning after the Second *Seder,* Adom fell ill and was rushed to hospital. The doctors diagnosed spinal meningitis. They did what they could, but had little hope of combating the dread disease. Bluntly, they told the Ratner-Staubers that the child would not survive.

As soon as the holiday ended, Rabbi Cunin called to tell the Rebbe what had happened, but received no answer. During this time, little Adom hovered between life and death.

Then one day, Rabbi Cunin rushed into Adom's hospital room. "The Rebbe gave his blessing," he told the Ratner-Staubers. And directly afterwards, as if it had been planned, a doctor entered with test results indicating that the baby's condition had taken a turn for the better.

Shortly afterwards, Aliyahu Simchah Adom recovered, and continued to develop normally, with no sign of what he had undergone.

⁂

The Baal Shem Tov initiated the custom of holding *Mashiach's Seudah* (the feast of *Mashiach)* on the last day of Pesach. At 770, this was always the occasion for a unique *farbrengen* at which, in keeping with the custom established by the Rebbe Rashab, the Rebbe and all those present each drank four cups of wine. At the conclusion of the gathering, the

Rebbe would lead the chassidim in the grace after meals while holding a fifth cup, and afterwards would distribute wine from this cup — "the cup of blessing" — to all the chassidim, as well as to Jews from all walks of life, who filed by to receive this blessing.

Reb Sholom Yeshaya Deitsch was one of the dedicated chassidim in the Crown Heights community who never missed a *farbrengen.* Even when his sons were very young, he would take them along, educating them to treasure time spent with the Rebbe. *Mashiach's Seudah* was surely no exception and so, on the last day of Pesach, 5727 (1967), Reb Sholom Yeshaya took his place at the *farbrengen,* positioning his youngest son Avraham Moshe, then a boy of 11, at one of the tables behind him.

The *farbrengen* proceeded, and the Rebbe delivered several *sichos.* In between, the chassidim sang *niggunim,* and some used the opportunity to say *LeChaim* to the Rebbe. At one point between *sichos,* Reb Sholom noticed the Rebbe looking intently in his direction, and holding up four fingers, a sign that someone should partake of the four cups of wine.

To whom was the Rebbe gesturing? Reb Sholom assumed that it was to another chassid nearby; he was certain it was not to him. But when, almost insistently, the Rebbe pointed to Reb Sholom's son, Avraham Moshe, and held up four fingers, the intent became clear: The boy should also drink the four cups.[2]

So Reb Sholom filled a cup and gave it to his son. The boy held it up to the Rebbe, received a nod of approval, recited the blessing and drank it to the bottom. The Rebbe smiled and began delivering another *sichah.*

After concluding that *sichah,* the Rebbe again turned to Reb Sholom and Avraham Moshe, holding three fingers up and one bent over. Again, the intent was clear, and the boy downed his second cup.

---

2. Since this time, the Rebbe encouraged that also women and children participate in *Mashiach's Seudah,* and partake of four cups of wine or grape juice.

Beyond Nature's Limits

As the *farbrengen* continued, young Avraham Moshe drank his third and fourth cups of wine. Shortly thereafter the *farbrengen* concluded, and the chassidim lined up to receive wine from "the cup of blessing."

Avraham Moshe, however, was not among them; the late hour and the four cups of wine had taken their toll, and the lad had fallen fast asleep on a table. One of the Deitschs' neighbors volunteered to carry him home while his father stayed behind to partake of "the cup of blessing."

When Reb Sholom approached the Rebbe, the Rebbe asked him where his son was. When Reb Sholom explained that the boy had fallen asleep, the Rebbe smiled understandingly. Reb Sholom then moved on, curious as to the meaning of the sequence of events.

Several weeks later, on the holiday of Shavuos, Reb Sholom suffered his first heart attack. When he had recuperated enough to take his place at a *farbrengen*, he approached the Rebbe and asked for a blessing for health. In reply, the Rebbe told him: "I gave your son the four cups to drink."

One Saturday night, shortly after the Sabbath ended, the phone rang in the home of Rabbi Leibl Groner, the Rebbe's secretary. It was an elderly chassid, asking for a blessing for his wife. She had been in hospital for several days, and her condition was critical.

"Would Rabbi Groner ask the Rebbe for a blessing?" the chassid asked.

Rabbi Groner offered some words of reassurance, but told the chassid that it was often difficult to establish contact with the Rebbe on a Saturday night. He would try, but if it was not possible, he would pass on the message first thing Sunday morning.

As Rabbi Groner had suspected, he was unable to contact the Rebbe that night. Sunday morning, as soon as the Rebbe came to 770, Rabbi Groner told him of the chassid's wife. The Rebbe listened, and told Rabbi Groner to call Rabbi Chodakov, the Rebbe's senior aide.

Rabbi Groner got Rabbi Chodakov on the line. After speaking to the Rebbe for several minutes, Rabbi Chodakov told Rabbi Groner to call the chassid so that he, Rabbi Chodakov, could communicate a message from the Rebbe.

Several moments after Rabbi Chodakov spoke to the chassid, the old man called Rabbi Groner back and told him the entire story.

His wife had been ill for several days. On Friday night, her condition had become so desperate that the doctors abandoned hope. Early Saturday morning, however, her condition took a sharp turn for the better. Nevertheless, as soon as the Sabbath ended, the chassid had called Rabbi Groner to ask for the Rebbe's blessing. During the interim, her condition continued to improve, and the doctors were confident that she would recover.

"Rabbi Chodakov said the Rebbe had instructed him to tell me that my wife's condition had begun to improve about 5:00 a.m. Saturday. He emphasized that, in case I might think this was due to other factors, I was to tell you that her recovery came about because someone had thought about her at that time."

※

It was one of those pleasant moments at which a *shliach* can sit back and take satisfaction in the success of his work. He had begun a day camp, and had been able to inspire the children and many of their parents to deeper Jewish involvement.

One couple in particular had shown an active interest, and were making steady progress in observance. The woman had just given birth, and the new parents were honoring the *shliach*

BEYOND NATURE'S LIMITS — 227

by choosing him as the *sandek*.[3] And so it was with feelings of calm satisfaction that the *shliach* took hold of the infant.

Suddenly, he was jolted out of his reverie by a look of alarm on the *mohel*'s face. The child was turning blue!

There was no thought of performing the *bris*. One of the guests knew first-aid, and administered artificial respiration until the ambulance arrived. The child was rushed to the hospital and placed in intensive care.

Startled by the turn of events, the *shliach* called Crown Heights and related the incident to the Rebbe's secretary, asking for a blessing. The Rebbe responded: "Apparently, the woman has not practiced the laws of *taharas hamishpachah*. What has happened until now is history. If she will promise to keep these laws in the future, her child will recover."

The *shliach* was somewhat hesitant about speaking to the woman; although he had developed a close relationship with the family, they had never spoken about such intimate matters. But did he have a choice? A child's life was hanging in the balance!

He called and found the mother resting after several hours at the hospital. He asked if she would like him and his wife to come over for support, and she said "yes." During their visit, the *shliach* found an appropriate opportunity to mention the Rebbe's comment.

"Have you ever heard about *taharas hamishpachah?*" he asked the woman.

"Yes," she responded, "my mother used to go to the *mikveh*."

"Well," he said, somewhat at a loss about how to continue, "when I asked the Rebbe for a blessing for your child, he responded by saying that your observance of these laws was lacking."

"How does he know?" exclaimed the woman.

---

3. The person who holds a baby while the circumcision is performed.

"He's a Rebbe," answered the *shliach,* "and he's promising that if you make a commitment to observe these laws in the future, your baby will recover."

The woman promised to observe the *mitzvah,* and shortly afterwards the baby was released from hospital. The *shliach* was again called to serve as the *sandek,* and this time the *bris* proceeded without incident.

≈

Mrs. Terri Naiditch, a member of the Lubavitch community in Pittsburgh, once received the following letter from her father:

"In the fall of 1985, I went for a check-up shortly before my crucial business season started, as was my habit in those years.

"I was referred to a dermatologist to confirm that a mole on my back had all the earmarks of a malignant melanoma — a potentially lethal affliction that can spread cancer throughout the body. He in turn sent me to the Mayo Clinic to see about having the mole removed.

"At the Mayo Clinic, I asked the head of the dermatology unit to tell me frankly whether the thing was malignant, for I was also suffering intense pain from a botched root canal, and was so discouraged by the pain and worry that I was considering early retirement. He not only confirmed that it was malignant, but even had his whole staff come in and look at my mole, evidently as a textbook example of a melanoma. (I had studied a pamphlet on this disorder, and had seen for myself that mine was identical to one of the most graphic illustrations.)

"Upon hearing of my planned operation, you and Pinky appealed to Rebbe Menachem Schneerson to intercede on my behalf, which he generously did.

"You know the sequel: When the operation took place, the tissue was sent out for the obligatory biopsy, and only moments after I was sewn up, the surgeon returned with the greeting: 'Boy, were you lucky! It's not malignant!'

"Now, you know that your mother and our dear friends the Dotys were there with me, and that their prayers and others were offered for me. The unique thing in my appreciation, though, was the help of the Rebbe. I do not make any claim — I do not feel qualified to do so — that G-d saved me from this life-threatening malady because of the Rebbe's intervention. Yet I have complete faith in the Mayo Clinic's staff and their diagnosis, and to me this experience cannot be explained in purely logical terms. I shall always feel a debt to, and a special affection for, the Rebbe — may his memory be a blessing to us all.

"Love,

"Dad"

Now, Mrs. Naiditch is a convert; her father, John Huff, is not Jewish. Nonetheless, when a blessing was requested for him, the Rebbe responded.

A tall, dark, good-looking gentleman walked into 770 and asked to see the Rebbe. Rabbi Groner, the Rebbe's secretary, asked him who he was and the purpose of his visit.

"I am a doctor from South America," the visitor replied, "and I would like to meet the man who can perform life-saving miracles from thousands of miles away."

The man was an obstetrician. A Jewish woman had entered his hospital to give birth, but he had immediately realized there were severe complications. He called the husband aside and told him that a major decision had to be made. Either the baby could be delivered, which would kill the mother, or the infant could be sacrificed to save the woman. The decision was the father's, but he had to make his choice quickly.

The father wept, not knowing what to do. Then a Jewish woman standing nearby, hearing the man's anguish, approached and gently asked if anything could be done.

The husband told her the choice that he had to make, and confessed that he simply didn't know what to do.

The woman answered that there was a great *tzaddik* in New York who could work wonders. She then took the initiative and called the Rebbe's office. When Rabbi Groner was told the story, he said he would consult the Rebbe, and that the person should call back soon.

The Rebbe told Rabbi Groner to find out if the mother-to-be would accept the *mitzvah* of *taharas hamishpachah*.

When the man called back and was given the Rebbe's reply, his sister-in-law (who was with him) promised that she would see to it that her sister kept the *mitzvah*.

When the Rebbe received this assurance, he told Rabbi Groner that the husband should instruct the doctor to deliver the baby, and that both mother and child would be safe.

The happy results so surprised the physician that on his next trip to the US, he made it a point to visit 770.

Chapter 14 —
Sparks of Greatness

The vintage chassid, Reb Mendel Futerfas, was wont to say: "There are chassidim who would say: *A dank der Oibershter far'n Rebbe'n.* "Thank You G-d, for giving us the Rebbe," expressing their genuine appreciation to G-d for giving them the opportunity to know and appreciate the Rebbe.

Others would say: *A dank der Rebbe'n far'n Oibersht'n;* "Thank you, Rebbe, for giving us the opportunity to know G-d." The intent is not merely that the Rebbe's teachings open up new windows of spiritual awareness. Although this is true, these chassidim meant more: Their intent is that from watching the Rebbe, and seeing his uniqueness, they were able to appreciate G-dliness.

R. Leib Sarah's would say that he went to Mezritch not to hear the Maggid's teachings, but to watch the way he tied his shoes. For everything that a *tzaddik* does is a lesson.

The chassidim of the early generations would ask: Why isn't there a tractate of the *Talmud* that focuses on the knowledge of G-d? And they would answer that this is unnecessary, because in every generation there are *tzaddikim* who, in our Sages' words:[1] "resemble their Creator," and thus enable us to perceive Him.

The understanding of G-d generated by observing a *tzaddik* is not abstract. On the contrary, it comes from watching how a person actually lives his life. This makes it possible for us to have actual awareness of the G-dliness which we possessed within ourselves and which is latent in every element of existence.

In this chapter, we have included various stories that did not seem to fit any of the others. Each one of them is, however, significant, for it sheds light on still a different element of the Rebbe's character, adding one more way to enable us to know him, and thus know G-d.

---

1. *Rus Rabbah* 4:3; *Bereishis Rabbah* 67:8.

A state senator from New York once asked for a private meeting with the Rebbe. After spending over an hour with the Rebbe, he came out excited. "Until now, I never realized what a great man your Rebbe is," he told Rabbi Leibl Groner, the Rebbe's secretary.

The senator explained that he had sought the Rebbe's counsel concerning certain issues involving the Jewish community. After offering advice with regard to these matters, the Rebbe asked if he could request a favor.

"'Here it comes,' I thought to myself," he told Rabbi Groner. "'Just like all the others, he's looking for the payoff.'

"But what did the Rebbe ask of me?

"He said: 'There is a growing community in Chinatown. These people are quiet, reserved, hard-working and law-abiding — the type of citizens most countries would treasure. But because Americans are so out-going and the Chinese are, by nature, so reserved, they are often overlooked by government programs. As a state senator from New York, I suggest that you concern yourself with their needs.'

"I was overwhelmed. The Rebbe has a community of thousands in New York, and institutions all over the state that could benefit from government support. I was in a position to help secure funding for them, but the Rebbe didn't ask about that. He was concerned with Chinatown. I don't think he has ever been there, and I'm certain that most people there don't know who he is, but he cares about them. Now that's a true leader!"

꣸

When the Rebbe suffered a heart attack in 5738 (1978), Dr. Ira Weiss of Chicago served as the head of the team of doctors who treated him. After the Rebbe recovered, Dr. Weiss would visit him several times a year, attending a *farbrengen* and then giving the Rebbe a physical examination.

One year, Dr. Weiss brought a friend with him, Dr. Gerald Dorros, a distinguished cardiologist from Milwaukee. After the *farbrengen,* Dr. Dorros waited in the foyer outside the Rebbe's room while Dr. Weiss conducted his examination. When he was finished, Dr. Weiss mentioned his friend and asked if he could introduce him to the Rebbe.

The Rebbe consented and invited Dr. Dorros into his room. "You should devote yourself to treating healthy people, not only sick people," the Rebbe told him.

"How can I improve on what the Almighty has done?" replied the doctor with a smile.

"You can," responded the Rebbe. "If a layman can't improve on what the Almighty has done — and if a doctor can't improve on what the Almighty has done — then what are we doing here?"

"Are you asking me to make man perfect?" asked the doctor.

"No, that is not what is asked of you," the Rebbe told him. And with a twinkle he added: "Leave that for *Mashiach.*"

※

Prof. Velvel Greene was employed by NASA in the early years of the space program. He once told the Rebbe that despite all their research, scientists had found no sign of extraterrestrial life.

"Shouldn't we stop looking?" the professor asked. "After all, is it not a point of faith that there is no life outside Earth?"

"Why put limits on G-d?" the Rebbe answered. "Continue looking! Whether or not there is life in outer space is a question for the scientists; it is not an object of faith."

※

The Rebbe once asked his secretary, Rabbi Yehuda Krinsky, to purchase a certain item for him. Rabbi Krinsky went to a store at which Merkos L'Inyonei Chinuch (the educational wing of the Lubavitch organization) had an account, charged the article to the account, and brought his purchase to the Rebbe.

When the Rebbe received the article, he said he wanted to pay for it himself. Upon examining the receipt, he noticed that sales tax had not been charged.

Rabbi Krinsky told the Rebbe that he thought the article was to be used by the organization, and that as a charitable organization, the item would be tax-exempt.

The Rebbe replied that the item was for his personal use. He asked Rabbi Krinsky to contact the store, cancel the original receipt, and pay the tax due.

≈

One day in the early 1970s, Reb Avraham Parshan was sitting in his office in Toronto when he received a call from Rabbi Chodakov, the Rebbe's personal secretary. "The Rebbe wants to know whether you have a valid passport."

Reb Avraham answered that he did.

"Would you be willing to fly to Milan?"

"Yes," answered Reb Avraham, without questioning why he was being sent. "When would you like me to go?"

"Today."

To this Reb Avraham also agreed.

"Ask your wife for permission," instructed Rabbi Chodakov.

Reb Avraham's wife consented, and he set off, still not knowing why the Rebbe wanted him to undertake this journey.

Upon arriving in Milan, Reb Avraham tried to contact the *shliach* there, Rabbi Gershon Mendel Garelik, but was unable to locate him either at home or at *shul*. Unsure of what to do, he took a taxi to Rabbi Garelik's *shul*.

Rabbi Garelik and Reb Avraham arrived at the *shul* at approximately the same time. "I'm sorry, I can't spend time with you today," Rabbi Garelik told Reb Avraham. He explained that the mother of Astro Meair had passed away that morning. Mr. Meair was a member of one of the wealthier families in Milan. He was also very involved in Israeli politics, and had taken a firm stand in favor of amending of the Law of Return to require a *halachic* conversion.

Despite a lifelong involvement with the secular Zionists who opposed such a revision of the law, Mr. Meair had advocated the position for which the Rebbe had fought so powerfully.

As Rabbi Garelik was explaining this to Reb Avraham, Rabbi Chodokov called from New York with a message from the Rebbe. The Rebbe said that since Reb Avraham was in Milan (he had left the previous day, before Mr. Meair's mother had passed away), it would be proper for him to represent Lubavitch at the funeral.

Because of the position of the Meair family in the city, many gentile dignitaries of the city also planned to attend the funeral, and it had been arranged that a delegation from the Catholic Church be present. When Reb Avraham heard this, he called Mr. Meair and told him that the Rebbe had sent him as a special messenger to attend the funeral in recognition of Mr. Meair's efforts to amend the Law of Return. Mr. Meair was greatly appreciative.

Reb Avraham continued, explaining that he could only attend if the funeral was carried out according to Jewish law, and thus no members of the Church could participate. Mr. Meair agreed, and the funeral was carried out in accordance with *Halachah*.

At the funeral, in the presence of many representatives of the Israeli government, Reb Avraham gave a stirring speech praising Mr. Meair's efforts to amend the Law of Return, and explaining that this would be counted in his mother's eternal merit.

⁓

Reb Nachum Rabinovitz, one of the vintage chassidim of Jerusalem, was once waiting for *yechidus*. Among those waiting was a young man, obviously wealthy, but wearing a morose and despondent expression.

A short while later, the young man entered the Rebbe's room, and when he emerged, his expression had changed. His face beamed forth energy and vitality.

Curious about this abrupt shift in emotion, when his own *yechidus* concluded, Reb Nachum inquired about the young man's identity from the Rebbe's secretaries and was able to arrange a meeting.

"I am a millionaire," the young man told Reb Nachum, "but recently, my only son died. At that point, I felt that my life no longer had any purpose. I saw no value to my wealth or my position.

"I went to the Rebbe for solace and advice.

"The Rebbe asked me what my feelings would be if my son went overseas and was living in a foreign country from which he could not communicate to me, but in which I could be assured that all his needs were being met and he had no suffering at all.

"I answered that although the separation would be difficult to bear, I would be happy for my son.

"'And although he could not respond, if you could communicate with him and send packages to him,' the Rebbe continued, 'would you do so?'

"'Of course,' I answered.

"'This is precisely your present situation,' the Rebbe concluded. 'With every word of prayer you recite, you are sending a message to your son. And with every gift you make to charity or institution which you fund you are sending a package to him. He cannot respond, but he appreciates your words and your gifts.'"

❦

In his diary, the Rebbe once wrote that on Kislev 12, 5693 (1932), the Previous Rebbe told him: "You should give *mashkeh* because of the dream I had today. Give me a kiss, give *mashkeh,* and begin studying *Chassidus.*"

The Rebbe wanted to kiss the Previous Rebbe's hand, but the Previous Rebbe motioned that he should kiss him on the forehead. Afterwards, the Previous Rebbe kissed the Rebbe on his cheek, and told the Rebbe that he had seen his own father, the Rebbe Rashab, in a dream. The Rebbe Rashab told the Previous Rebbe: "Why are you heartbroken? It's bright in your home!"

The Previous Rebbe awoke and saw that the moon was shining into his room, but he understood that his father had not been referring to physical light. He then entered his library and saw the Rebbe studying.

❦

It was a *yechidus* night and, as usual, the Rebbe had received people until the early hours of the morning. When the last visitor had departed, he did not tidy up his desk and go home. Instead, he asked his secretary, Rabbi Groner, for the day's mail.

Obediently, Rabbi Groner brought in several piles of letters that had been received that day. When he saw that the Rebbe was not merely interested in seeing how much mail had arrived, but began reading each letter and penning answers, Rabbi Groner found himself in a quandary.

He knew how taxing *yechidus* was, and he saw that answering these letters would take time. He wanted to suggest that the Rebbe go home and rest, leaving the letters until the next day, but he hesitated to interrupt the Rebbe and make his suggestion.

Finally, he had an idea. He wrote his suggestion on a note and put it on top of the next pile of letters.

The Rebbe read the note and looked up with a smile. "Would you like me to put off answering this question until tomorrow as well?" he asked Rabbi Groner, and went on to the next letter.

The *tefillin* campaign was central to Rabbi Moshe Feller's activities when he first arrived on *shlichus* in the Twin Cities. He would frequently go to the Hillel building at the University of Minnesota campus and put on *tefillin* with the students.

One day, as he was busy giving students the opportunity to perform the *mitzvah*, Lewis Milgrumb, the Hillel rabbi, approached. "You're helping so many others," he told Rabbi Feller. "What can you do for me?"

Aware that Rabbi Milgrumb was orthodox and put on *tefillin* daily, Rabbi Feller answered: "For you, we will bring *Rabbeinu Tam's tefillin*, or maybe four pairs of *tefillin*?"

"Do you mean that there are people today who put on four pairs of *tefillin*?!" Rabbi Milgrumb asked.

Rabbi Feller explained that the Rebbe and certain select chassidim would don four pairs of *tefillin* daily, so that their observance conformed to the conceptions of *Rashi*, Rabbeinu Tam, the *Raavad* and the *Shimusha Rabbah*.

As the two men struck up a friendship, "four pairs of *tefillin*" remained their buzzword. "I'll do it when I put on four pairs of *tefillin*," Rabbi Milgrumb would tell Rabbi Feller. And for his part, Rabbi Feller would quip: "Come on, Rabbi Milgrumb, it's a lot easier than putting on four pairs of *tefillin*."

Rabbi Milgrumb was chosen by the B'nai Brith to open a Hillel House at the university campus in Melbourne, Australia. Before departing, at the suggestion of Rabbi Feller, he wrote to the Rebbe asking his advice and blessing.

The Rebbe answered, telling Rabbi Milgrumb that in Australia, he should feel freer to introduce more religious programming. "There," the Rebbe wrote, "the students are more traditional than in America, and will welcome the opportunity for religious experience."

"Did you tell the Rebbe what to tell me?" Rabbi Milgrumb asked Rabbi Feller.

"Of course not," answered Rabbi Feller, explaining that such a thing would run contrary to the entire thrust of the chassid-Rebbe relationship.

"I am sure you did," said Rabbi Milgrumb. "Look at the next line."

The Rebbe's letter continued: "I am not asking you to have the students put on four pairs of *tefillin*, but merely to give them the opportunity to observe those Jewish practices that they are accustomed to performing at home and in school."

꙰

At the burial of his mother, Rebbitzin Chanah, the Rebbe looked very disturbed. Initially, he would not allow the pallbearers to lower the coffin into the grave. No one understood why he was so upset.

Reb Avraham Parshan saw the gentile gravediggers watching, and it occurred to him that they might be the cause of the Rebbe's discomfort. He took out a $100 bill and gave it to them, telling them to take a break. As soon as they turned their backs, the Rebbe motioned for the pallbearers to continue.

A few days later, Reb Avraham received a receipt from Machne Israel (the central Lubavitch charitable organization) for $100. Rabbi Chodakov called and told him that the Rebbe had sent a check for $100 to Machne Israel, explaining that this was for his mother's burial expenses.

Rav Shmuel Shneid is a scribe living in Monsey, N.Y. He is not a Lubavitcher chassid, but nurtures a growing relationship with the Rebbe. His feelings are shared by many in his community, as evidenced by the countless occasions on which neighbors have come, asking him to check their *mezuzos* on the Rebbe's instructions.

Once a woman who had come to him because the Rebbe told her to have her *mezuzos* checked was upset when Rabbi Shneid did not detect any problems. She had been experiencing several difficulties, and was hoping that correcting her *mezuzos* would alleviate these hardships.

Rabbi Shneid explained that checking *mezuzos* is in itself a positive activity which brings blessing. The woman accepted his explanation and waited, but her difficulties persisted. She wrote the Rebbe again, mentioning that her *mezuzos* had been checked. The Rebbe advised her to have them checked again.

She went back to Rabbi Shneid, who agreed to check the *mezuzos* again without charge. When the woman brought in her *mezuzos* this time, however, Rabbi Shneid noticed two wrapped in wax paper. Now, after checking a *mezuzah*, Rabbi Shneid always wraps it in saran wrap. Obviously, he had not checked these two.

He asked the woman about them. She replied that she had not wanted to leave her home totally without *mezuzos* while they were being checked, and had therefore left one on the front door and one on the back door. She had forgotten about them, and so was bringing them in now for the first time.

While checking the *mezuzah* for the front door, Rabbi Shneid discovered that it was invalid.

~

It once happened that Reb Nissan Nemanov, the renowned *mashpia* from the Lubavitcher *yeshivah* in France, emerged from *yechidus* in tears. Rabbi Leibl Groner, the Rebbe's secretary, was puzzled. Reb Nissan was known for his self-control. What had happened to provoke such an outburst?

After ushering the next person into *yechidus,* Rabbi Groner took Reb Nissan into the office of the secretariat, gave him a chair, and asked him the reason for his tears.

"I came to the Rebbe with a problem," explained Reb Nissan. "The *bachurim* studying at the *yeshivah* today cannot be compared to the *bachurim* of previous years. In previous years, when I would tell *bachurim* to spend hours *davening,* to practice *iskafia* (control of one's natural desires), and to carry out all the other dimensions of *avodah* (the Divine service of mastering oneself), they would listen; they would try. Today, even the terminology is foreign to them.

"On the other hand, I don't know what other message to give. *Chassidus* is *avodah;* there is no alternative. I asked the Rebbe what to do.

"The Rebbe answered: 'Learn from my example. When I think of a new directive, I consider who my followers are. If half of them are capable of putting the directive into practice, I speak of it.'

"I'm crying," Reb Nissan continued, "because of those directives the Rebbe withheld because he thought that less than half of his chassidim could follow them. Who knows what they could have been?"

~

Once the Rebbe and the Previous Rebbe were discussing the *tefillin* mandated by the *Shimusha Rabba*.[2] The Previous Rebbe asked the Rebbe if he possessed such *tefillin*.

The Rebbe replied that he did not and asked the Previous Rebbe whether it was appropriate for him to begin putting them on, for our Rabbis had counseled that only those most fastidious in their observance should put them on.

The Previous Rebbe answered: "For you, every Jewish practice is appropriate," and promised that he would have them ordered for the Rebbe so that the matter would not be publicized.

(Significantly, years later, with the publication of *HaYom Yom*,[3] the Rebbe publicized the order in which all four pairs of *tefillin* should be put on.)

~

In the 1960s, Rabbi Asher Zeilingold was one of the graduates of the Lubavitcher *yeshivah* who accepted Rabbinical positions in what were then far-removed Jewish communities. Serving as the Rabbi of the Adath Israel Congregation of S. Paul, Minnesota, Rabbi Zeilingold combined energy, erudition and commitment in his efforts to spread *Yiddishkeit* in his congregation and in the community at large.

These efforts frequently attracted the attention of the local media. Methodically, Rabbi Zeilingold would collect any write-ups of his activities, and on his trips to New York, or when the pile became uncomfortably large, he would send it to the Rebbe.

---

2. There are four opinions regarding the order to place the passages in the head *tefillin*: that proposed by *Rashi* which are worn during prayer, that proposed by *Rabbeinu Tam* which are put on by many after the prayer service, and those proposed by the *Shimusha Rabba* and the *Raavad* which are worn by a select few.
3. Entry 19 Menachem Av; see also *Sefer HaMinhagim*: The Book of Chabad Lubavitch Customs, p. 37ff.

One year, Rabbi Zeilingold visited Crown Heights on Lag BaOmer, taking a package of clippings. This time the package was larger than usual, because Rabbi Zeilingold had been honored by his congregation and the local papers had made much of the event.

Before Rabbi Zeilingold left for New York, one of his congregants had entrusted him with a question for the Rebbe. The man was observant, and the head office of the corporation for which he worked was threatening to fire him unless he removed his beard. He wanted the Rebbe's advice. Rabbi Zeilingold submitted this question to the Rebbe together with his package.

Before leaving for Minnesota, Rabbi Zeilingold asked Rabbi Chodakov, the Rebbe's personal secretary, if there was an answer for the man. Rabbi Chodakov replied that the Rebbe had not answered yet, but to wait a short while and inquire again.

A little later, Rabbi Chodakov came out with a letter of a page and a half, advising the man to keep his beard, and supplying various explanations that he could give his company. Together with the letter was a picture from Rabbi Zeilingold's clippings. In the letter, the Rebbe noted that the picture showed the mayor of S. Paul, who was also bearded. "Tell your company," the Rebbe wrote, "that if this is acceptable for a mayor, who does not wear a beard because of religious beliefs, surely it is acceptable for a Jew who does so out of religious commitment."

What amazed Rabbi Zeilingold was not the Rebbe's argument, but the fact that he had singled out the mayor of S. Paul. The picture had been in the middle of the package which Rabbi Zeilingold had sent. Only in the small print of the caption was the mayor mentioned. He understood that the Rebbe had not merely skimmed the clippings, but had read them all, even the captions.

On another occasion, Rabbi Zeilingold visited Crown Heights for *Chaf Av*, the *yahrzeit* of the Rebbe's father, Rav Levi

Yitzchak. He brought a copy of his *shul's* bulletin announcing the coming High Holidays, and submitted it to the Rebbe.

Shortly afterward, Rabbi Zeilingold received a message from Rabbi Chodakov that the Rebbe would like to see him. "After the *Minchah* service, wait in the corridor outside the Rebbe's room. When he buzzes, open the door and enter."

Rabbi Zeilingold was unnerved, not knowing what to expect. As he entered, the Rebbe pointed to the upper right hand corner of the bulletin. Inadvertently, the traditional greeting ב"ה, *Baruch HaShem,* — "with G-d's blessings" — had been omitted.

"Ever since you accepted the position in Minnesota," the Rebbe said, "I have read every one of your publications. This is the first time the *Baruch HaShem* is missing."

Chapter 15 —
More Than During His Lifetime

"When a *tzaddik* departs he is to be found in all the worlds more than during his lifetime."[1]

In *Tanya*,[2] the Alter Rebbe explains that this does not refer only to the spiritual realms. That is obvious. The intent rather is that even in this material world, a *tzaddik's* presence is more powerfully felt after his passing than during his lifetime. For during his lifetime, his physical body, however refined it might be, restricts the extent to which his disciples can be nourished by the contact of their souls with his. After his passing, those restrictions no longer exist.

This means that the stories related above are not merely past history. Instead, they reflect an ongoing initiative that is as powerful as during the Rebbe's lifetime, and indeed more powerful.

After the death of the Previous Rebbe, the Rebbe Rayatz, the Rebbe told the chassidim to continue directing their requests for blessings to the Previous Rebbe. "He will find a way," the Rebbe explained, "to communicate his response."

---

1. *Zohar*, Vol. III, p. 71b.
2. *Iggeres HaKodesh*, Epistle 27.

What the Rebbe told us about the Previous Rebbe certainly holds true with regard to himself.[3] As the stories to follow indicate, he finds a way to respond. Be it through dreams or visions of the Rebbe, prayers at his holy resting place (called by chassidim "the *Ohel*" or "the *Tziyun*"), or by placing written requests for guidance randomly in any one of the many published volumes of the Rebbe's thousands of letters (*Igros*),[4] the chassidim and the Rebbe have maintained their relationship.

Anyone who spoke to the Rebbe had the feeling that, at the time the Rebbe was speaking to him, the Rebbe's concentration was focused solely on him. No matter how petty that person's concerns were, the Rebbe invested himself in them, showing that person the utmost care and attention. Today that motif continues.

But that is only part of the story. Perhaps most significant is the fact that the Rebbe's work — Jewish outreach, and performing this in the most complete way, so that it will lead to the coming of *Mashiach* — is still going on, and indeed, has continued to grow. It is hard to believe, but the number of new *shluchim*, young couples going to outlying places to put the Rebbe's mission into practice, has grown year by year in greater numbers. New Lubavitch centers are continually springing up and the existing centers are widening their scope of activity. His influence is being felt — more than during his lifetime.

3.. See *In the Paths of Our Fathers*, the commentary to *Avos* 3:16.
4. One might add that in the interests of honesty, the writer's subsequent search for a reply explicit or implicit in the letters appearing on the randomly chosen pages should perhaps be made in consultation with a mature and objective friend, one who is experienced and familiar with the Rebbe's style of response.

More Than During His Lifetime

In 1995, Jeremy Jordan underwent extensive surgery. During his recovery, he developed a severe infection, which necessitated an additional operation.

His own surgeon was out of town at the time, and so Dr. S. — a man whom he had never met before — was commissioned to perform the second surgery.

Dr. S had Jeremy put under general anesthesia and began surgery.

Then, while still on the operating table, Jeremy woke up! He felt no pain, and was aware of his surroundings. As he looked up at the ceiling, he saw a clear vision of the Rebbe. In this vision, the Rebbe told Jeremy that he wanted to give him a message for the doctor who was operating on him!

The Rebbe then told Jeremy to tell Dr. S that if he began to put on *tefillin* every day, the difficulties he was experiencing with his daughter would cease. The Rebbe stressed that although something was very wrong with the man's daughter, it would be rectified if he performed this *mitzvah*.

Jeremy told the Rebbe he would pass on the message. Imagine the consternation in the operating room when the "anaesthetized" patient began to speak! The nurse told Dr. S that the patient had awakened, and asked what she should do. Dr. S replied that she should give him additional anesthesia.

Before this could be done, however, Jeremy spoke up and asked Dr. S to come close so that he could see his face. Dr. S complied, asking Jeremy if he was in any pain, and curious to know if his "unconscious" patient truly understood what was going on around him. Jeremy made it clear that he did.

Then Jeremy told the doctor: "You may think I'm crazy, but I have a message for you. Do you know who the Lubavitcher Rebbe, Menachem Mendel Schneerson is?"

Dr. S replied: "I've heard of him, why?"

"Well," Jeremy continued, "He just appeared to me in a vision and told me to tell you that the difficulties with your daughter will be solved if you put on *tefillin* every day."

The doctor was dumbfounded, but remembering where he was, he managed to say that the surgery was almost finished, and that he would have Jeremy out of the operating room soon.

During the remainder of the procedure, Jeremy remained conscious, feeling a unique peace of mind as the Rebbe's words echoed in his thoughts.

While Jeremy was in the recovery room, Dr. S came over and closed the curtain around the bed. He took Jeremy's hand in his own and, with tears in his eyes, whispered: "I believe you!

"The last time I was in a synagogue was at my *bar mitzvah*. I hadn't prayed or acknowledged G-d since then.

"My daughter happens to be gravely ill. Since I am a physician, I feel doubly helpless that I can't help her.

"This morning, I prayed for the first time in over 30 years, pleading with G-d to heal her. And I added: 'If You really exist, please show me a sign.'

"Then you awoke during surgery and gave me that message from Rebbe Schneerson! It's incredible."

After this experience, Dr. S purchased a pair of *tefillin* and began attending synagogue. Within weeks, his daughter recovered completely.

Rabbi Dovid Goldwasser is a sensitive Rabbi in Flatbush who has dedicated himself to enhancing *shalom bayis* (peace and harmony between husbands and wives), and securing help for *agunos* (women whose husbands refuse to give them a *get,* a Jewish divorce). In many instances, he has been able to convince recalcitrant husbands to enable their ex-wives to remarry.

These efforts have gained him a reputation, and *agunos* from all over the world appeal to him for help.

In the winter of 5756 (1996), a well-known Jewish philanthropist called. "A woman has been separated from her husband for six years," he said. "There is no hope of restoring marital harmony, and yet the husband refuses to give a divorce. Could Rabbi Goldwasser help?"

Rabbi Goldwasser told the philanthropist that he would make preliminary inquiries and contact him when he had more information. Upon investigating, however, he found that he was not the first Rabbi who had been contacted about this case. The woman had spoken to several, and they had tried all the channels which Rabbi Goldwasser would usually employ. The husband was unusually stubborn; no one had been able to budge him.

Rabbi Goldwasser called the philanthropist back and told him that he didn't see what he could do. "Believe me, if there was anything I could do to help, I would. But I'm stumped. I wouldn't know where to start."

Several months later, the philanthropist called again. "Would the Rabbi at least sit down with the woman and hear her plight?"

Rabbi Goldwasser could not refuse such a request, and so an appointment was arranged. The philanthropist came with the woman, and for two hours, she told her tale of woe. When she finished, the philanthropist called a cab for her and remained with Rabbi Goldwasser.

"What do you say now?" he asked the Rabbi.

"What *can* I say?" answered Rabbi Goldwasser. "After hearing such a story, can I say No?! But what can I do, if I say Yes? I don't see any openings. Nevertheless, I'll try to do what I can."

Thus began several months of protracted dealings between the woman, Rabbi Goldwasser, and the woman's husband. At first it appeared that some headway was being made, but then suddenly, the door slammed shut. The husband absolutely refused to cooperate.

Throughout this time, the woman had been in touch with another woman in Australia who was experiencing similar difficulties. She too had been separated for many years, but her husband refused to give her a *get*. Over the years, the two woman had become friends, each one commiserating with and supporting the other.

At this time, the Australian woman was able to achieve a breakthrough. Her husband consented to give her a *get*. Overjoyed at this sudden and fortunate change, the first person she called was the woman with whom she had shared so much suffering.

Needless to say, the woman shared in her friend's joy, and showered warm wishes for continued good fortune. When she hung up, however, she broke down and cried. Now she was truly alone.

Struggling to maintain her composure, she called Rabbi Goldwasser. She told him the good news she had received, but then could not hold herself back. All the pent-up suffering and anguish she had been feeling over the years exploded.

At first, Rabbi Goldwasser had nothing to say. He had no new suggestions for this woman. She had been told — and she had internalized — many teachings about *bitachon,* trust in G-d. What more could he tell her? And yet he felt the woman should not be left without an answer.

Over the years, Rabbi Goldwasser had maintained a relationship with the Rebbe, and had heard of the miracles that had happened in response to prayers at the *Ohel.* "There is a place," he told the woman, "where people from all over the world go to pray. And their prayers are answered. Go there and pour your heart out to G-d."

More Than During His Lifetime

The woman agreed, so Rabbi Goldwasser arranged to have two attendants take her to the *Ohel*. She prayed there for an hour.

On the way home, she received a call on her beeper. An acquaintance had a message from her husband. He was prepared to give her a *get!* The woman quickly made her way to a pay phone and contacted the caller. She also called Rabbi Goldwasser, who immediately arranged for a scribe. The husband was called, and he also agreed to come.

But Rabbi Goldwasser was not yet ready to celebrate. He knew of too many incidents when a husband had agreed to give a *get*, but had not shown up at the appointed time.

This time, however, there were no difficulties; the husband arrived at the *Beis Din* even before Rabbi Goldwasser. The *get* was composed and given to the woman.

Within five hours after she had prayed at the *Ohel*, a woman who had waited seven years for a divorce had her *get* in hand.

Rabbi and Mrs. Eliezer Lazaroff are the live-in directors of the *Chabad* House at the Texas Medical Center, a world-famous facility with two medical schools and 10 hospitals, including the M.D. Anderson Cancer Center and the Texas Heart Institute.

Patients come from all over the world for treatment at these hospitals, and the *Chabad* House provides an apartment for them and their families, supplying them with kosher food if necessary.

These activities and the day-to-day chores associated with a growing family made it almost a necessity for the Lazaroffs to hire a housekeeper so that Mrs. Lazaroff could focus on her responsibilities as co-director of the *Chabad* House and raising her children. In 5753 (1993), they hired a young woman on a two-year contract. She shared in all the activities of the *Chabad* House during that period.

In the winter of 5755 (1995), the Lazaroffs spoke to the woman about renewing her contract, for they were pleased with her work and her dedication. While it could not be said that she was indispensable, she was intelligent, reliable, and knew the ins and outs of the *Chabad* House. It would take weeks to train a replacement.

The housekeeper was hesitant about making a renewed commitment. Although she appreciated the way she had been treated, the work was not very stimulating, and she thought she should start planning for her future.

At about this time, she took ill and spent a week convalescing in her apartment at the back of the *Chabad* House. That Friday, the Lazaroffs had many guests for *Shabbos,* a *kiddush* was scheduled, and many meals had to be sent to the hospitals. For the first time in almost two years Mrs. Lazaroff had to do all the preparations herself. This caused her to realize anew how much of a help her housekeeper was. After *Shabbos,* she discussed the matter with her husband, explaining the vital role the housekeeper played.

Her husband agreed, and said he would do everything in his power to keep her, but the decision was not his. The housekeeper would have to make the choice.

The following morning Mrs. Lazaroff sat down and wrote a letter to the Rebbe, describing the difficulty and asking for his blessing. She put the letter into a volume of *Igros Kodesh* and resumed her work.

The housekeeper, meanwhile, was still sick. Alone in her apartment, she was thinking about her future. Should she continue working with the Lazaroffs, or should she go on to something else?

That Sunday night, she dreamt that she heard someone knocking on her door. At first, she thought it was the Lazaroffs checking on her health, but then she looked at her clock. It was three in the morning! She knew her employers would not come by at that hour.

Although she tried to ignore it, in her dream, the knocking persisted. Finally, she opened the door. There stood a venerable man with deep eyes and a warm smile. The housekeeper felt she recognized him, but couldn't place him.

"Do I know you?" she asked.

"Yes," the man answered.

"From where?"

"From the *Chabad* House. I'm always here, making sure that everything is all right."

In her dream, the housekeeper felt that her visitor was a wise man, so she asked him about her dilemma.

The man answered her: "Don't you know that the people around you are good, and very nice to you? The *Chabad* House needs you more than any place else that you could go. And there is no place where you could do as much good as you could do here."

"But the work is very monotonous," the woman protested.

"If you must," the man answered, "go away for a vacation. But not permanently."

Startled by the dream, the housekeeper awoke and could not go back to sleep. She wrote down everything the man had told her.

The next morning, she walked into the *Chabad* House. There, hanging in the hallway was a large picture. She was stunned; this was the man who had given her advice the night before!

Elozor Plotke works as a project manager for a California company that builds, launches and operates communication satellites. His job is to procure sophisticated and reliable electro-optical sensors which "lock" on to and track the Earth as the satellite circles the planet in geo-synchronous orbit. A small company in Connecticut builds the sensors.

Ron Carmichael is a California expert who helps companies reduce costs and lower risks so that they can meet critical budget and deadline goals. The company in Connecticut needed those services, and so Elozor and Ron had often worked together with that company on various projects.

A few weeks before Pesach in 1996, Elozor arranged to meet Ron at the Connecticut firm. Elozor's plan was to fly to New York, go to the Rebbe's *Ohel*, and then drive to Connecticut. The plane trip was uneventful, until Elozor looked up to see Ron. The latter had a big smile on his face and was striding down the aisle towards him. In that split second, Elozor thought: "Oh no! What about my plans to visit the *Ohel*?!"

Ron greeted Elozor warmly, and explained his presence: "You know I really don't like to drive, and even if I did, I always get lost. And by driving together, we can save the company some money." Ron had (without Elozor's knowledge) learned of his travel arrangements from his secretary and had purposely made reservations to be on the same flight.

Elozor was disappointed; he did not see how he could explain the importance of a visit to the *Ohel* to Ron, who is a gentile. Besides, Ron was probably hungry and would not have the patience to wait for dinner. Rather than broach the matter, Elozor kept his disappointment to himself.

On the same flight was a dapper gentleman who kept looking at Elozor and smiling. It seemed a little strange, but Elozor smiled back. After they left the plane, the gentleman came over and introduced himself as Amos from Tsfat, Israel. He asked Elozor if he knew of a way to get to the Rebbe's *Ohel*.

At this point, Elozor decided to stop hesitating. He asked Ron if he minded making a slight detour to stop off at the grave site of his spiritual mentor, the Lubavitcher Rebbe. To his great satisfaction, Ron said: "Sure, Elozor. Anything you want to do is fine with me."

Elozor felt very positive about the Divine Providence at work, as he, Ron, and Amos rented a car and drove to the *Ohel.*

On the way, Ron kept asking questions. Who was the Rebbe, he wanted to know, and what would they be doing at the *Ohel?* Amos answered all of Ron's inquiries. Amos had served as deputy mayor of Tsfat a few years before, and because of the large Lubavitch community in that city, had developed a long-standing relationship with the Rebbe, often visiting on Sundays to receive dollars, advice and blessings.

While they were traveling, he spoke of some miraculous events that had come to pass thanks to the Rebbe. He also explained the procedure at the *Ohel* — how they would write notes asking for blessings and requesting that the Rebbe intercede with the Almighty on their behalf. Ron was interested; he wanted to write his own note!

So at the *Ohel,* Elozor, Amos and Ron each wrote and read their notes to the Rebbe, and said some *Tehillim.* Afterwards, Elozor and Ron said farewell to Amos, drove to Manhattan for a kosher dinner, and then proceeded to their destination in Connecticut.

Several weeks after Pesach, Ron and Elozor needed to return to the vendor in Connecticut to present a company-wide seminar and workshop. Ron knew Elozor's travel plans, but was not on his flight this time. Since Elozor's plane was scheduled to arrive in New York very late in the evening, he did not think of going to the *Ohel* on the way to Connecticut. Instead, he had decided to take care of his business first, and go to the *Ohel* on the way back.

After his flight landed, Elozor called the rental agency to send over a courtesy van. He was very surprised when the rental agent asked for his name, but nevertheless identified himself.

The receptionist replied: "Oh, Mr. Plotke, it is so good that you are here. There are three gentlemen waiting for you in the lobby."

Elozor thought to himself: "It must be Ron."

Sure enough, Ron and two of his associates were in the car rental office waiting for Elozor to arrive. Ron quickly strode over and declared: "Elozor, you must take me to the *Ohel* to see the Rebbe again!"

"Why, Ron? What has happened?" replied the startled Mr. Plotke.

Ron grinned. "In the note that I wrote the last time, I asked him for help with my job, health and livelihood. You see, for the past few months, my managers have been threatening to lay me off because they no longer need me full time. All the uncertainty had been very stressful, and I was having a lot of stomach problems. In addition, living in Los Angeles is so expensive that I can no longer afford it."

"I explained all this to the Rebbe and asked for his help. A few days after I got back to Los Angeles, I received a call from a hiring manager at Hughes Training in Texas. He was looking for a person with my extensive experience. Not only did he offer to pay my moving expenses, but he gave me a bonus for accepting the offer, and a 20% raise in base salary! Since the cost of living in Texas is about 20% less than in Southern California, this meant the equivalent of a 40% raise!

"I already feel so much better that I want to go back to the Rebbe to thank him and ask for more!"

Since then, whenever Elozor and Ron get together, the first thing Ron mentions is his desire to visit the *Ohel.*

❧

One of the *shluchim* in Belgium, Rabbi Shabsie Slavatizki, was conducting a Purim feast at the Antwerp Chabad House in 5755 (1995). This was the first Purim since the Rebbe's passing on *Gimmel* Tammuz, and all the participants felt that that event had diminished their ability to celebrate.

One of those present, a diamond dealer named Arnon Zak put into words what everyone was thinking. "How can we rejoice when we are living in a vacuum? After the Rebbe's passing, is it possible to feel joy?"

Reb Shabsie was touched by Arnon's words. "Questions like these," he responded, "can be faced, but can't be answered. The pain we feel because of the Rebbe's passing cannot easily be soothed, but it's not a negative thing. On the contrary, the pain reflects powerful energies that should be channeled toward bonding with the Rebbe and furthering the mission with which he charged us."

"Moreover," Reb Shabsie continued, "we should not think that the Rebbe has forsaken us. Though now in the spiritual realms, he continues to care for all those who seek his assistance."

To illustrate his point, Reb Shabsie read a story from *Kfar Chabad*, a weekly Lubavitch magazine, which related how, after the Rebbe's passing, a person with a difficulty had written a letter to him and placed it in a volume of *Igros Kodesh*[5] (a collection of the Rebbe's letters). When the person read the letter printed on the pages between which he had placed his note, he found an answer which gave him guidance concerning the problem confronting him.

---

5. The placing of a letter to the Rebbe in a volume of his teachings when there is no way to deliver it to him personally is a long-standing chassidic custom. The concept of looking at the place where the letter is placed is a new development. Nonetheless, there is precedence for it in Torah sources, as reflected in *Sichos Shabbos Parshas Bamidbar* 5749, where the Rebbe refers to the long-standing Jewish custom of clarifying doubts regarding certain questions by opening a *Chumash* or other holy text and acting on the directive one understands from that text.

The practice of this custom is not limited to the chassidic community. On the contrary, we find it also described in the notes of the *Birkei Yosef* to *Shulchan Aruch (Yoreh De'ah)* and it lies at the core of the *goral HaGra*, the procedure established by the Vilna Gaon to seek guidance in times of distress.

A genuine chassid, Reb Shabsie continued, does not need stories like this to prove the Rebbe's ongoing concern, but if a person feels that he *does* need proof, such stories can serve the purpose.

Reb Shabsie was interrupted. One of the participants, an Israeli, and from his style of dress obviously non-observant, challenged him: "Would you mind putting that statement to a test? According to what you're saying, if one of us were to write a letter to the Rebbe and place it in a volume of *Igros Kodesh*, he would receive a pertinent answer. Can we try that now?"

All the listeners were stunned, and waited anxiously to see how Reb Shabsie would react.

Reb Shabsie turned to his son and asked him to go to his library and bring back a volume of *Igros Kodesh*. He turned to the questioner and asked him to write out a question for the Rebbe.

Somewhat unnerved by Reb Shabsie's acceptance of his challenge, the skeptic took a pen and paper and wrote: "When will we return to *Eretz Yisrael*?" He then signed his name, Shuki ben Yehoshua.

"Place your question in the volume," Reb Shabsie told him.

Reb Shabsie's son had brought the first volume of *Igros Kodesh*. Reb Shabsie opened the book and reported that the questioner's letter was between pages 264 and 265. The letter on those pages is dated Purim, 5704, and begins with the greeting: "Happy Purim."

The assembled crowd felt an immediate connection. Here they were on Purim, listening to a letter written on Purim! And the Rebbe concluded that letter with a blessing:

"On that day, G-d will be one, and His name one."[6] [May we proceed] immediately to *teshuvah*, and immediately to the Redemption."

---

6. *Zechariah* 14:7-9.

There were those who considered the answer obvious proof of the effectiveness of asking the *Igros*. Here was a letter which seemed to provide a direct answer to the question which had been asked. Even the more skeptical had to admit the uncanny coincidence.

Reb Shabsie then asked Shuki if he would mind hearing the entire letter the Rebbe had written.

"Of course not," Shuki answered.

"Even if it reflects on your personal life?"

"Why not? I'm an open person. Let the chips fly!"

So Reb Shabsi proceeded to read the letter in its entirety. It spoke about an Israeli youth who had studied in *yeshivah*, but who had abandoned that lifestyle. The Rebbe asked that contact be made with him, and efforts undertaken to encourage him to identify with his roots.

Upon hearing the whole letter, Shuki became very embarrassed, and asked to be excused, for his personal history was similar to that described. For years, his parents had encouraged him to return to observance, but with no success.

Reb Shabsi refused to let him go. "Don't run away, Shuki! Look yourself in the mirror. Face who you are!"

The *farbrengen* continued until late in the morning, and had a profound effect on Shuki's life, inspiring him to confront his past and return to it.

———

Mr. A. came from a poor Russian family that had moved to Israel while he was still a child. Lubavitch in Israel had taken care of the family's material and spiritual needs.

This kindness was never forgotten, so when Mr. A. emigrated to the United States as a young man, he maintained close contact with the Rebbe. At every step in his business or personal life, he kept the Rebbe informed.

When he started his business, he wrote to the Rebbe for a blessing, and committed himself to giving one tenth of his earnings to charity. His ventures were blessed with success, and in keeping with his commitment, he made generous donations.

He married, and some time afterwards his wife gave birth to a baby boy. But the child weighed only 2 lb. 3 oz! The doctors were not certain the infant would survive. If he *did* live, they told the worried parents, it was quite probable that he would neither see nor speak.

Mr. and Mrs. A. asked the Rebbe for a blessing for their son. The Rebbe assured them that the baby would develop normally, and his blessing was realized.

Not surprisingly, Mr. A was one of the many whose grief at the Rebbe's passing was personal. Though not a chassid, he felt as if he had lost a father.

Several years later, the A.'s doctor noticed that their son's muscles weren't developing correctly. Somberly, he told the parents that the boy might never be able to walk properly. Mr. A. knew only one address from which to seek help, so he went to the *Ohel* (the Rebbe's resting place) to pray for the health of his son.

Soon afterwards, he had a puzzling dream. In his dream, he approached the Rebbe for a blessing for his son. The Rebbe replied by telling him to visit Rabbi Leibl Groner, his secretary, and follow his instructions. Also, there was an implication that Mr. A had fallen behind in his gifts to charity.

Then, still dreaming, Mr. A visited Rabbi Groner, who told him to go and inspect a *mikveh*. As the dream continued, Mr. A. watched himself go to the *mikveh* and, seeing that it was incomplete, grow more and more angry, outraged at finding an unfinished *mikveh* in America.

When Mr. A. awoke, the dream came back to him, and he checked with his accountant. Sure enough, his contributions to charity had fallen behind in the amount of $40,000. Mr. A.

decided to go to Rabbi Groner. If Rabbi Groner told him of a *mikveh* that needed about $40,000, he would know his dream was significant.

While Mr. A's personal drama was being played out, a drama of another sort was taking place. Rabbi Yosef Carlebach, director of *Chabad* of Middlesex/Monmouth counties in New Jersey, was in the process of constructing a new *Chabad* House that would provide a home away from home for the Jewish students of Rutgers University. The five-million dollar facility was almost complete, ready to house more than two dozen women, provide kosher meals to thousands of students a week, and serve as a center for the vibrant Jewish life which *Chabad* has built at Rutgers.

But Rabbi Carlebach had a problem. In mid-July he still needed $800,000 to pay the contractor to complete the project. And he could not receive a Certificate of Occupancy until the building was virtually complete.

By August, the situation looked bleak. The contractor had walked off the job and wouldn't return unless more money was forthcoming immediately. Time was growing short — the center was scheduled to open by the first of September — and there was still a good deal of work to do before the certificate could be issued.

As the summer days passed, Rabbi Carlebach labored non-stop to obtain the necessary funds. His supporters had already donated generously, and could not give any more large sums. Rabbi Carlebach had called Rabbi Leibl Groner (who had spoken at the groundbreaking ceremony) for some fundraising leads, but Rabbi Groner had also been unable to provide substantial help.

The frustration and stress were taking their toll. One Sunday afternoon in mid-August, in the middle of making calls to solicit funds, Rabbi Carlebach fell asleep with the phone in his hand.

At that moment, the two dramas began to intermesh. Mr. A. entered Rabbi Groner's office to tell him about the dream. "Do you know of a *mikveh* that is in the process of completion?" he asked.

Rabbi Groner thought of Rabbi Carlebach, and called him immediately. Startled out of his sleep, Rabbi Carlebach was surprised to hear Rabbi Groner's voice asking: "How much money is needed to complete the *mikveh* in the *Chabad* House?"

"Forty thousand dollars," was Rabbi Carlebach's immediate response; he knew the figure only too well. When Rabbi Groner conveyed this information to him, Mr. A.'s face turned white.

Rabbi Groner called Rabbi Carlebach back on Monday morning with the news that a New York businessman might be able to help. Time was of the essence, so Rabbi Carlebach called Mr. A., and offered to drive into New York, pick him up, and bring him out to the unfinished *Chabad* House. Mr. A. agreed, and Rabbi Carlebach picked him up late Tuesday afternoon. Mr. A. sat quietly for the whole drive.

As Rabbi Carlebach showed Mr. A. around the *Chabad* House, he seemed only mildly interested. When the two men entered the area designated for the *mikveh,* however, Mr. A. just stood and stared, transfixed.

Five minutes passed, then 10. After 15 minutes, Rabbi Carlebach told Mr. A. that he would be upstairs saying the afternoon prayers. When Rabbi Carlebach finished praying, he heard Mr. A. downstairs, talking excitedly on his cellular phone.

On the way back to New York, Mr. A. told Rabbi Carlebach about his dream. "It's not only that the dollar amounts match," he told Rabbi Carlebach, "but the unfinished *mikveh* in your *Chabad* House looks exactly like the one I saw in my dream!"

On Thursday, Mr. A. brought Rabbi Groner the $40,000. Although it was 10:30 PM, Rabbi Groner called Rabbi Carlebach at once, and the latter immediately drove into New York to pick up the money.

Early next morning, Rabbi Carlebach met with the contractor and the workers. Of the $800,000 he needed, Rabbi Carlebach had $500,000 readily available and the envelope from Mr. A.

The meeting was filled with tension, and the contractor was prepared to storm out until Rabbi Carlebach stopped him and handed over the envelope from Mr. A. When the contractor realized that funds were indeed available, and after hearing the story of the dream, he ordered his workers back to the site.

Within a week, the building was ready for occupancy.

The following Friday, the city officials and the Board of Health gave their approval, and that night, hundreds of Jewish students were able to celebrate *Shabbos* in the new *Chabad* House.

―――

For ten years, Rabbi and Mrs. Moshe Menachem Mendel Liberow, *shluchim* in Porto Alegre, Brazil, have run the only Jewish day school to offer Torah education in a radius of several hundred miles.

Operating a school that provides a program from kindergarten to eighth grade is always a challenging financial undertaking. Nevertheless, Rabbi Liberow is not one to compromise on quality, and he has always been able to find a way to stay fiscally afloat, while providing the best education possible for his students.

Brazil is in the southern hemisphere, and the summer vacation begins in January. This is the time which Rabbi Liberow uses to make an accounting and take stock of his financial position.

In 5755 (1995), after checking over his ledger sheet, he discovered that there was a deficit of $26,000. Now in Porto Alegre, that is a large sum, a figure which would require adjustments to be made in the operating budget in the coming year.

That night, Rabbi Liberow shared the unpleasant news with his wife. She was disturbed; she had hoped to implement several new programs in the coming year, and now she had to contemplate cutting back.

She had one natural reaction; she wrote a letter to the Rebbe, faxing it to the *Ohel* and placing it within a volume of *Igros Kodesh.*

The letter was written Wednesday, night. On Monday morning, Rabbi Shabsi Alpern, the director of *Chabad-Lubavitch* activities in Brazil, called Rabbi Liberow. He had just completed a meeting with a leading Jewish philanthropist. A year previously, Rabbi Liberow had asked this philanthropist for a donation. He had not been able to accommodate him at that time, but now he had made a substantial profit on a recent business transaction. Although neither Rabbi Alpern or Rabbi Liberow had contacted him concerning Porto Alegre; indeed, Rabbi Alpern wasn't even aware of the Rabbi Liberow's deficit, the philanthropist promised he would make a donation to the school — for exactly $26,000.

Afterword

AFTERWORD

My brother-in-law is a *shliach* in a suburb of Paris. On one of our trips from *Eretz Yisrael* to the Rebbe, my family and I stopped midway and visited him for a *Shabbos*. At the *farbrengen* after *Shabbos* services, the main speaker was a longhaired young man of Moroccan descent who had spent the previous *Shabbos* at 770.

He was speaking with deep emotion. I don't understand French, but my brother-in-law translated for me.

The young man was saying that he knew now that there was a G-d, that the Torah is true, that he had a *yetzer hora* (a natural inclination), and that he had to conquer it. All this, he said, he had learned from the Rebbe.

What did he mean, "he had learned from the Rebbe"?! Though he had attended the Rebbe's *farbrengen,* he didn't understand Yiddish, and had not heard a translation. Yes, he had passed by the Rebbe on Sunday morning to receive a dollar for *tzedakah*, and the Rebbe had given him a short blessing. But nothing more.

So how did the Rebbe teach him?

This is not an isolated incident; it has repeated itself time and again with people from many countries and backgrounds. When people met the Rebbe, they began to believe.

For a person who was not yet observant, meeting the Rebbe often prompted that vital first step toward Jewish awareness and practice. If a person was already observant, ideas which he knew and accepted would suddenly be felt as actual truth.

This is not to say that on every occasion, the Rebbe told people something which dissolved their doubts and hesitations. Certainly the Rebbe taught, but often the most powerful effect he had on people was experienced without their comprehending or even hearing a word he said.

In *Chassidus*,[1] we learn that the core of every person's soul is *yechidah*, that dimension which is one with G-d. When the level of *yechidah* manifests itself, a person believes, not because he suddenly has a "reason" to believe, but because at that plane, G-dliness is the only reality; there is nothing else. This truth is so powerful that even as the person exists within our material frame of reference, he must acknowledge this ultimate truth

Just as every individual soul possesses a *yechidah*, in every generation there is an individual who constitutes the *yechidah* of the Jewish nation as a whole. G-dliness is as real to this individual as ordinary material existence is to us.

When people come into contact with such an individual, they cannot remain unmoved. On the contrary, meeting a person whose *yechidah* is openly revealed stirs their own *yechidah* into expression. This is why people began believing when they met the Rebbe.

Mashiach is described as the *yechidah* of history itself.[1] At the time of his coming, this innate awareness of G-d will spread throughout the world. This is intimated by Maimonides at the end of his discussion about the era of *Mashiach*,[2] with his quotation of the verse:[3] "And the earth will be filled with the knowledge of G-d, as the waters cover the ocean bed."

A multitude of creatures inhabit the ocean. Nevertheless, when looking at the sea, what we see is the ocean as a whole, and not the countless entities it contains. Similarly, in the era of *Mashiach*, every individual creature will be suffused with the knowledge of G-d. This will become our frame of reference.

This helps explain why the Rebbe pressed so powerfully for the coming of the Redemption. It was not only that he was a visionary, able to appreciate that the spiritual climate of the

---

1. See *Kuntres Inyono Shel Toras HaChassidus*, and the sources mentioned there.
2. *Mishneh Torah, Hilchos Melachim* 12:5.
3. *Yeshayahu* 11:9.

Afterword

times is changing, and that "the time for your Redemption has come."[4]

There was something more fundamental involved. Since the Rebbe was identified with *yechidah*, *Mashiach* was his mission. He was a harbinger of the future, already possessing the mindset that will characterize the era of *Mashiach*, and he shared that mindset with others.

This sharing was more than a contact between minds; it was a connection between *souls*. When you came face-to-face with the Rebbe, you believed, you felt, you *lived Mashiach*.

Tzaddikim possess a certain dimension of immortality. It is our hope that after reading this book, you will feel that you have encountered the Rebbe.

---

4. Cf. *Yalkut Shimoni*, Vol. II, sec. 499, interpreting *Yeshayahu* 60:1.

Glossary and Biographical Index

GLOSSARY AND BIOGRAPHICAL INDEX

An asterisk indicates a cross reference within this Glossary.
All non-English entries are Hebrew unless otherwise indicated.

"770": 770 Eastern Parkway, N.Y., the address of Lubavitch World Headquarters

Adar: the twelfth month of the Jewish year when counting from Nissan (or the sixth when counting from Tishrei); the joyful month in which the holiday of Purim is celebrated

aliyah (lit., "ascent"): immigration to **Eretz Yisrael*

Anash (acronym for *anshei shlomeinu*): the chassidic brotherhood

Aron HaKodesh (lit., "the holy ark"): the repository for the Torah scrolls in a synagogue

Av: the fifth month

baal teshuvah (pl., *baalei teshuvah;* lit., "master of return," i.e., a penitent): in contemporary usage, one who has discovered his spiritual heritage and its responsibilities when already an adult

bachur (pl., *bachurim;* lit. "young man"): a **yeshivah* student

badchan: jester at weddings, etc.

bar-mitzvah: (boy celebrating his) religious coming of age at 13

behiddur: enhanced or meticulous observance of a **mitzvah* beyond the demands of the letter of the law

Beis HaMikdash: the (First or Second) Temple in Jerusalem

berachah: blessing or benediction

bitachon: trust in G-d

bris (lit., "covenant"): circumcision

bubbe (or: *bobbe;* Yid.): grandmother

Chabad (acronym for the Hebrew words meaning "wisdom, understanding, and knowledge"): the approach to Chassidism which filters its spiritual and emotional power through the intellect; a synonym for *Chabad* is *Lubavitch, the name of the town where this movement originally flourished

Chabad House: an outreach center established by the *Chabad*-Lubavitch chassidic movement

chassid: adherent of the chassidic movement and follower of a Rebbe

Chassidus: chassidic thought

cheder (pl., *chadarim*): school in which young children learn reading skills and begin the study of the Torah

Chessed: the Divine or mortal attribute of lovingkindness

chinuch: education

Chol HaMoed: the semi-festive intermediate days of *Pesach or *Sukkos

chutzpah: nerve

daven (Yid.): to pray

Elul: the sixth month of the Jewish year when counting from Nissan (or the twelfth when counting from Tishrei); a month devoted to repentance and soul-searching in preparation for the Days of Awe

emunah: faith

Eretz Yisrael: the Land of Israel

erev: the day preceding

farbrengen: a gathering of chassidim

gabbai: the person responsible for the proper functioning of a synagogue or communal body

gartl (Yid.): belt worn during prayer

gmach: an acronym for the Heb. words *gemilus chessed* which mean "deed of kindness," esp. an interest-free loan, or a fund which distributes such loans

get: bill of divorce

Gevurah: the Divine or mortal attribute of strict justice

halachah (pl., *halachos;* Eng. adj.: halachic): (a) the body of Torah law; (b) a particular law

Havdalah (lit., "distinction"): the blessings recited over a cup of wine at the conclusion of a Sabbath or festival to distinguish it from the ordinary weekdays that follow

ikvesa diMeshicha (Aram.): the era in which the approaching footsteps of *Mashiach can be heard

Kabbalah: the mystical dimension of the Torah

kashrus: the state of being *kosher

Kiddush (lit., "sanctification"): (a) a blessing recited over a cup of wine expressing the sanctity of the Sabbath or of a festival; (b)

Glossary and Biographical Index

refreshments served in the synagogue after the recital of *Kiddush*, the occasion being usually graced by the sharing of Torah thoughts and song

Kiddush Levanah (lit., "the sanctification of the moon"): prayers recited in the first half of each month and related to the appearance of the New Moon

Kislev: the ninth month of the Jewish year when counting from Nissan (or the third when counting from Tishrei); the month in which Chanukah begins

kohen: priest, descendant of Aaron

kollel: *yeshivah for advanced adult students

kosher (lit., "fit for use"): (of food or religious articles:) meeting the standards prescribed by Torah law

kos shel berachah: the cup of wine over which the Grace after Meals has been recited

Lag BaOmer: the thirty-third day of the *Omer,* a minor festival falling between *Pesach and *Shavuos

LeChaim! (lit., "to life"): toast exchanged over strong drink

lekach (Yid.): cake

lishmah (lit., "for its own sake"): altruistically

Lubavitch (lit., "town of love"; Rus.): townlet in White Russia which from 1813-1915 was the center of *Chabad *Chassidism, and whose name has remained a synonym for it

maamar: a formal chassidic discourse first delivered by a *Rebbe

Maariv: the evening prayer service

Machzor: prayer book used on holidays

Mashiach (lit., "the anointed one"): the Messiah

Mashiach's Seudah: festive meal instituted by the Baal Shem Tov and held on the Last Day of Pesach in anticipation of the coming of *Mashiach

mashpia (lit., "source of influence"): spiritual mentor serving in a *yeshivah or chassidic community

matzah (pl., *matzos*): the unleavened bread eaten on Passover

mechitzah: the partition separating the men's and women's sections in a synagogue

Melaveh Malkah: festive meal held on Saturday night to usher out the Sabbath Queen

mem: thirteenth letter of the Hebrew alphabet

Menorah: (a) the seven-branched gold candelabra in the Temple; (b) the eight lights lit on Chanukah

mesirus nefesh: self-sacrifice

mezuzah (pl., *mezuzos;* lit., "doorpost"): a small parchment scroll affixed to a doorpost which contains the first two paragraphs of the *Shema (Devarim* 6:4-9 and 11:13-21*)*

Midrash: classical collection of the Sages' homiletical teachings on the Torah, on the non-literal level of *derush*

mikveh (pl., *mikvaos*): a ritual bath used by women for purification after emerging from the state of *niddah,* and used by both men and women in their endeavors to attain spiritual self-refinement

Minchah: the afternoon prayer service

minyan (lit., "number"): the quorum necessary for communal prayer

mitzvah (pl., *mitzvos;* lit., "command"): a religious obligation; one of the Torah's 613 Commandments

Modeh ani: first two words of a Jew's daily statement of faith and thanksgiving immediately upon wakening

mohel (pl., *mohalim*): circumcisor

Moshe Rabbeinu: Moses our teacher

Motzaei Shabbos: Saturday evening after the close of **Shabbos*

nadn (Heb./Yid.): dowry

Negev: the south of **Eretz Yisrael*

neshamah: soul

niggun (pl., *niggunim*): melody, esp. one figuring in divine service

nigleh (lit., "the revealed [knowledge]"): the study of the Jewish law as reflected in the **Talmud,* and in the works of the subsequent commentaries and codifiers; cf. **nistar*

Nissan: the first month of the Jewish year according to certain reckonings, or the seventh when counting the months from Tishrei; the month of the Exodus from Egypt

nistar (lit., "the hidden [knowledge]"): the Jewish mystical tradition, viz., the *Kabbalah;* cf. **nigleh*

GLOSSARY AND BIOGRAPHICAL INDEX

Pesach: Passover, festival of seven days (eight in the Diaspora) beginning on 15 Nissan, commemorating the Exodus from Egypt

Pesach Sheni (lit., "the second Passover"): opportunity given to certain persons who were unable to offer the Paschal sacrifice to do so one month later, on 14 Iyar

pnimiyus haTorah: the inner (i.e., mystical) dimension of the Torah, viz., **Kabbalah* and **Chassidus*

Purim (lit., "lots"): one-day festival falling on 14 Adar and commemorating the miraculous salvation of the Jews of the Persian Empire in the fourth century B.C.E.

Rabbeinu Tam: R. Yaakov Tam, grandson of Rashi; one of the earliest authors of the *Tosafos* commenting on the **Talmud*

Rambam (acronym for Rabbi Moshe ben Maimon; 1135-1204): Maimonides, one of the foremost Jewish thinkers of the Middle Ages; his *Mishneh Torah* is one of the pillars of Jewish law, and his *Guide to the Perplexed,* one of the classics of Jewish philosophy

Rashi (acronym for Rabbi Shlomo Yitzchaki; 1040-1105): author of the commentaries which have become the classic guides to the Torah and **Talmud*

rav ("rabbi"): halachic authority and spiritual guide of a community

Reb (Yid.): Mr.

Rebbe (lit., "my teacher [or master]"): saintly Torah leader who serves as spiritual guide to a following of chassidim

rebbitzin: the wife of a rabbi or Rebbe

Rosh HaShanah (lit., "head of the year"): the New Year festival, falling on 1 and 2 Tishrei

rosh *yeshivah: academic head of a Talmudic academy

Seder (lit., "order"): the order of service observed at home on the first night (first two nights in the Diaspora) of Passover (see *Pesach)

semichah: Rabbinic ordination

Shabbos: the Sabbath

Shacharis: the morning prayer service

shaliach (pl., *shluchim;* fem., *shluchah*): an emissary of the Lubavitcher Rebbe involved in Jewish outreach work

Shalom Aleichem (lit., "Peace upon you!"): (a) a common greeting; (b) hymn of welcome to the ministering angels who visit every Jewish home on Friday eve; see *Siddur Tehillat HaShem*, p. 144

Shalosh Seudos (lit., "three meals"): i.e., *Seudah Shelishis*, the Third Meal of *Shabbos

Shavuos (lit., "weeks"): festival commemorating the Giving of the Torah at Sinai, in *Eretz Yisrael* falling on 6 Sivan, and in the Diaspora on 6-7 Sivan

Shema: first word of the verse beginning *Shema Yisrael* ("Hear O Israel..."), the daily declaration of faith in the Unity of G-d; see *Siddur Tehillat HaShem*, p. 46

Sheva Berachos: the seven blessings recited at a wedding celebration and after the Grace after Meals at the festivities held during the following week

Shimusha Rabbah: author of one of the views as to the order in which four prescribed Scriptural passages should be placed within the *tefillin

Shivah: the seven-day period of mourning following a bereavement

Shlita: an acronym for the Hebrew words meaning, "May he live a long and good life"

shochet: ritual slaughterer

Shofar: ram's horn sounded on *Rosh HaShanah

shomer Shabbos: Sabbath-observant

shtetl (Yid.): an Eastern European township of the kind in which many Jews lived in recent centuries

shul: synagogue

Shulchan Aruch (lit., "a set table"): the standard Code of Jewish Law compiled by R. Yosef Caro in the mid-sixteenth century

sichah (pl., *sichos;* lit., "a talk"): an informal Torah discourse (as delivered by the Rebbe)

Siddur (pl., *Siddurim*): prayer book

Simchas Torah (lit., "the rejoicing of the Torah"): a day appended to the festival of *Sukkos (in *Eretz Yisrael*, the eighth day; in the Diaspora, the ninth), on which the annual cycle of weekly Torah readings is completed, and celebrated exuberantly

GLOSSARY AND BIOGRAPHICAL INDEX 281

Sivan: the third month of the Jewish year when counting from Nissan (or the ninth when counting from Tishrei); includes the festival of *Shavuos

Sukkos (lit., "booths"): festival of seven days (eight in the Diaspora) beginning on 15 Tishrei, taking its name from the temporary dwelling in which one lives during this period

tallis: prayer shawl fringed with *tzitzis* and worn by men during prayer

Talmud: the basic compendium of Jewish law, thought, and Biblical commentary; when unspecified refers to the *Talmud Bavli*, the edition developed and edited in Babylonia at the end of the fifth century C.E.

Tammuz: the fourth month of the Jewish year when counting from Nissan (or the tenth when counting from Tishrei)

Tanya: the classic text of *Chabad* chassidic thought authored by the Alter Rebbe

tefillin: small black leather cubes containing parchment scrolls inscribed with the *Shema* and other Biblical passages, bound to the forearm and head and worn by men during weekday morning prayers

Tehillim: the Book of *Psalms*

tekios: the blasts of the *Shofar*

teshuvah (lit., "return"): repentance

Teves: the tenth month of the Jewish year when counting from Nissan (or the fourth when counting from Tishrei)

Tiferes: the Divine or mortal attribute of beauty, fusing *Chessed* and *Gevurah*

tish ("table"; Yid.): i.e., the ceremonial Sabbath meal which a chassidic Rebbe conducts in the company of his chassidim

Tishrei: the first month of the Jewish year according to certain reckonings, or the seventh when counting the months from Nissan; the month which includes *Rosh HaShanah, *Yom Kippur and *Sukkos

Toldos Yaakov Yosef: the earliest written record of the teachings of the Baal Shem Tov, by his disciple R. Yaakov Yosef of Polonnoye

Torah *Shebiksav* (lit., "the Written Torah"): Scripture

tzaddik (pl., *tzaddikim*): righteous man, often used as a synonym for Rebbe

tzedakah: charity

tzitzis: fringes on the corner of a **tallis* (see *Bamidbar* 15:37-40)

Ufaratza (lit., "and you shall spread out"): the Biblical word that has become a byline for Lubavitch outreach efforts

yahrzeit (Yid.): anniversary of a person's passing

yarmulka (Yid.): skullcap

Yechidah: the highest of the five levels of the soul, the rung at which the soul is in absolute unity with G-d

yechidus: private meeting with a Rebbe

yeshivah (pl., *yeshivos*): Rabbinical academy

Yid (Yid.): Jew

Yiddishkeit (lit., "Jewishness"; Yid.): the Torah way of life

yiras shamayim: the fear (or awe) of heaven

Yom Kippur: the Day of Atonement, fast day falling on 10 Tishrei and climaxing the Days of Awe

Yom-Tov: a festival

Yud-Beis Tammuz ("the Twelfth of Tammuz"): the Previous Rebbe's birthday (1880) and the anniversary of his release from capital sentence and imprisonment in Soviet Russia in 1927

Yud Shvat ("the Tenth of Shvat"): anniversary of the passing of the Previous Rebbe in 1950

Yud-Tes Kislev ("the Nineteenth of Kislev"): anniversary of the passing of the Maggid of Mezritch in 1772, and anniversary of the release from capital sentence of his disciple, the Alter Rebbe, in 1798

zeide ("grandfather"; Yid.)

Zohar (lit., "radiance"): classical work embodying the mystical teachings of the **Kabbalah*

Made in the USA
Columbia, SC
14 October 2018